MW00575326

RED LOVE

ALSO BY DAVID EVANIER

THE ONE-STAR JEW
THE SWINGING HEADHUNTER

RED LOVE

DAVID EVANIER

Charles Scribner's Sons
New York

Collier Macmillan Canada
Toronto

Maxwell Macmillan International
New York • Oxford • Singapore • Sydney

Excerpts of RED LOVE have appeared in *The American Spectator, Commentary, Confrontation, Journal of Contemporary Studies, New American Writing,* and *Witness,* and in *Congregation: Contemporary Writers Read the Jewish Bible,* Harcourt Brace Jovanovich, 1987, edited by David Rosenberg.

Charles Scribner's Sons
Macmillan Publishing Company
866 Third Avenue, New York, NY 10022

Collier Macmillan Canada, Inc.
1200 Eglinton Avenue East, Suite 200
Don Mills, Ontario M3C 3N1

Library of Congress Cataloging-in-Publication Data
Evanier, David.
Red love / David Evanier.
p.   cm.
ISBN 0-684-19191-1
I. Title.
PS3555.V212R44   1990
813'.54—dc20   90-35364   CIP

10 9 8 7 6 5 4 3 2 1

Printed in the United States of America

To Dini, Tom Sgovio, Robert Gladnick,
Cherie and Buddy Smith, Bill Buckley,
and Abraham Foxman

Whether it happened so or not, I do not know. But if you think about it, you can see that it is true.

—BLACK ELK

Acknowledgments

The author gratefully acknowledges the generous support of the Yaddo Corporation and the MacDowell Colony.

With special thanks to Erika Goldman, Michael Congdon, Richard Gid Powers, Judith Liss, and Alan Schwartz.

RED
LOVE

Gerald Lerner's Prologue

I

This is a novel about the joys of espionage. I wrote it with fear, sanity, and guile.

Dolly and Solly Rubell were executed for spying for the Russians in 1954.

I began this book about the Rubells ten years ago by placing ads in the *Jewish Daily Forward*, the *Morning Freiheit*, *Screw*, the *Jerusalem Post*, and the *New York Times*. I wanted to speak to anyone who had spied for the Soviets or who knew anyone else who had. My ad read: IF YOU DID IT, OR KNEW SOMEONE WHO DID. . . .

Did I expect a line forming around the block in response to this?

I lack common sense.

As I near fifty, I grow more self-aware, less shy.

Obsession! I was obsessed!

I have fucked the Rubells in this book. I have fucked this gentle, peace-loving couple. And I feel very much better.

My involvement with the Old Left began in the mid-1950s, when I started to hang around the Communist Party. I had problems. I felt like I was only a guest here, and I expected to be treated like one. My parents were . . . problematic. My father claimed he'd given up women to raise me. Did I appreciate this? I thought the Soviet Union could teach my parents a lesson they wouldn't forget. I was in search of a family, any family. Girls, any girls.

My first girl friend, Rachel, had parents who looked exactly like the Rubells. They were Jewish Communists and they were obsessed with the Rubell case. They sang a song on spring evenings: "We wanna die like the Rubells, with a hard-on and a smile; just can't wait to walk that long, lonely mile." They fed me (food they could not afford to share: spicy pasta and chili), gave me a place to go, let me listen to their laughter and hard good times and watch Danny Thomas while holding hands with Rachel. And they let us close Rachel's bedroom door so I could play the upright piano while Rachel perched tragically upon it in a black tuxedo jacket and bow tie, Judy Garland singing "You Made Me Love You." And behind that door we smooched until one day we took a blanket up to the roof and made love.

Yes, the Communists were nice to me.

Then I discovered the freaks among them, and this was really great.

Robert Strugin, a redhead with wild, boiling eyes. Took me under his wing, asked me to evaluate his manuscripts. He was about forty-five, a man of delicious extremes. He'd fought for civil rights in the South when it was deadly dangerous.

He was pure, upright, incontrovertible, brilliant, almost overcome by internal fury. He had a furious smile. Khrushchev had just given his speech about Stalin's dementia. Things were falling apart and people were leaving the Communist Party in droves. But there was Strugin at the Party school, intense, boiling, insanely intelligent, speaking with measured fury to his classes. A pleasure to watch; you never could be sure if he might not murder a questioner. His favorite word was "indubitably."

Strugin would pause for many minutes to turn his back on the class (droolers, fat boys in shorts, white socks and sneakers, F.B.I. agents, Communist singles) to look out the window. On the blackboard in large letters he had written quotes from Stalin. Slogans from the master like: Ferret Out, Eliminate, Destroy. True blue Strugin. Weaklings might be deserting the master, but not Strugin. He was a rock. He had Scientific Reasons.

And unlike other Party bureaucrats who spoke very, very carefully, afraid they could be expelled any moment for a deviation (at one point looking Negroes in the eye was a deviation, at another not looking was one), Strugin reveled in naming the enemy with words like "scum," "human animals," "faggot honeybuns," "vermin," "garbage," and "trash." Said with gusto and spit. I got a big kick out of this as a kid. There was a revolutionary purity to Strugin. With him you just closed your eyes and got on the roller coaster. If I could be a Commie, I thought, that's the way to go. And Strugin has kept the faith over the years. Just recently I heard him refer to Social Democrats as "pen prostitutes, lice, vermin, bedbugs." I love Strugin to this day.

I arrived on the scene at the right moment: the Party had been decimated. There were more F.B.I. agents than real comrades. Strugin felt lonely and abandoned. He had taken to drinking bourbon and miming to Sinatra records. It was a thrill for him to see me, a "representative of the youth." He threw a blanket around me the first time he saw me, lest I catch cold and die. I appreciated his fervent response. Strugin took me into the inner Party orbit, introduced me to top leadership, read aloud his manuscripts to me and asked for my "dialectical criticism," and introduced me to his pretty daughter, Passionara. I wanted for nothing, rode around in taxis and treated underlings like shit.

And yet . . . the Party's lapdog attitude toward the Soviet Union was impossible to swallow. Were tractors, gray poverty, and slave labor camps that appealing? I wondered. Was it really necessary to use mushy Soviet condoms? To import expensive roses from the Soviet Union? All you got in your airmail package were withered stems. Comrades would pretend the flowers were abloom—"How beautiful!" they would scream, sniffing and pretending ecstasy, throwing their hands up in the air.

The Soviet connection was fascinating. Like being wired to a murder machine. Yet how they loved to deny the thing they loved. Earl Browder denied the Party's connection to any underground apparatus to the end of his life. His room on the ninth floor of Party headquarters at 35 East 12th Street in Manhattan adjoined that of J. Peters, who helped coordinate the underground of the Party across the United States. They passed each other in the hall every day, but were ships in the night.

"I pledge myself," said Earl Browder in 1935 to two thousand new Party members taking the oath, "to remain at all times a vigilant and firm defender of the Leninist line of the Party, the only line that ensures the triumph of Soviet Power in the United States."

And there were frustrations. The granddaughter of the famous Mother Minerva, who had been a Party legend, traveled from a Dakota farmstead to New York to join the revolutionary struggle and fuck her head off. Yet the bitch wouldn't fuck me. Winona was already thirty but had that youthful look that some Party dreamers kept most of their lives. She was pretty; she exuded sex. Winona permitted me only kisses, but she fucked every F.B.I. agent in sight. True, there were almost no Party members left around her age, and the few Communist males who were didn't fuck, work, or change their socks—ever. They were eaters, shouters, screamers, slurpers. Healthy revolutionary males in their thirties had to be F.B.I. men.

I tenderly see myself then, boiling with hatred and anxiety. But it wasn't just revolutionary. I was prematurely bald and I couldn't walk down the street without my hair turning into string. It drove me crazy. It made me want to kill. (Strugin promised to send me to the Soviet Union soon, where, he said, natural hair grew back "as a matter of course.") With Communist girls I could explain the hatred away as progressive. I'd say I was burning with hatred of the country, the system, the president: what America was doing to the world, bringing war and devastation and fascism to peace-loving peoples and systems. I said I couldn't take it one more minute, putting my hand on her knee. I added that I was involved in some kind of secret work—a white lie—and that if I were to suddenly disappear (a fierce look tinged with fatalism, incredible courage), well, that's what the risks were under fascism. Obviously my love life would be crushed soon and we'd better fuck now.

I still didn't get laid.

I did very, very well with old ladies, as you will see in this book.

Then, in June 1961, I traveled to "reactionary" Israel and worked on a kibbutz. I saw the tattooed numbers on the arms of the Israelis as they pitched cherries into bags in the golden sunlight. The comrades in New York had said, "What do you want to go there for?"

There are moments, like the sight of those arms in the sun, that slide into our consciousness, taking us unawares when we seem to be sleeping. And we are altered forever.

The thread had snapped.

RED LOVE

II

Ah, the Rubell case. The marches, the rallies. On the stage were marionettes of Dolly and Solly Rubell, political prisoners. The left side of the stage was captioned, Political Left: Rosy Dawns, Solidarity, Bread and Roses. The right side of the stage was captioned, Political Right: Fascism, McCarthyism, Heartlessness. The marionette figures of Dolly and Solly, their hearts filled with compassion, moved to the far left of the stage. Their heads were chopped off by a man in a black mask and bounced off the stage into the audience. A woman grabbed the heads, screamed, and raced down the aisle with them and out of the hall.

Music, chorus lines, fainting fits, screaming family members. Money was collected immediately after the most wrenching speech.

Then a leader of the Rubell Committee confided to me (I was thirteen at the time) over lunch that he had just read the trial transcript of the Rubell case for the first time. He asked me—of all people—"What if they are actually guilty?" This was the guy staging these rallies, and he was asking me?

A reporter later told me: "The most persistent mystery about these people is their seeming self-righteousness even though they knew they were guilty. Their public stance had fervor, sincerity, the passionate outrage of a brokenhearted man who was wronged. Their outrage—the position that the charges were all 'accursed lies.' The genuine feeling of being put upon even though they knew they did it. That's the essence of it. It's beyond politics." Then he said, "If you can handle that, you will write an outspoken book."

Look, it's simple: you take a dirty, rotten, filthy system like ours: the *worst* imaginable system, right? It's polluting the world, poisoning the flowers, turning innocent children into Zionists, etc., etc., you know the spiel. If a brave, selfless, little couple endeavor to *prick* that big-cocked monster for humanity's sake, for bread and roses, for children's laughter, what are they *guilty* of? Hold the image, and move the clock back to the 1940s, when Stalin was the little father, the role model for progressive humanity, the feeder of the hungry, and the gentlest, kindest, most noble human being in the world. What if that little couple is allowed the opportunity to help Stalin achieve his goals?

Guilty? Fie, fie! A thousand fies!

5

III

But I needed to hear it from them. Out of their own mouths, if you will. The Rubells were gone, but others were still here.

How do you deal with guile? With guile. And a sweet, soulful, trusting expression.

I interviewed hundreds for this book. I believed everyone as long as I was chatting with them. But a click would register in my head when I was home free. I'd gotten what I wanted. A wonderful feeling. They told me because they felt I was on their side. Was I? No, but I loved them and they knew that.

They were my family.

I called President Reagan to tell him the good news, but I didn't get through to him. Howie Mowshowitz called me back. He was the president's representative to the Jews of Borough Park.

"I told the president of your message," he said. "And the president said, and I quote, 'God bless you.' "

Then I met one of the Rubells' prosecutors, Hy Briské, in 1982. He was dressed in an oriental bathrobe at his mansion on Sutton Place. He was escorted by a younger man who remained silent and hovered somewhat behind him.

Hy Briské was dusty; he seemed to have an incapacity for the human experiment. Later I would learn he was being nice to me. I connected him to the Central Park West Jewish boys I knew in the 1950s, kids I met at the Concord in the Catskills at the Ping-Pong tables. I was poor and they were rich. (My father took me there to make me feel I was as good as the next kid. Afterward I would race back to Union Square and resume my other life.) Frequently father-less, these boys had the run of large apartments with servants and enormous quantities of frozen food (I had never seen it before) because their mothers lay in distant bedrooms with headaches and lovers. They were presidents of the Young Democrats; they didn't even want the civilized, gorgeous, adorable girls they met at Miss Wishrop's Dance Class; their bathroom cabinets were filled with astounding creams, colognes, and talcums.

But these were back-room boys, premature old men, lonely. Hy Briské was like that, absolutely. At our first ninety-second meeting, I made the mistake of telling him I wanted to write about him.

RED LOVE

He didn't show up for our second appointment. I wrote him. I'm sure my letter was bristling with controlled rage. He replied:

Dear Mr. Lerner:

Your letter arrived today. I want to set you straight. I'm a very busy man. I run a major law firm. I administer some worthy charities (Foundation for the Sicklies, Scumbunnies Anonymous, Prisoners' Self-Expression League, Jewish Punchers, Dog and Cat Club, etc.) and a score of other patriotic efforts. Plus I am deeply committed to my writing, most of which is of best-seller quality.

I am also at work on a posthumous pastel of Senator McCarthy which will reveal him as the true blue Joe I knew who fought to uproot the scab of Communism before it proved fatal for our country.

Considering all this, why should I take on the projects of others less handsome than myself? Nobody does my work for me.

I have been incredibly good to you, Lerner. My life has been complicated by a recent virus. I'd never been sick a day in my life before.

There's no doubt I should have told you to fuck off in the first place, but I have tried to find time for you. And you know, I'm still going to, despite your pretentious letter. Contact my colleague, Fifi Dorsay, to set things up.

Sincerely,

Hy Briské

I didn't answer him. Being a hysterically sensitive fiction writer and not a hard-boiled reporter type, I didn't think it was a nice letter. The "handsome" line enraged me for several years. Now I think it was, and I regret my silence. I saw him one more time, a year before his death, at a party. No one came near him because of the nature of his illness, although there were many whose ideologies matched his own.

I was afraid for much of my life.

When I was called down to my draft board, I feared they would find out about my connections to the Party. On my way there I carried three red leather volumes of Stalin's collected works which I wanted to destroy. I had tried to set them on fire at home, but they wouldn't catch. In my anxiety I forgot I was still carrying them until

I got within a block of Whitehall Street. Looking around to see if any nuts were watching me, I tried to casually drop them through the grates of sewers, but they were too thick. I picked them up again, garbage and litter falling off them, and hurled them into a stairwell.

That was 1958.

To this day I am the kind of fellow who, if he really *detests* other guests at a dinner party, may love them to death. I recently sat next to a poet over dinner who loved to write poems in honor of dictators she admired, like Castro, Assad, Qaddafi, and Ortega. She referred to Israel each time she had to mention it as, "that client state of the United States."

She asked me what the book I was writing was about. I felt that if I said one honest word to her, all my real feelings would come tumbling out or that even the one honest word would give me away. Even a word like "really?" or "wow." And that she would get me. So I told her only that this book was about "political radicals in the 1930s," plied her with admiring questions, gave her a fairly expensive set of pearls, and grinned when she toasted the Palestinians.

On my way out I heard her ask the host, "Why does that little guy hate me so much?"

It's difficult to get up in front of the world. Christ, it's even difficult to get up in a saloon and sing "Heart of My Heart" and do a little dance. I wanted to be a song-and-dance man in a high hat. Until life encroached.

Yet I wrote this book. I got the story of the true believers. I walked up to their front doors, rang their bells, and walked in when invited. Life became emotionally charged and rich.

Maury Ballinzweig's sister (Maury was codefendant with the Rubells) read a chapter from this book before she would see me. She criticized me for writing that the sister of the executed Solly Rubell said it was a tragedy that Solly "didn't live to experience the joys of television." I asked her about all the "nice" things I quoted Solly's sister as saying about him. She replied, "Yeah, but you pricked the balloon with that one." At another point, I told her that Maury had felt I was too "anti-Communist." She said, "What does this have to do with Communism?"

I stared at her, and smiled. "I don't know."

"I read your other books," she said. "You nitpicked your characters to death. You just spat them out. You know, you can get at the truth and be sympathetic, or you can get at the truth the way the F.B.I. tries to get at it. I can't give you any information."

"Your criticism of my books is marvelous, by the way," I said. "But I'm not looking for information. I'm looking for family background."

"That's information," she said. "From that information you draw your own conclusions."

"Maury talked to me," I said.

"Yeah. And he told me he was sorry." She laughed and kissed me.

I went to those who were most directly involved. They talked out of the need to talk, out of loneliness, because they wanted to be understood. Sometimes they jarred my understanding. When I heard that a grandson of the Rubells wrote in a creative writing class of his father's guilt about their death—that he had been unable to prevent it—I was stopped in my tracks and left alone with the human story.

IV

How I ever got Maury Ballinzweig, "the prince of progressive humanity" himself, to talk to me—that was exhilarating and impressive. Maury was convicted along with the Rubells. He had once been called one of the most dangerous espionage agents in America.

What happened was this: he was sensitive. I was sensitive. And we liked each other tremendously.

It was a case of sensitivity rewarded.

Maury had been photographed, taped, wired, spat upon, condescended to, despised, and generally screwed in every orifice. He should have awaited my visits with machine guns and barbed wire and baby tape recorders in corners. Instead he sat in his bare room waiting for me in his slippers, fortified by apricots, his radical publications, his picture of his father, his ideology. Maury was the pied piper of ragamuffin espionage. Lee Harvey Oswald wrote him a fan letter. The Weather people looked up to him as a mentor. In the

1980s he visited them in prison. When he entered the prison corridor, a hush descended as if the pope had arrived.

I worked up to calling Maury on the phone and then meeting him over the course of two years. I cultivated his former wife Linda and his other friends, learning all I could about him.

First I called Linda Ballinzweig. "Turtles get a great deal of satisfaction sitting and getting sunned on a rock," Linda told me, explaining how she had always been "attracted to a profound respect for things in and of themselves." She was sitting in my living room talking and darning socks. She went on to point out that this society did not have that "profound respect," and she traced it back to Columbus, who "came to this continent, looked at these people who welcomed him, and the first thought he had was how to use them." That was why, she said, she now conducted anti-Columbus celebrations in her classroom.

And Linda used Maury but good, while he was in prison, to make herself the toast of progressive society, a celebrity from coast to coast and continent to continent.

I wanted to understand more, I told Linda in my living room. The idealism, the hope, Spain, antifascism in the thirties and forties.

"You want to build a bridge over the Holocaust," she said.

Sure, why not? "Yes," I said simply.

"I was in Washington," Linda said, "in the park, picketing, when we heard that the Rubells were murdered. Shit on a stick! We lined up to put away our signs on the truck. As each sign was lowered on the truck, into a huge growing pile, it was as if a part of the world's virtue were being destroyed and savagery were winning sway.

"Maury was meant to testify against Dolly and Solly," she said. "Dolly and Solly were meant to testify against others. Concentration camps were ready, you know. The F.B.I. came to Maury and told him he was a patsy for not testifying. After the Rubells' death, they wanted someone to wash their hands for them."

I asked her: "How would you describe Maury?"

"He's a hedgehog: a prickly outer shell which he uses to protect his soft inner self."

"I would like to meet him," I said, as if it were a new thought.

"You can try," she said. "Here is his number and address."

She was leaving New York to teach the art of software in Cleveland.

When we said goodbye, she said, "I want to help you." Then she kissed me on the mouth. She raised one orthopedic shoe behind her as we clinched.

I wrote a heartfelt letter to Maury Ballinzweig and made out my will in case he decided to have me bumped off. Weeks passed. Heartbroken, I wrote him again and told him how depressed I was about not hearing from him.

And then a letter came:

Dear Gerald,

Mea culpa! Yes, I was touched by your letter.

You mustn't get so depressed. Keeping busy and active helps.

But so many years have passed. I'm not sure my memories of Dolly and Solly will have the clarity you need. But I'll try. The question is when. My daughter is coming to see me next week so I'll be busy. Soon after that. Call me?

Again, I'm sorry. But you were very much on my mind. Your name, "Desperate Gerald," is on my bulletin board in big letters.

Maury

358-9704

What a sweet letter! I decided Maury was innocent after all. But those moods don't last.

I called Maury after a martini, a tranquilizer, and black coffee. The first phone conversation took place in December 1982. Maury's voice on the phone was Brooklyn Jewish with little curls of refinement. There was whining in it, weeping, and a bubbling joy. And such sophistication—Maury knew psychology! Art exhibits! Hemingway's male chauvinism! There was also an alacrity in his response to me, openness, suspicion, curiosity, and friendliness. But he was not willing to schedule a date for our meeting yet.

Three weeks and ten phone calls later, we set a date, and I met Maury at his apartment for four hours. After I left, I stood in a freezing doorway and wrote in my notebook:

When we said goodbye, we shook hands, and when I began to pull away, Maury held my hand for a moment longer.

This is a very lonely person. A sweet person.

The inner man is very close to the surface. Maury wants to make himself known to someone who can understand.

Wasn't he lucky he found me?

And so my novel began.

When I called Maury for a second appointment, he seemed upset. He said he had spent the weekend visiting two "friends": one of the Weather people and a Roumanian convicted on espionage and conspiracy charges for supplying classified information to Cuba.

The Weather lady had killed several innocent passersby during a holdup. Maury told me that the impact of visiting her had been so traumatic that afterward he'd had to stop his car on the side of the road and close his eyes. He told me the Weather lady had been moved by his example, and she kept his picture on the wall of her cell.

Maury said he hadn't been sleeping well and that his work was going badly. He seemed to relate these problems to our meeting. He said he'd been reading some of my stories in my earlier books, *Hot Pastrami Sandwich* and *Kosher and Topless*, and that he "envied" my ability. But while he admired the writing, he said, he did not always care for what my writing was *saying* politically.

"The problem," Maury said, "is that, really, Gerald, I am a political person, and the humanist side of things does not really turn me on."

My voice trembled as I said, "I wish you wouldn't close me out, Maury."

"You're not closed out! *Believe me*, Gerald, believe me, you're not closed out. Let me solve my problems of the moment. I'll try to—look, look—I'm putting you up on my bulletin board again—up you go—so I won't forget."

When I called Maury next, he said, "Ah, bad news, bad news. I mean I still got all this other stuff to do." Maury said he was working as a technical adviser for Nicaragua, Cuba, and Vietnam. "Look," he said, "maybe we'll get together in the springtime when it's nice and sunny."

I didn't speak.

"Gerry? Gerry? Are you there? Listen to me. I promise. When the sun comes out in Riverside Park, when it's nice and sunny, we'll find a pleasant bench and we'll talk."

V

I had discussed everything with my psychiatrist in Chicago, who analyzed Maury for me and told me how to approach him. Now I was desperate, yet it had become difficult to fly to Chicago from New York more than once a week to see him. My debt is staggering. I called Dr. Goldberg again and said I had to see him to talk about my problems with Maury.

Dr. Goldberg sighed. "You promised me."

"What?"

"You promised you wouldn't talk about your problems anymore."

It was true. After seeing Dr. Goldberg for thirty-three years, years during which we had both aged, had our ups and downs, and gone through many changes, Dr. Goldberg had told me he wanted to only talk about himself from now on.

For years Dr. Goldberg invited me to visit him in Maine in the summer. He had a summer house there. Even when we walked in the woods, in his gray shirt, shorts, and little argyle socks, Goldberg was alert to human grief. He would turn our walks into brief therapy sessions, which he interspersed with bird-watching.

"I have needs too," he said now. "My patients become my healers. It's your turn, Gerald.

"I was always shy as a young man," he said. "My father would say that suffering is the law of life . . ." he began, and I couldn't get a word in edgewise from then on. I think he felt I owed him since I never paid him for my therapy. Dr. Goldberg talked to me for eight months on how Ronald Reagan was ruining his life. "All therapy is pointless until we get rid of him," he said.

"A blind girl knocked at my door," Dr. Goldberg continued. "She was looking for a room. She wore dark glasses. She came by at the suggestion of a patient, Bob Starr, who said she was a witch. Before I could decide whether to let her stay, the doorbell rang again, and a bunch of people came in and trudged upstairs with boxes of her stuff. I said 'wait a minute,' and she said, 'You wouldn't want to be known as a doctor who put a blind girl out on the street.'

"Now I can't get rid of her. She's taken over the house. She has a malign presence, an aura, and a vast network of people who are devoted to her. I told her she had to leave, and a lawyer's letter

13

arrived several days later. It had the same refrain: 'You wouldn't want a news story that says a noted doctor put a blind girl out on the street.' Even Bob Starr, who used to hate her, comes to see her now. I see him disappearing into her room. He says, 'She has a way of moving her body.' "

"But what about Maury—" I shouted at him.

He sighed. "From what you tell me," he said, "Maury is a very warm, affectionate person. Especially for a former spy. He wants to carry on this relationship with you, but he doesn't really know quite how to do it.

"There's an essential conflict," Dr. Goldberg said. "He has to deny that he's important on a personal level, since he's only important in his own view if he furthers his political ideology. He feels his heroism is in his martyrdom. By letting him know you think his own story is important, you're telling him that *he's* important. Maybe he's beginning to sense there's something important about him that no one else realized. In a way you are re-creating him, establishing him as a person of significance in a world that rejected him. You may be the only one who's communicated this to him. He isn't going to let you go, Gerald, but he isn't going to make it easy for you to get to him either. Now can I talk about myself?"

The next time we talked, Dr. Goldberg said, "You've got to realize he'll only be willing to talk on a superficial level at first. He's glad to find somebody who doesn't see him just as a political entity, but he'll never admit that. That's his armor.

"He sees you as a person with genuine feeling for him. That's very moving to him. But when he's alone afterward and begins to think it over, he must have reservations about what he's doing. He may feel guilty about the extent to which he thinks he's betraying the memory of people he felt a very strong tie to."

"He has good reason not to trust anybody," I said.

"Yes, the story is one of betrayal, and he is not at all persuaded that he won't be betrayed again."

I said, "Maury commented to me about the Rubells, 'I can't compete with death.' "

"Maybe that's the important thing," Goldberg said. "They got more in their death, while he was neglected because he only had to spend sixteen years in prison. By comparison it seems trivial. He sounds to me as if he may be on the verge of disillusionment with his ideology, and you, by making him reflect, may push him over. He's already too close to cynicism—that's what he has to protect himself from."

Goldberg continued: "You say Maury's joyful, but his gaiety sounds too forced to me. You don't know where it's coming from. Where is his bitterness? What is he so cheerful about? I wish I could be that cheerful.

"By the way, I'm not sure that girl is blind."

In the spring, in early May, when it was nice and sunny, as he had promised, Maury saw me again.

And despite what Dr. Goldberg said, Maury did let me go—as you will learn.

At our parting he said: "You are too full of feeling."

Dr. Goldberg commented about this: "You remind Maury of himself as a vulnerable young man. To deny that part of himself, he takes it out and places it in you."

VI

I received many responses to my ads. One was a warning. Mailed from one of the laboratories in New York State where some famous people accused of spying for the Soviets worked in the 1950s, and using the pseudonym "Ravichaux," the letter contained a crude drawing in red of a hammer and sickle, and the words:

WEBBER—SPOOK—CAREFUL

Michael Webber was a respectable figure, a reputable character who had lectured about the innocence of the people I was writing about. I took the letter to the F.B.I. The agent, fending off my kisses, looked at the letter and said it could have been sent by a nut, but maybe not. (He also looked me over for a long time.) I began to look into Webber. What I learned about him suggested that the letter was not sent by a deranged person.

Another came in a perfumed pink envelope:

I tingle when I say this: I am a great-niece of Solomon and Dolores Rubell. And it's not because death turns me on that I feel this. I am a third generation Leninist. And I am the star of a goodly number of hardcore films.

I know by heart the fabled story of how Solomon Rubell was a yeshiva boy, a wimpish lad with a yarmulke planted firmly on his head. One day he read Stalin's *The Kidneys of Leninism*, and it freaked him out. He became an internationalist, and realized that we are all One.

Because of this, I am what I am today. I do not consider myself a deep thinker like Solomon or Dolores, but more a socialist of the heart. But when I pass the Soviet embassy, to this day I feel a tingle.

I began stripping at the blessedly early age of seventeen at Dapper Dan's Burlesque in New York City. My father, who is now a Zen Master, turned me on to Alexandra Kollontai's Glass of Water theory of sex. Sex, to Alexandra, was as natural as drinking a glass of water. It was as simple, and profound, as that. And she was one of Bolshevism's stars.

Dolly and Solly are part of me: they followed their own star. The legend has come down the annals of time on how advanced they were about eating the pig at a time when such conduct subjected them to ridicule by all the "yarmulkes" around them. I simply have taken their example one step further as the *pièce de résistance* of my latest film—and deeper.

My theatrical name, Suzie Sizzle, was chosen because it is simple and even the tourists from Hong Kong can say it. I have always been a perfectionist: my male partners must be horny rabbits.

One day I will retire to the shadows, pursuing my other passion, library science. I want to practice it somewhere it would truly be appreciated, like Cuba or Libya.

But before I go, my dearest wish is to stick progressive and feminist concepts into my movies and give them sex appeal. I'd love to do the relationship of George Jackson and Fay Stender (before things got tacky), and other hot items in the great progressive panoply.

But the story I want most of all to bring to the world is the love story of Dolly and Solly. I would call it *Red Love*.

VII

Getting this story right was like leaving betraying parents behind, looking at the naked body of a woman without fear—like leaving a false family. I remember the trap to this day, the lull of the Communists. They were so ridiculous, yet they offered a love-starved boy the world, or at least the trappings of it. (Delicious food anyway, a job, open arms). If I'd sacrificed my sanity, I would have had all that.

So this book was an act of sanity. I have, instead, sacrificed the innocence of the Rubells—of that strange family—forever.

Family.

One Monday night in spring, I was with the gang at my favorite Italian bistro in the Village, Frankie D's. I play the tambourine if no one else feels like it. Frankie D's was a place that was integrated before America was.

That night Big John was there, Big Bob, Big Joe, Big Carlo, Big Nate, Big Earl, Big Chaim, Big Ernest—and me, Big Gerald. Big Norm, who calls himself a soul dancer, moved his head—only his head—to the music, back and forth with increasing ecstasy. When he was really moved, he flung his high hat and his leather jacket on a bar chair, and, holding his nose lest it fall off, whirled around and around in a circle.

I love this place with my life, and especially Vinnie Cardinali. Vinnie sings and orchestrates the night. There is a great picture of Frank, Dean, and a monsignor behind him. He is a waiter the other days of the week. Monday is his big night. Vinnie is a devout Catholic. On rare occasions he will say "God bless you." And you do feel blessed.

If this had been my family, oh man, would I be whirling around the room—all of me, hitting those high notes, like Jimmy Roselli, or those powerful nuanced phrases, like Francis Albert or Tony Bennett. Not just timidly tapping the tambourine.

Vinnie once told me, "I want to be like Alan Freed, gathering in all these souls. I go on there like a volcano. It can be too much. If I'm depressed I can bring them so low."

That Monday night we all gathered expectantly. Vinnie had told us a month ago that on that night the daughter he hadn't seen for fifteen years, since she was three, would be coming to Frankie D's to see him.

We waited: Billy the bellhop, Charlie the cop, Julie the teacher, Art the labor arbitrator, Vito the construction worker—the whole gang. Vinnie and his father sang "Heart of My Heart." Vinnie's Aunt Nina took pictures. We waited. She had to show. Everybody roots for Vinnie: to find another wife, to go beyond Frankie D's. He's forty-two and seems to want nothing for himself. He's had two. "In my religion, the Catholic religion," he said, "it's for life."

"It's crazy," he said. "Which is the real marriage—the first one, that the Church said was real but I was scared to death, or the second one, when I really loved her?" He still wears the ring, although his wife has been gone for years.

A blond girl came through the swinging door. Big Dan from Wall Street took her arm and escorted her to Vinnie. She smiled. Vinnie sang "Baby Face." We stood on table tops.

"To all of you," Vinnie said, "who have told me of wanting to find your heart's desire—now I understand what you meant."

And he took his daughter in his arms and danced with her.

Then Vinnie sang "Cheek to Cheek," and he remembered that when he was six, he was watching Fred and Ginger dance to it on TV and that suddenly his Aunt Nina and Uncle Mario were whirling around the room in front of the TV. Big Dan bowed to Aunt Nina then, and while Vinnie played and sang "Cheek to Cheek," Aunt Nina dipped and whirled in the arms of Big Dan.

I watched Vinnie, his daughter Maria, his father Rocco, his Aunt Nina. At 1 A.M. Vinnie's new girl came off work. Red-haired and nurturing, a good, solid face; she pressed up behind Vinnie and put her arms around him.

Around 3:30 Big Lou, the bartender, did his specialty, but he did it differently; he sang it to Maria at the bar—"Slow Boat to China." We were rocking, we were whirling; Maria had come home.

I began to write this book in 1980 and have published sections of it in *Heartless*, *Get a Job*, and other reactionary literary magazines. Yet for eight years I continued to walk through the front doors of "progressives" without incurring suspicion or hostility. Sometimes I was afraid. But my fears were usually unjustified. These people never read anything that contradicted their world view.

But in 1988, at Fat Tuesday's, a club in Manhattan, I ran into the "progressive historian" of the Rubell case I had written about in the chapter called "The Prince of Progressive Humanity." This was the scholar who believed the Soviet Union had never once engaged in espionage because the Soviet constitution forbade it. I had had such a streak of luck all these years that I may have been a little giddy by then. On the way out, I shook the historian's hand, and reminded him who I was.

"How dare you shake my hand?" he screamed, his face livid. "Fie! Fie! You wrote that horrible story. Get outta here. Such a terrible betrayal!" He shouted to everyone around him: "Don't talk to him. Don't say a word! That's Gerald Lerner! He wrote that story in *Heartless*! You'll wind up in the files of the F.B.I.!" His shouts followed me down the street.

His feelings were understandable: I nailed him in the story with his own words. I did not, however, quote one thing he told me: that when he took a date to a Rubell rally in the 1950s, with emotions so high, he always got laid.

Wait a minute. This is not what he actually said. I softened it. What am I afraid of? The Rubells left a legacy of love, didn't they?

What he said was that he always took a date along with him when he took the Rubell children to see the Rubells at Sing Sing. Afterward, he said, he always got laid.

Catch me some Monday night at Frankie D's. The little guy at center stage, in the spotlight, singing "Heart of My Heart."

The F.B.I. Log

The F.B.I.'s version of events. If you have a
warm bone in your body, you will disregard it.

—G.L.

Teletype June 20, 1950. The following information obtained by Special Agent Tabackin on subject Solomon Rubell. Born November 3, 1919, New York City. Father: Ben Rubell, same address, born Russia. Came to U.S. at age fifteen and naturalized five or six years before World War I. Mother: Sarah Rubell, née Goldberg, came to U.S. and naturalized through husband.

First job: Frederick Electric Company, 25 East 63rd Street, New York City. Next job: soda clerk, 1938, Joffe's Pharmacy, Seventh Avenue and 132nd Street, New York City. May to June 1942: tool designer, Richards Company, 42nd Street and Sixth Avenue, New York City.

Married Dolores Stern, April 1942 in New York City. First marriage for both. Her parents, both born in Russia, are naturalized. Subject claimed to own no property and to possess personal property worth $180. Maintains joint savings account with wife at Manhattan Savings Bank, Delancey and Essex streets, New York City. 1942 balance about $203. Only income is from salary. No debts. Avocations of subject given as aviation, radio, attending movies, folk dancing, playing checkers and chess, Ping-Pong and tennis. Physical description: 5 feet 7½ inches, weight 142, no physical defects.

Subject denied membership in the Communist Party or any subversive group, though admitted sometimes feeling "moony" about the contributions made by the Soviet Union to the war effort.

Teletype June 23, 1950. Interview with Hershie Stern. Solomon Rubell asked Hershie Stern's wife, Jelly, if he, Hershie Stern, would give information to the Soviet Union. The USSR was fighting the enemy and was entitled to the info.

Hershie Stern is the brother of Dolores Rubell, Solomon's wife. Stern has stated that on or about October 3, 1944, his wife Jelly arrived in New Mexico from New York City and advised him that Solomon had requested that he furnish information to the Soviet Union. Hershie agreed.

Hershie Stern advised that Rubell had two apartments for micro-filming in New York City, one in Greenwich Village. Joe Klein rented the apartment at 29 Perry Street from Rubell, maintaining it until 1947. Klein turned it over to Robert Metzger in 1947.

Stern identified Sid Smorg from newspaper pictures as the individual who contacted him sometime during the summer of 1945 for information. Hershie admitted to having received $800 from Smorg on this occasion. Hershie furnished Smorg with a list of persons who he thought could be approached for information. Hershie said he gave Smorg a sketch of the bomb. Smorg advised Stern that he would come back to see him again. However, no further contact was made by Smorg.

Stern furnished the following information regarding Solomon Rubell: he resides at 110 Catherine Street with his two children and his wife Dolores (or Dolly), who is Hershie Stern's sister. Rubell is the owner of Great Machine Products, 389 Madison Street, New York City. Solomon Rubell is thirty years of age, a graduate student in engineering at City College. Stern knows that Smorg has positively identified himself as the soldier he met in June 1945 in New Mexico.

Teletype July 5, 1950. Solomon Rubell interviewed by agent Tabackin for 80 minutes. Rubell appeared to be frightened but was unresponsive. After calling his lawyer and being advised he could leave, he politely departed.

Teletype July 7, 1950. In view of Hershie Stern's confession and Solomon Rubell's imminent arrest, it is deemed advisable to interview Robert Metzger, Joe Klein, and Jed Levine regarding their possible involvement in espionage as part of Rubell's network. With respect to these three, it is desired you give careful consideration and preparation for these interviews and institute them as soon as possible. You should in the course of these interviews attempt to secure consent to search individuals' residences. You should bear in mind that these individuals do not know that Rubell has not confessed. They should be utilized by attempting to have them furnish us details concerning their espionage activities with Rubell.

Teletype July 7, 1950. 7 P.M. Supervisor Webster of the New York office telephonically furnished the complaint which had been drawn up against Rubell, charging him with a violation of Section 34 of Title 50, U.S. Code. The complaint was sworn due by Special Agent Tabackin before Federal Judge John F. McCuddihy. Thereafter issued a bench warrant for Rubell's apprehension. The warrant was issued at 5:35 P.M. and Special Agents Tabackin and Steiner were dispatched to apprehend Rubell, who has been under intensive surveillance for the last several hours following a determination by the department that he should be apprehended.

8:35 P.M. Sergeant O'Neill called to advise that the subject had been apprehended at his home at 7:18 P.M. and the agents were conducting the search of his apartment incidental to arrest. At 8:30 Sergeant O'Neill called to advise that the search would be completed at 8:45, at which time Rubell would be brought to the office to be arraigned before a federal judge.

9:15 P.M. Special Agent Steiner advised that the search was practically completed and Rubell would be brought to the office promptly.

Addendum: at 9:48 P.M. A.S.C. Burwell advised that Rubell had been brought into the U.S. courthouse for fingerprinting and photographing. As a matter of record, he advised that the agents entered Rubell's apartment at 7:18 P.M. and completed the search at 9:25 P.M. No trouble was encountered. Dolly, Rubell's wife, made typical Communist remonstrances, demanding a warrant and wanting to call an attorney. She was told to keep quiet and get in the other room with the children, which she did. Inasmuch as the children were making a considerable fuss and Dolly Rubell refused to talk, she and the children were dispatched to her mother's home in the company of two agents. At 9:32 P.M., Special Agent Tabackin advised that they would attempt to talk with Solomon Rubell for about an hour to see if he would cooperate, after which he would be brought before Judge McCuddihy.

At 10:10 P.M. Special Agent Steiner advised that Dolly Rubell had called attorney Henky Rubin, who is well known for his Communist connections. Rubin contacted U.S. Attorney Marv Duboff, and Rubell would not talk without consulting his attorney. Therefore agents are going to arraign him.

At 10:25 P.M. Special Agent Tabackin advised that the subject was being taken down to Mr. Duboff's office. Duboff had come in from New Jersey for the arraignment.

At 11:55 P.M. Special Agent Tabackin advised that Rubell was arraigned before Judge McCuddihy and remanded to the custody of the marshal in lieu of $100,000 bail. The hearing was set for July 25 with the right to make motions between now and that time. Special Agent Tabackin advised that considerable data, such as checkbooks, papers, cameras, etc., resulted from the search, and the agents are going over them carefully to see what is pertinent.

Inasmuch as it appears that Rubell will not be cooperative and the indications are definite that he possesses information concerning the identity of a number of other individuals who have been engaged in Soviet espionage, New York should consider every possible means of bringing pressure on Rubell to make him talk. A careful study should be done of the involvement of Dolly Rubell in order that charges can be brought against her if possible.

Teletype July 20, 1950. Mr. Stevens called from New York at 12:20 A.M. to advise that the interview with Jed Levine had been completed. He said Levine appeared to be cooperative. A signed statement regarding what he knew had been obtained from Levine, and he voluntarily consented to a search of his premises, which has been done.

Levine contended that Rubell contacted him several times beginning in 1944. Levine was working for the Bureau of Ordnance in Washington, D.C., on fire control equipment for naval vessels. Rubell spoke of the Russian war effort and the sacrifice of the Soviets and said some people were contributing to the Russian war effort by giving them info on secret material and developments. He asked Levine to contribute by giving reports and drawings concerning the projects on which he was working. On about eight occasions Rubell solicited Levine for information. But Levine maintains he never gave it, either orally or in writing. He finally told Rubell he had thought the matter over and could not go along with him.

He then told Rubell he was contemplating going to New York City to work for the Howland Instrument Company on fire control equipment. Rubell expressed his disappointment and said he would prefer that Levine stay with the Bureau of Ordnance.

Levine advised that Rubell told him that Maury Ballinzweig, Levine's neighbor, who was employed at the Howland Instrument Company at the time, was one of the persons furnishing information to the Russians. Ballinzweig left the Howland Instrument Company about the beginning of July, 1950, and failed to return. His whereabouts are unknown. He left his residence on about July 5, 1950, with his wife and child, and his sister-in-law, who is now occupying his home, advised Levine that Ballinzweig "has gone to the farm to recuperate."

Levine said that recently Ballinzweig appeared to be very nervous. Bureau files state that Maury Ballinzweig was born on June 3, 1917, in New York City. His parents were born in Russia. He is married to Linda Ballinzweig, and resides directly in the rear of the Levine home.

Ballinzweig is a graduate of the City College of New York, with a bachelor's degree in engineering. He was employed by the Navy Department, Bureau of Ordnance, in Washington, D.C. from 1939 through 1941, when he resigned to enter the University of Oregon. He and Levine roomed together in Washington, D.C. Earlier they had attended the City College of New York together. He was active in the American Youth Congress and the American Peace Society.

A complete review of all our references on Ballinzweig has not been made as yet. This will be done immediately.

Every effort should be made to locate Ballinzweig immediately.

Teletype July 25, 1950. In connection with espionage activity of Solomon Rubell, recently arrested, he operated a network probably including Robert Metzger, employee of National Advisory Committee for Aeronautics, Pittsburgh, Pa.

Every attempt should be made to locate and thoroughly interview Joe Klein, last known address—23, rue Lagore, Paris. Klein formerly worked in the Army Signal Corps, Fort Monmouth, New Jersey. In 1949 he went to Holland to study butterfly art. Visited Finland, thereafter went to France. Stern said that Rubell told him Klein had left because he feared his espionage activities would be exposed. Klein should be closely questioned re apartment 29 Perry Street on whether photo equipment maintained in that apartment was for espionage purposes. He should be questioned re his ownership of Leica camera and where he obtained it. He should be asked when he intends to return to U.S.

The Death House, 1954

Solly Rubell near the end of the road.

       —G.L.

If Solly Rubell were asked before that week if he were sure of what he had done, he would have said yes. There was always the terror of dying. But the worst thing was this dot of doubt.

A former comrade who'd fought in Spain had written him in the death house. He had been taken off guard.

> Dear Comrade Solomon:
> I'm a Lincoln vet.
> I want to tell you what you're dying for.
> This letter is going to light a firecracker up your ass.
> Here is what I know . . .

The vet had a foul mouth, but the letter clanged in his head. Then he'd wanted to burn it, but he had to keep reading, until the world seemed to be turning upside down. He couldn't keep it out of his headaches and nightmares at night.

The vet wrote of Spain. And of the Soviet Union: starving men and women, peasants and workers, sores oozing from their faces and legs, gathered at garbage cans looking for food during collectivization. Rounded up by guards with whips and guns. The stoned pavement scraping their bare feet, tossed like sacks of flour or bales of hay into freight cars, weeping and screaming for help. Taken to areas where they would starve unseen.

Tens of millions tortured to death in concentration camps.

Then the vet told him of the Jewish doctors' plot, the murder of Peretz Markish and the other Yiddish poets, the Slánský trial in Czechoslovakia.

> Comrade Solomon, I come from where you come from. Once I thought I knew the score too. I put my body on the line for Stalin, that putz, that sadist, like you are doing now. But this is fascism, comrade. This is the most anti-Semitic regime on earth—shit and filth and torture and human suffering like you can't believe.
>
> Is this worth dying for? Sacrificing your children for?
>
> Sammy Kuznekov

He tried to tell Dolly about the letter. She rose up, proclaiming, "What? You too? Methinks you're beguiled by their offers of forty pieces of silver!" She told him to leave her cell.

She never spoke to him again.

How Sammy Kuznekow Became a Vacillating Element in Spain

Avoid foreign places.

—G.L.

Sammy Kuznekov had been an orphan since the age of two. He came to America from Russia in 1928. He was hungry all the time. He'd ridden the rails, worked on a gas pipeline in Montana, hung around the Wobblies, shipped out as a seaman, and later was an organizer for the farm workers and the Marine Workers Industrial Union. He joined the Young Communist League in Houston, Texas.

He had sung with the Wobs:

> Shall we always slave and work for wages?
> It is outrageous.

In North Dakota he'd seen A. C. Townley, preacher and Silver Shirt, spread straw on the floor at the start of a meeting. As the farmers came in Townley said, "You goddamn bunch of cattle, I hope you feel at home." They loved it.

Sammy, Jewish, looked like a handsome Nordic devil. A six-foot-two-inch, chestnut-haired, broad-shouldered man, the Party could use him anywhere. J. Peters himself told Sammy, "You look a thousand percent American."

In 1935 Sammy came to New York City and became secretary of the Young Communist League on the waterfront. He took part in the famed action against the SS *Bremen*, a Nazi ship. Dressed in a tuxedo, he mingled with the hoi polloi, his brass knuckles hidden. When the signal came, the comrades ran across the deck and up to the front where the Nazi flag waved. The Nazi soldiers, not knowing who was who in the elegant crowd, hesitated. Then they struck out blindly. The Y.C.L.ers, kicking off the Nazis, cut the lanyard and the Nazi flag fell. They sang the "Internationale" as they ran.

When the Party moved like this, Sammy was sure of his path and his destiny.

Sammy was recruited by J. Peters for the Party's antimilitary work. Peters's office on the ninth floor of Party headquarters adjoined those of Brown, the Comintern rep, and Earl Browder.

He attended Peters' course on "How to Organize Party Cells in the Armed Forces." Peters urged the comrades to join the National Guard or to get into the Brooklyn Navy Yard. The route to getting into the guard was first to join the Citizens Military Training Camp at Fort Dix.

Sammy remembered going to City College's campus and seeing the demonstrations against the ROTC. He had looked at the ranks of the ROTC, and thought, my God, they're all Y.C.L.ers! Then who were the demonstrators? The Party had mobilized outside elements as protestors. The real comrades going to CCNY were right there, on the way to becoming officers.

His course completed, Sammy went to see Peters. "You'll drop your waterfront work. I want you to be one of our key contacts," Peters said.

"There's one problem, comrade," Sammy said. "I'm not a citizen. And I've been arrested a few times."

"Eh! American police. They're *schlumperei*. Don't worry about it. I want you to go to San Antonio, Texas. We have contacts at Kelly Field."

Peters took out a copy of *Smith and Wesson Magazine* and taught Sammy how to write messages to him. One, three, four, he explained, meant first page, third paragraph, fourth word. Whenever he wanted to send a message to Peters, he was to go to the local library and use the magazine. "It's so simple, it's beautiful," Peters said. "If you don't know what magazine to use, you're lost. Simplicity is best."

Almost fifteen years later, when the Rubells were arrested, Sammy would read about an Ex-Lax box top cut in half, and Solomon Rubell's alleged words, "The simplest things are the cleverest."

Ah, Peters, Sammy thought.

Sammy Kuznekov eased himself out of antiwar work. He left Kelly Field and returned to New York, telling Peters his effectiveness was compromised by his inability to join the armed forces. He was ready to ship out to sea again.

At the May Day parade in Union Square in 1936, a Spanish navy cadet training ship, the *Juan Sebastián Elcano*, representing the Popular Front government of Republican Spain that had been elected that February, came rolling by on wheels. The officers and cadets were greeted with wild applause by the demonstrators. A Spanish seaman made a speech. Sammy was struck by their proud presence, their commitment. They had *grundschaft*, they came right out of the Spanish revolutionary tradition.

Working a private ship off the coast of Cuba, the radio operator, Sparks, told Sammy, "Well, the war is starting." The military had risen against the Spanish Republican government; civil war was breaking out. Sammy thought of those seamen he'd seen in the May Day parade, and a shiver passed through him.

Hurrying back to New York, he went to see the Comintern rep, Brown, on the ninth floor of Party headquarters. "I hear the time has come," Sammy said. He drilled with the other recruits at Ukrainian Hall, helped recruit for Spain on the waterfront, and slept at night on a cot at the Seaman's Church Institute on South Street.

Sammy and the other boys were given a farewell party at a movie theater near Union Square. Earl Browder, the "quiet man from Kansas" with the soul of a file clerk, stood by the door saying goodbye to the boys. Puffing a big cigar, Browder shook Sammy's hand, and for a long time after Sammy couldn't get the feel of that fat, clammy hand off of his skin.

He sailed December 26th on the *Normandie*, a stowaway in a cabin with two others because he wasn't a U.S. citizen. There were one hundred and six men secretly bound for Spain and thirteen Lebanese rug merchants.

From Le Havre they took the night train to Perpignan. The men all sang the "Internationale" in their own languages. They traveled through Avignon and Narbonne, and from train windows they raised the Popular Front clenched fist to the natives. "*Viva la republica!*" they shouted as the train clambered across the frontier into Spain.

At Figueras, the people cheered them and pelted them with al-
monds. Barcelona, then Tarragona, where almond trees blossomed
pink and orange trees shone in the sun. Spaniards clenched fists,
calling out "*Salud*" to them.

On January 8th they reached Albacete, headquarters of the International Brigades, and marched behind a German band to the Guardia
Nacional barracks. They stood together in a courtyard, with all the
windows and doors facing inward.

Toilets were four holes on each floor of the building. As the men
defecated on the lower floors, there was a curtain of feces falling
behind them from all the other floors. It was constantly coming
down in all four corners of the building. The smell was intense.
They did not care; they were finally in the headquarters of the
brigade.

In the morning they were told to line up in the bullring. As they
stood there, they heard an operatic bugle call from the iron balcony.
They looked up. The door swung open and a huge character with a
big white moustache and a giant black beret walked out. It was
André Marty, supreme commander.

Six foot three, the splendid Marty approached the French recruits
and said in a foghorn voice, "The glory of France will endure
forever." Approaching the Americans, he bellowed, "Now that the
Yanks have arrived, the war will soon be over." The British: "Who
can ever forget the courage of the English square?" The Germans,
Roumanians, Hungarians, and finally the Italians: "All the greatest
soldiers in the Grand Army of Napoleon were Italians." Sammy was
probably the only man who understood almost every language (he
did not know Roumanian).

The bugler blew once more, Marty made a grand gesture of
salute, shouted, "*Viva la republica!*" and was whisked into his limou-
sine decked with small flags by his chauffeur and aides.

Sammy and all the other men felt the buttons flying off their
chests.

They arrived at the training camp at Villa Nueva de la Jara after a
week at Albacete. There was almost no target practice because there
was no live ammunition. There were no trench mortars. There were
three rifles, but they jammed after each shot. The men knocked
open their bolts with a rock. Each man gave the next a chance with

the gun. They passed around a defused Mills "to get a feel of the hand grenade thing." They were taken by truck at night for their first shooting exercise. Permitted five rounds, they fired into the hills and then were taken back to camp.

The Americans opened the battalion clinic to the civilian population as a free hospital. They produced a musical in which a black man recited Langston Hughes's "Scottsboro," and they sang the "Marching Song of the Lincoln Battalion." The villagers had been antagonized by the previous group of French volunteers who had raped women and seized wine cellars. These Americans, who did not drink, recited poetry and sang songs, won them over.

Sammy's expertise in Russian got him a post as a runner for the brigade commander, and he got to Albacete frequently.

One day he walked out on to the second floor of the Albacete Guardia Nacional and heard a familiar voice. As he stood by the railing, above the putt-putt of feces from the graduated toilets, he heard Marty declaiming. He looked up. Marty was addressing a new group of volunteers.

"The glory of France will continue forever . . . Now that the Yanks have arrived, the war will soon be over . . . All the greatest soldiers in the Grand Army of Napoleon were Italian. . . ."

Putt-putt, putt-putt.

On February 15th, the American volunteers were assembled at the Albacete bullring again. André Marty stood on the floodlit bandstand. He told them that the Republican front along the Jarama River had caved in. It was up to them to save Madrid. *"No pasaran!"* they shouted with clenched fists.

They were given rifles, fifty rounds of ammunition, Mills bombs, and triangulated bayonets. The battalion climbed aboard the trucks at midnight and headed toward Madrid, one hundred and fifty miles northwest. They dismounted at Morata de Tajuña, where suddenly a squadron of Italian bombers appeared. Many of the men stood and gawked as the bombs exploded, instead of taking cover. At that moment six Russian planes appeared and chewed away at the Capronis, knocking them out of the air. The Americans cheered, slapping each other on the back, firing their rifles into the sky.

A German Interbrigader led them up the mountain. Looking back, they looked at the pear trees and poplars along the river.

When they reached a flat-topped knoll, the German told them to dig in. The ground was almost pure rock. Their officers had not told them to bring picks and shovels. They shoveled the dirt with their helmets and bare hands, stabbing at it with their bayonets. Working all night, they made very shallow trenches and fell onto the ground exhausted at daybreak.

In the daylight, the nationalists immediately spotted the Americans' trenches, since they had been dug against the skyline. The bullets cracked overhead. Grabbing their bayonets and helmets, they desperately tried to dig deeper. As the bullets kept coming, two men were so curious about what was happening that they peered up. One of them, a tool-and-die maker in his forties, was the oldest man in the battalion. Both men were shot in the head. Sammy stared at the broken skulls.

The men stayed in the trenches for four days.

Lieutenant Colonel Milovan Pohoric was the new commander of the International Brigades. A thick Yugoslav of forty-six, he appeared in an outfit of many straps and belts holding his pistols, binoculars, and map case. A former opera singer, he had been a competent commissar. He was at his best in relaxed moods when he might perform an aria. But he knew nothing about military matters and followed orders from his superiors unquestioningly. Vacillating elements among the Americans said of Pohoric, "When a Moscow button gets pushed, he lights up."

Pohoric was not half bad. Above him was a Hungarian, General Lotz, a Red Army veteran, who liked to receive the men while lying on a couch. His staff was not allowed to speak except when he addressed them. His boots were the glossiest in the brigade.

That week, seven new Americans arrived in street clothes. More Y.C.L.ers from the Pinky Rodman branch in Brownsville, holding copies of the *Daily Worker* and Y.C.L. pamphlets like *Make Your Dreams Come True* by Gil Green and *Life with a Purpose* by Joe C. Clark. Sammy gave them their only training: one hour of rifle instruction.

One of the new boys, Abe Gold, spent his time writing home:

Now, on the Jewish question, the real international language here is Yiddish. Jews from Germany, Roumania, Poland, England, Hungary, all the front ranks of their movements have come to fight the common enemy of the proletariat, and of the Jews as a special oppressed minority.

We've been marching all day long. Guys kept dropping all along the line. Full pack, ammunition, heat took their toll and trucks picking them up. I felt like dropping too but thought, if the other guys can do it, so can I.

Any hour now we'll be off. You know what I mean. It will be a long action and if things go well we'll crack into enemy territory. While our forces are incredibly powerful compared to the enemy and we absolutely anticipate victory—accidents can and do happen to individuals. I'll sign off for now.

Don't show this letter to my folks. Take care of them.

Salud and love,
Your comrade
Abe

The officers had no maps.
Four machine guns worked, sporadically.

The Lincoln Battalion had been moved south of the San Martin Road. On February 26th, Pohoric told the commander of the battalion, Woodhouse (ex–college football player, recent graduate of the Lenin School in Moscow) that the Lincolns were to be part of the offensive against Hill 693, the highest point on the plateau between the Jarama and Tajuña rivers and protected by nationalist machine gun nests. Lotz and Pohoric believed that if Hill 693 were retaken, they could drive the fascists back across the Jarama. The Lincolns were to create a diversion by attacking enemy lines along the San Martin Road.

Pohoric said that at 6:45, a battery of Republican artillery would bombard the fascist trenches four hundred yards away. At 6:55 the Republican Air Force would attack. After that, a tank company would grind down the enemy barbed wire and prepare the way for the Americans.

*   *   *

It was gray, damp, and cold on the morning of February 27th. The four hundred and fifty men peered out at the fog and ate breakfast.

Woodhouse, constantly smiling, briefed the officers. He said to Sammy, "You stay behind and if anybody remains in the trenches, shoot 'em. Then come over."

At 6:45 a battery of Republican artillery briefly opened fire, but at the Americans instead of at the fascists. They dove for cover, cursing and screaming.

Seven o'clock arrived, without the air force or the tank company. The men looked at each other. Machine gun slugs pounded into their sandbags.

Woodhouse kept looking at his watch. He phoned Pohoric and asked about the air and tank support. Pohoric said there would be a short delay.

Pohoric phoned Woodhouse a few minutes later and asked why the Americans had still not attacked. Woodhouse again asked for help. He said it would be hopeless without support from the flanks. Pohoric ordered him to move the men out. Just then three Republican planes flew overhead and dropped a light packet of bombs nowhere near enemy lines.

Woodhouse blew his whistle, and the men scrambled up the trench wall. Woodhouse waved them out. As he waved, a bullet broke his shoulder in five places. The dead and wounded lay everywhere. Those who were unhurt hid behind olive trunks and fired at the enemy trenches.

The attack was over within ten minutes.

The wounded lay immobile, waiting for the stretcher-bearers who could not get through the enemy fire. The snipers kept firing. In no-man's-land bodies caught fire; the wind carried the smell of burning flesh.

When Sammy finally climbed over the top with his bayonet, he saw them: the newly arrived young comrades from Brownsville, all dead, piled on top of each other. Abe was in the middle. Sammy crawled in behind them, and he could hear the bullets hammering an inch above him. Sammy lay there terrified from noon to midafternoon.

Then the freezing rains came.

The chill of fear and the chill of the rain.

Sammy overcame his terror and made a dash to pull in one of the wounded men. The trench was filled with bleeding, vomiting, coughing men, and with corpses. Many of the wounded drowned in the bottom of the trench in puddles of red mud and ice water. The exhausted men stepped on the wounded and the dead or fell upon them as they slipped in the ice and mud.

They waited for medical care and food. There was none.

The men cried aloud and sobbed and shook with rage. And yet they could not help thinking as they stared at their comrades in the bloodied water, "Better him than me."

Sammy Kuznekov and a Franco-Belgian, Robert, slid down a hill, filed up another hill, and down to the cookhouse where they found two men, Stahl, the cook, and Koch, an officer. They were both drunk.

"Why didn't you bring the rations up front?" Sammy asked them.

"Well, nobody came," the cook said.

"Give me the food for the battalion."

"Hold on," Stahl, a blond Minnesotan with a moustache, said. "I heard there were a lot of casualties. I gotta know the exact figure."

Sammy stared at him. "How many rations did you prepare for today?"

"Four-fifty plus."

"*Well, that's exactly what I want.*"

"Now under brigade rules you only get rations for each man you got."

Sammy picked up his bayonet. "Stahl, you're gonna give me the food. I'm not gonna carry it, you're gonna put it on your mules. And you and Hill are coming with me—"

"Please! Don't take me!" Stahl cried.

"You bastards, I'll blow your heads off. Do you know that most of the boys are dead or wounded?"

"Well, we don't know, we have no records," Stahl said.

"Fuck you," Sammy said. "I want you to load up your mules with two barrels of rum, if there's any left after you bastards got through with it. Plus the cognac. And all the goat chops—"

"You can't order me. I'm a lieutenant," Koch said.

Sammy put his bayonet to the man's stomach. "You're gonna be a dead lieutenant in a minute."

The men loaded up the mules with the bags of food and drink.

It took more than an hour and a half for Sammy and Robert to get back to the men. He could hear the moaning, and in the trenches the wounded wailed in pain.

He passed out the rum and goat chops and the men drank and ate them like the elixir of life.

Whenever they heard a cry, Sammy and the other survivors tried to locate the man and drag him in. But many of them were too weak to carry the stretcher cases. "Look," Sammy said, "two of you guys take a wounded man between you and let your body heat try to keep him warm." They crawled under the blankets of the wounded to give them warmth and protection from the rain until the stretcher-bearers came.

The stretcher-bearers arrived at daybreak, when most of the wounded were dead.

Before they arrived Sammy and the others took their little half-tents (they hadn't had time to build them) and put them over themselves. There were no holes to crawl into. They passed out on the ground.

They awoke at daybreak and peered over the top. Dead bodies were strewn everywhere in the trenches.

Sammy passed out the remaining food and cognac.

The surviving eighty men made a mass grave for the dead. They dragged the bodies from the trenches onto a spur and placed rocks and earth on top of them.

The dead were not counted or identified.

Sammy looked around at the furious faces. There was only one officer left, Stern, who had been a sergeant in the U.S. Army. Sammy went over to him. "Kuznekov, don't come near me. I don't want *any* command here. From now on I'm just a plain fucking soldier. Because this is a slaughter that no army would permit and I don't want any part of it. So I'm just a soldier, man."

Sammy led the men to the first-aid station, a kilometer behind the lines. A group of Russian cavalry, former Cossacks with lances, approached them.

Sammy said in Russian, "Devil take you, why are you pointing lances at us?"

"Oh!" the first man said. "He's one of ours."

He said to Sammy, "We've received orders from the brigade to bring all of you in."

They were taken to the brigade in the field. Most of the men were so exhausted they lay down on the ground. Sammy and eight others stood. Pohoric suddenly appeared with General Krauss, a German.

"You Americans are a goddamn disgrace," Pohoric said in English, and added in German to Krauss: "They're nothing but shit."

Speaking in Russian, Sammy said, "Comrade Commander, that isn't true. Do you know that we're the only remnants of the entire battalion?"

"Well, it's too goddamn many," Pohoric said. "You guys came here to play with your social theories about revolution. You don't even know basic principles. Soldiers must learn how to die! And I'm going to teach you, friends. I'm making an example of you." He turned to Krauss and said, "Arrest all the men who are standing."

The men were taken to the wine cellar. Sammy and the eight other men were separated from the others and locked up. Exhausted and almost delirious, most of them screamed with delight when they saw the huge jars of wine. They drank and laughed and reeled and threw up. Sammy did not drink. He sat silently in a corner.

General Krauss came down to visit them. Krauss was a typical German military officer: tall, very well built, and clean cut, with glasses. He stood straight as a ramrod. He greeted the nine men with a smile. He handed them a pack of cigarettes.

Sammy refused.

"How come?" Krauss asked.

"Young Communists don't drink, smoke, or screw around," Sammy said, looking at him steadily.

"Oh," Krauss said. "I see."

Krauss paused. "Remember, whatever happens, be proud."

He turned to the others and added, "You will all be sentenced to death. And I wanted you to know that this is nothing personal. This will be an objective trial. In fact, I can personally assure you that the balance of your subscriptions to the *Daily Worker* and other progressive literature will be transferred to your families in the States."

The men had stopped drinking. It was very quiet in the room. Krauss continued. "Listen, this is a revolutionary necessity, so please act correctly. Be solid Communists."

As there were no questions, Krauss put the package of cigarettes on the floor, waved, and marched out the door.

The nine men were taken upstairs to a high-vaulted cave lit by sooty lamps and candlelight. They saw their own shadows on the walls and heard their comrades below in the basement, laughing and retching and throwing up the wine. General Krauss sat hunched over a little table raised on a platform with a group of judges: the Spanish commissar, who knew only Spanish; the French commissar, who knew only French; the Russian commissar, who knew only Russian; and the Bulgarian commissar, who knew Russian well. Four interpreters sat beside Krauss. Pohoric sat off to the side.

The men waited in the flickering light for the trial to begin. The minutes passed, and many of the men sprawled on the floor and began to snore. Sammy, sober, remained alert.

Krauss began to speak in German. After each sentence, the first interpreter translated into Spanish, the second into French, the third into Russian, and the fourth into Bulgarian.

Krauss said, "Comrades, the reason these Americans are so weak is that they do not have any proletarian history whatsoever, whereas the German working class, the European working classes have a mighty proletarian tradition developed over the centuries. It's simple. These poor Americans are not individually culprits—"

Sammy raised his hand. "*Tovarishch*," Sammy said, "look, you're trying a group of Americans. The language of America is English. Now the least any court could do is provide an interpreter for the defendants. Am I asking too much?"

"Ach, not important," Pohoric said, wriggling his fingers.

But the jury conferred for a moment. The Bulgarian addressed Sammy. "Look, you understand Russian. That's enough. We're not going to cater to you damn Americans."

Sammy leaned down to the other men and told them what the Bulgarian had said. He had to shake some of them to make sure they heard him. "Aw, fuck this shit," said Rob Mason, a steelworker from Youngstown. "Let them get it over with."

Krauss cleared his throat and continued. "Comrades, I was con-
trasting the measly American working class with our splendid German
workers. The German progressive tradition goes back to the *Bauern-
Kriege*, the peasant wars. As early as the sixteenth century and the
time of the Reformation, the peasants and artisans of Germany
formed their own militias and fought against the city bourgeoisie,
yah. That, comrades, is tradition. Let me describe for you the nature
of the battles throughout our glorious German history that illustrate
my thesis."

Krauss spent an hour and a half on his illustrations, pointing his
finger at the Americans, concluding his sentences with "*Yah!*" and
occasionally stamping his foot, making the candles shudder. Some of
the interpreters also stamped their feet. The men beside Sammy
were snoring, and from below in the basement, he heard chairs
thrown and dishes breaking and the roar of voices drunkenly shouting.

"*Viva el ejercito popular!*"
"*Viva las Brigadas Internacionales!*"
"*Viva la victoria final!*"

"It is illuminating, comrades," Krauss droned on, "that the German
working class and the German general staff were one and the same,
for one reason, holding to the current ideological perspective: it was
in the interests of the bourgeoisie, and in the interest of the nobility
to keep the motherland united, *yah yah yah!* You get it? The only
elements that stood for German unity were the peasants and workers
of Germany! This advanced consciousness continued all through the
eighteenth century."

Whatever Krauss was saying, Sammy noticed that each interpreter
diluted it further until little of his meaning, such as it was, came
through. Thus, the Spanish translation was: "Krauts are all pals, yah
yah yah! They stick together, always, Bolsheviks and Stalin's goody-
goodies. So get on the wagon and push!"

The French version went: "The *boche* bastards are all the same.
What else is new?"

Sammy thought, Well at least I'll live until morning at this rate.
Yet he too had trouble staying awake.

"And at the time of the Napoleonic Wars, dear comrades," Krauss
continued, "there were young revolutionaries who later formed the
German general staff. Up until 1848 it was only the revolutionaries

that wanted a united Germany. It was the *Fichtebundler*, because Professor Fichte believed in a just state. Fichte, Fichte, Fichte, comrades! Remember Fichte! Fichte can be considered the father of German nationalism and German socialism all in one! Fichte was a Hegelian, and it was Hegel who believed that in order to bring about social justice, you must have a social state. And that social state, must be a *strong*, *a very strong*, advanced state, which is the state of Marxism. In all of these phases of history, the German working class took a progressive part.

"And what did beloved Hegel say? He said world history occupies a higher ground. . . . Moral claims which are irrelevant must not be brought into collision with world-historical deeds and their accomplishments. The litany of private virtues: modesty, humility, forbearance, and philanthropy, must not be raised against them. . . . So mighty a form as the State must trample down many an innocent flower—crush to pieces many an object in its path. *Yah ha hah!*"

A very tall Soviet general, Pashin, walked into the room and looked around. Pashin sat down beside Sammy. Krauss droned on. Sammy realized that Pashin had to wait for the Russian translation, which followed the French version. That took some time, since it was translated into Spanish first, and Sammy could understand it immediately. What the hell, he thought, and leaning over, he interpreted for the general. "Regarding then the *Fichtebund*," Krauss continued, "many of the German nationalists, especially the Prussians, escaped from Germany, *yah*. Let us not forget Scharnhorst, *yah*, let us not forget how he advised Pavlov, the commander in chief of the Russian Army who fought against Napoleon at the battle of Borodino. How Scharnhorst advised Pavlov about every move he made before and after the battle—"

Sammy noticed that as he interpreted for the general, the man was getting red in the face and breathing heavily. He suddenly stood up and bellowed in a rage: "*Swallich! What? Goddamn sausage-suckers*—no goddamn sausage-eater is going to tell me that General Pavlov had to be told anything. Maybe he let the little Kraut creep wipe his boots—"

The French commissar shouted, "*Sacrebleu!* I'm not going to listen to this bullshit that a filthy *boche* had anything to do with defeating our great emperor Napoleon!"

"Hey Sammy, what's going on?" A couple of the Americans were jabbing Sammy on the shoulder. The noise had awakened them.

"Well, actually, guys," Sammy said, "Krauss's political line is kind of stale. Where's the Popular Front in all this? I think he's gotten himself into a little hot water."

The Russian and the Frenchman shouted at once until the Russian announced that he was Pashin, commander of the Soviet tank corps. When the French commissar realized who the man was, he shut up.

The commissars bolted to attention, standing on their toes.

General Pashin turned to Sammy. "What's going on here? This is the most stupid bullshit session I've ever heard. Don't they have anything better to do with their time?"

"Well actually, sir," Sammy said. "This is not a bullshit session. I'm on trial, and will probably be executed by morning."

"*You* are being tried—by *them*?"

Pashin pushed himself to the front of the room, pushed over the table, picked up the five-foot-six Pohoric in his arms and threw him against the wall. Pohoric fell over. "You son of a bitch. You have the nerve to try one of our boys?"

"He's an American!" Pohoric screamed.

"Don't tell me. I know one of our boys when I hear him and see him." Pashin pointed to the commissars and asked Sammy, "Who are these monkeys?"

Sammy answered, "They're the judges, and the German is the prosecutor."

Pashin's face had turned beet red. "I heard what you did today," he shouted at Pohoric. "You slaughtered a whole battalion *uselessly*, uselessly. And these are the few remnants, huh? And the only thing you can think of is killing them. Don't you know what you do with demoralized young troops, you asshole? You bathe them, you clothe them, you give them a few drinks, get 'em all fucked, and then you reorganize them. If you don't understand these elementary facts of life, you should be ashamed of yourself."

The Americans were poking Sammy in the shoulder and asking what was going on, but he was too busy to answer.

General Pashin had turned back to Sammy. "And as for you, bastard, this is what you get for associating with foreigners. What's a nice Russian boy like you doing associating with all these scum?" he said, pointing at the Americans.

The commissars had slunk out of the room, including Krauss. Pohoric was left leaning against the wall. Pashin said to him, "I don't want to hear anything more about trials or executions for now. If you don't take my goddamn advice, I'll have your head."

Pashin headed for the door. He stopped and turned back to Sammy. "You ought to be ashamed of yourself," he said. "A young man from the motherland, associating himself with these *bastards*."

The day after the trial, Sammy, flea-ridden and filthy, was ordered to report to brigade headquarters. When he arrived, a sidecar scooted up to him and a mousy man with red hair shouted at him to get in. He drove with insane speed to Madrid and deposited Sammy at a bathhouse for the exclusive use of the Russians. No Spaniards, whatever their rank, were permitted to enter. Two women undressed Sammy, put him in a hot tub, sprayed eau de cologne on him, bathed him, and gave him a manicure. The redhead appeared and handed Sammy silk underwear, a polo shirt, a leather jacket, an elegant pair of trousers, a beautiful pair of Russian boots, and a Russian tank uniform. Then Sammy was driven back at the same speed to headquarters and presented to a Major Vorov, who asked him to fill out a biographical form. When Sammy came to "nationality," he hesitated for a moment and almost wrote "Jew." Then he made the smartest move of his career in Spain. Sammy wrote, "Russian."

Vorov asked him, "What did you do when you lived with these foreigners in America?"

"I was a seaman, Comrade Major."

"First mate, second mate, or captain?" Vorov asked.

"No, just a seaman," Sammy said.

Vorov looked astonished. "You left the motherland to become a common seaman?"

"Yes, comrade, but I was an organizer of the union," he replied.

Vorov registered no reaction.

"And I was secretary of the Young Communist League on the waterfront of New York City."

Vorov beamed. "Ah, *now* I understand." Then he told Sammy of the high honor in store for him. Sammy was to join the Soviet tank corps. "Well, comrade," Vorov said, "how does it feel to be back with your own?"

"Very good," Sammy replied.

He was now stationed with the Russians.

Sammy was driven to Alcalá de Henares, the secret headquarters for Russian tank operations located behind an eight-foot whitewashed stone wall. Soviet sailors relayed messages to Russia from mobile equipment in the curtained backseat of a Buick with three retractable fifteen-foot antennas.

Vorov called him in for another pep talk. "You'll get along fine," he said. "Of course, be careful of the Jews."

Sammy had a conversation with Vorov about the purges of the Red Army that had taken place in Moscow. He was especially curious about how Vorov felt about the purge of Marshal Tukhachevski, who was after all the commander of the tank corps. Vorov had praised Tukhachevski to Sammy many times.

"Well, there's a silver lining in this thing," Vorov said.

"What is it?" Sammy asked.

"I'm not a major in Russia. I'm a captain. *Here* I'm a major. But who knows, now maybe they'll even skip me over some ranks. Now that they're getting rid of all these Jews, who knows?"

"Uh huh," Sammy said.

A new group of Russian soldiers arrived at Alcalá de Henares. They talked freely with Sammy, since he was one of them. They marched with the goose step, an innovation. They talked about these aliens, the Jews, constantly. Jokes about the little kike who sold things and robbed things. About the one Russian Jewish officer who always tried to show off and was killed at Brunete.

Vorov liked to drink and talk with Sammy until three in the morning. Vorov was also an orphan, one of the thousands of waifs in the early 1920s—the kids whose parents were killed in the civil war. They lived in the streets, stealing, always running from the cops. Vorov had never known his parents. The Bolsheviks had taken the orphans and made them the proletarian guard of the revolution, used them to put the old Bolsheviks in their place. They were given education and power, and the beauty of it was that they had no morals. They were placed in the NKVD or became guards in the concentration camps.

"Boy," Vorov told Sammy, "in the old days no one could swipe a wallet as good as me. I was like a wild animal. Sometimes I'd cut and not just the coat; I'd even cut into the asshole of some old broad. One time a regiment of soldiers showed up at a railroad yard where a bunch of us were sleeping. They rounded us up and said, 'You guys are going to have a punishment worse than death. You're going to school.' One day they gave us spoons to eat with. I threw mine away. The next day, the bowl of kasha was on the floor instead of on the table. The teacher said, 'Get down and eat it.' He rubbed his foot in it and spit on it and said, 'Eat it, goddamn it. That will teach you to throw spoons away.' And I ate it, in front of my friends. I didn't mind that, but the laughing and snide remarks and humiliation. But I took it like a man, and then I got to do the punishing.

"In the G.P.U. we didn't have any sympathy for the bastards who didn't know how to outrun the cops. We had these old blabbermouths, these damn Jews we arrested who would tell you about the old days: 'I was a great revolutionary. I went to jail.' Piss on them if they had served time.

"They cried to us, and I'd say to them, 'You son of a wolf—how could you be a great revolutionary?' They'd cry, 'I fought with Lenin.' And I'd say, 'So I was a great pickpocket. So what, asshole?' " Vorov roared with laughter, throwing the empty vodka bottle at the wall.

Sammy, the only American tank commander in a Russian unit, served with the Russians for fourteen months in Spain. His rank was second lieutenant. His Soviet B.T.-5 tank weighed twenty tons and could easily jump over a fifteen- to twenty-foot ditch and land smoothly.

In May, the Soviet commander, Lieutenant Colonel Buslov, called Sammy into headquarters and explained his plan to frontally attack Fuentes del Ebro with fifty Russian tanks and head for Saragossa.

"But Comrade Colonel," Sammy said, "the terrain there is green on your map. In Aragon that means irrigation ditches. We'll never get across."

Buslov glared at Sammy. "Second lieutenants in the Red Army are seen and not heard."

Sammy was silent.

*   *   *

The tanks moved slowly across the rocky stubble field. Sammy's riflemen clawed to the rear railings. Within fifty feet, Sammy saw they were plowing through a field of high vegetation. The weeds were higher than the turrets. The dust was impenetrable. The only way to orient themselves was to keep in sight of the church steeple in Fuentes del Ebro three thousand feet ahead. Sammy's tank fell down into a ditch. It was saved by its fluid shock absorbers.

Sammy was able to turn the tank around, but suddenly he heard hail hitting all around. Machine-gun bullets were burning down upon them. Sammy looked around. His infantrymen had disappeared. He would never see them again. The tank cleared an irrigation ditch twelve feet wide. It jumped again, landing in a dry ditch fifteen feet deep. Turning right, Sammy found a breach in the right wall, a shell hole, and climbed back. He passed the burning tanks, their front ends blown open.

Almost all the tank riders died.

Lying beside his tank, Sammy fell asleep. In the morning, he learned that out of fifty-three tanks, twenty-two were lost.

It was the end of the Aragon offensive. Later in the morning, Buslov summoned Sammy and told him that some of the Russians could not be accounted for. No one knew if they were dead or wounded. He asked Sammy to check the local hospitals.

Sammy went first to the warehouse of the Hijar railroad station, which was being used as a hospital. It was a charnel house. Over four thousand wounded were lying on the ground and on stretchers. There were two doctors, four nurses, and one ambulance. The wounded lay with open chests with intestines exposed, moaning and calling out to him for help. The smell was unbearable. He saw the indifference of the staff. Wounded soldiers were no longer useful.

Sammy found a Ukrainian from Canada and two Russians. The three men were taken away in an ambulance which was reserved for the Russians.

The Americans heard Sammy speak in English to the Ukrainian.

"Please, please," the Americans cried. "You're an American and you won't help us." They cursed him.

He fled, his heart beating fast.

*   *   *

I'm trapped. What do I do?

He lasted for fourteen months, and he got out. Before he had gone with the Russians, he had thought, we've got to get their hands off the American Communists. When he got to know them, he decided, we've got to fight them, they're even worse than the Nazis. With the Nazis, you knew where you stood. The language was plain.

When he arrived in New York, he kissed the ground.

Now he is seventy-five years old, retired, living in Florida with his wife. Behind him on the wall perches a small American flag. He hopes that the Israeli Army will allow him to serve as a replacement for a young soldier for a month in the summertime. He has limited funds, and partakes of some of the activities that are offered to retirees at little cost. But watching him at these affairs (obese women in pink bunny suits singing at costume parties) his apartness and dignity are clear.

He takes courses in philosophy at the local college, wears a bracelet for a Soviet Jewish political prisoner, and eagerly accepts a few invitations to speak about Spain. There aren't many, because of what he has to say. The producer of a film about Spanish Civil War veterans comes to interview him. The producer stops in the middle and says, "I can't use any of this. I never heard anything like this in my entire life. You're a cold warrior."

On the day of the T.W.A. hijacking in which Jews were again the victims of a selection process, he walks on the beach with his wife. He hears the gentle sounds of elderly Yiddish voices singing, the sounds of balalaikas and familiar Russian melodies and songs of the Spanish Civil War. He hears "The Peat Bog Soldiers" and "The House I Live in" and the World Youth Festival Song and "Freiheit." The old Communists are seated together on the beach in their regular corner. In their seventies and eighties, many of them have the peculiar resilience and strength that ideology provides. They are peacefully sewing P.L.O. flags in anticipation of the upcoming Party dinner in honor of General David Dragunsky, head of the Soviet Anti-Zionist Committee and instructor of P.L.O. troops in Libya. One of them is writing a slogan in crayon: "Condemn American Terrorism." Some are reading *Soviet Life*, which has on its cover soldiers skipping along in a meadow, grinning and gathering daffodils. He recognizes two Spanish war vets, but they do not see him. He passes by them, shaking his head. Their humming and strumming and singing gradually fade as he moves on.

He remembers the wounded crying out to him at the railroad station in Spain. He remembers going to Spain as if going to an optometrist with blurred vision, and emerging with clear sight.

He remembers.

Street Scenes, 1930

The lollipop salesman.

—G.L.

When he was eleven, Solly Rubell sold lollipops for a penny apiece on the roof garden of an apartment house on Stanton Street.

A skinny boy, he stood on the roof, waiting for customers. Then, dressed up in a black suit and Stetson hat, Solly went to *shul* with his father, mother, sister, and cousins.

It was the thick of the Depression. At night, after work, his father cut lace to make a little extra money. Everyone did it, even though it was against the labor laws. If strangers entered the building, people went running from floor to floor calling out, "Lace inspector!"

Solly and his family lived on the top floor. It was a cold-water flat. Water dripped from the roof, and the toilet in the hall had no light. In winter the wind swept through the rattling windows. But in summer they kept the front door open so a breeze would waft through the apartment, and put bowls of ice in front of the fan.

The candy stores were cool, dark, and dank, with their smells of pretzels, malteds, lime rickeys, and sawdust. Baseball cards with gum, pink candies, and watermelon slices cost a penny. A big chunk of ice surrounded the sodas in a metal box; on the floor around it was a growing puddle.

Solly and the other boys caught fireflies and bottled them. He tried to read *The Motor Boys Under the Sea* by the fireflies' light.

At ten in the morning, the junk peddler with his horse and wagon rang his cowbell and called: "Old clothes, old rags, old newspapers, old springs, old junk." Later a singer in a top hat appeared in the courtyard. Pennies fell from windows, rolled in small packets of paper.

When the cool wet sheets hanging on long ropes in the laundry were drying, Solly and his friends ran through and hit their steaming faces against them.

Solly's Sister, 1986

Solly was blowing his top.

—G.L.

Solly moved to Alabama with my father. Solly was eleven. He loved our father so much. Mama and I stayed with a relative on Pitt Street while they tried to make ends meet. Then, two years later, our father's business failed and they came back to the Lower East Side. Something happened to Solly. He became a radical. It was a wrench for our father. Solly went to an extreme. He kept shouting against any unjust factor; he came right out with it. He was just blowing his top about it. In the yeshiva—he went afternoons after school—he had been a hundred percent religious. Took a keen interest in Hebrew. Put his whole heart into it. When Solly did something, he did it with a full feeling. He was a prone leader, a brilliant boy.

Solly had faith in everything at ten, just like young girls who haven't reached maturity or gone out into the world yet. But he lost all his faith after a while. I think Dolly was his first girl friend. He was her first and she was his first. These boys were so pure, these Yiddish *boyeles*.

We had culture from my father. He was a self-educated man. He educated himself to read the *Forward*. My mother didn't have an education, she couldn't read, but she knew to *daven*, which amazed me. In *shul*, the way she *davenned*! You'd think she was reading from the book, but she knew it by heart.

My father told us stories about his childhood. His parents died from hunger in Bialystok. They had eleven children. Eight died.

The three survivors were sent to America, my father and his two brothers. He told us stories, how they discriminated against Jews, the hardship they went through. I couldn't believe these things; I was American-born. We didn't see this in America.

Welfare came to investigate us when my father was out of a job. They refused us. But we got along. My mother used to make a hard-boiled egg, divide it, and we'd share.

We lived first on Stanton, then Pitt, and then Delancey. A step upward—you had hot water and steam. The radicalism was so common among the poor children.

Solly's children. After the arrest, I took them to the park, bought them candy, ice cream. When I'd leave, the little one—she was afraid, you could see the fear—she'd jump up at me. With her little ruffled pants. She was only four years old.

Dolly was a super-duper person. She won't talk against anyone. I was with her when a man undercharged her for some merchandise. She said, Mister, you didn't charge me enough. She couldn't afford to pay that extra two or three cents, but she paid it. That was Dolly. And they were so in love with each other.

I would come into her cell. Her apple would be on the metal window, a round of toilet paper, pictures of the children. She was short. Without shoes, she was even shorter. Everybody said they were supposed to have money from the Russians. But my brother and Dolly were so poor. If our mother didn't give Solly money to fix his soles, he would go without shoes. They ate dinner at our mother's house and he took a roll from my father to take home. They didn't have anything. I mean, they were *schleppers*.

Imagine, the very last day, I went to see Dolly, then I went to see Solly. The stay had come through. They were so happy. She had a little can of chicken she had set aside to celebrate; they shared it. But we didn't know the stay had been suddenly overturned that day. Solly evidently got wind of it over the radio. I was with Solly. Mama was with Dolly. And Solly said to me, "Take Mama home, take Mama home." He cut it short. He didn't want to see his mother, because he would break down. But I didn't know what was happening. "Just take Mama home," he kept saying. "I don't want Mama to come here this afternoon." That's all he said to me. So I took our mother home. When I got home, I heard the news.

This here was my brother's Hebrew book from the yeshiva. June 12th. Twelve o'clock. Four o'clock. Room seven. Five o'clock. He was a little boy then. Written by Sol. That's his handwriting. Upside down. Why did he write it upside down? No, wait, Sol's right. This is the way to hold it. I forgot, this is the way it goes, he was right! My brother's Hebrew book . . . held in my brother's hands.

I had envelopes addressed by him to their friends. I kept them. Where did I put them? Goddamnit. I'll find them . . . I'll find them. . . .

Saturday-Afternoon Parade, 1930

Solly sees strange fruit.

—G.L.

Solly and his father moved to Mitchell's Dam, Alabama, when Solly was eleven. Solly's father opened a work-clothes store on the railroad track from Red Mountain. His father had done everything from loading pig iron on railway cars to selling tombstone insurance. They lived in one big room behind the store. The mountain was thirty miles long, with solid iron ore. The track from the steel plant went straight on a level past the highway crossing where they lived.

Behind the store was the large shanty area called Niggertown. The store became the Jewtown corner of Niggertown. The white community lived on the other side of the tracks.

Most of Solly's new friends were black: Ray, Louie, Smitty, and Ronnie. Their mothers fed him at lunchtime. They called him their honey. A little Jewish boy. He could not insult them by refusing and telling them he was kosher.

At a crossing point of the tracks, Solly would hop the freights from the steel mill with the other kids. They fished and swam in a rock quarry. They shot marbles. Pitched horseshoes. Chased water moccasins, cottonhead rattlers, down the creek together in the running rapids. At the base of the mill, where the water came through the sluice, there were huge rocks. The water moccasins lay under the rocks. Solly and his friends would run barefoot on the rocks, holding clubs in their hands.

Solly's friend Ray was always writing (his mother had taught him). Ray wrote out a sheet in pencil which he distributed weekly to

the other kids: *The Journal of the Sleeping Hollow Home for Blind Mice.*
The journal dealt with the problems of the blind mice trying to cope
with life in a civilized world, trying to get attention for their special
problems.

At night, when the mill was closed, the slag that had been poured
into the huge slag pots all day had to be emptied. It was still red hot.
The slag pots were on enormous hangers. When the six pots were
tipped over, the hot slag would light up the sky like a volcano. Solly
loved to watch it at night from his bedroom window.

In school, the first exercise was to recite the Pledge of Allegiance.
About everyone being equal. The words were odd to him. His black
friends were not starting school. Then the teacher asked each student to tell the class about himself or herself. Solly didn't say very
much. The teacher asked him who his friends were. He said, Smitty,
Louie, Ray, and Ronnie.

At recess, the kids formed a tight little circle around him in the
yard. The tallest of them took him by the shirt and said, "Hey
Slopbucket, Slopfuckit, your friends ain't Smitty, Louie, and Ray.
Your friends ain't got no names. Your friends is Niggerbaby, Tarbaby,
and Smokerack. They're dirty and stupid and they smell of rat shit.
That's why there's no school for 'em. We're gonna beat you up,
nigger lover."

They knocked Solly to the ground and jumped all over him. They
rolled him over and jumped on his back. They kicked him and spat
on him. When the class bell rang, they ran back to the schoolroom,
laughing and shouting.

Solly's teacher, a pretty young woman named Bessie Stuart, came
out looking for him and saw what had happened. She touched him
and said, "Now you know, Solly: niggers are just dirty and ignorant
and stupid. That's why there's no school for them, and that's why
you got no business playing with them." She put her arm around
him and walked him back to school. She said, "I'm sure the boys and
girls are sorry for what they did to you. But now you know why
they did it."

A month later, some of the kids followed him home. One boy told
him to knock the chip off his shoulder. Solly refused. Another boy
said, "Well, I'll show him what we do with cowards." He twisted
Solly's arm and threw him into a ditch.

The next day, Solly went back to the school, smiling. He was scared, but he smiled. He didn't tattletale, but he didn't play up to them, either.

In the afternoon, he still played a little with his black buddies.

And on the Sabbath, he didn't play with anyone.

The work week in the town stretched until Saturday noon. Saturday was payday. There was drinking, whoring, blackjack, and poker, and a movie house for whites. Gambling was off limits for blacks.

On Saturday afternoon, the sheriff would pick a half-dozen cronies, appoint them deputy sheriffs, give them revolvers, which they jammed in their pockets, pin badges on them, and head with them for Niggertown.

In Niggertown, the men fanned out, looking for a crap game. Every crap game had a pot on the ground with a large sum of money in it. The sheriff would spot a big pot among a bunch of blacks and shout, "All right! Fan out. Get away from there." He confiscated the money, which he shared with his deputies, and aimed his revolver at the blacks. "Now march," he shouted.

The Saturday-afternoon parade had begun. The sheriff and his men marched the blacks who had been involved in the game—men, women, and children—down the railroad tracks, to the crossing, down a rampway in the dirt road, into a large open enclosure beside the jailhouse. It had a barbed-wire fence around it and a locked gate.

They opened the gate and herded the blacks inside. They locked the gate.

The blacks would remain there until they could get a dollar somehow and buy their way out. They huddled in the heat, without sanitation.

The Saturday-afternoon parade took place year-round.

The Declaration of Independence was celebrated in Brightwood Park on July 4th. It didn't take place in Niggertown.

There were many contests, including watermelon eating. The white participants wore aprons. The watermelon was sliced for them.

The nigger show came next. Blacks were hired for the day. In the watermelon-eating contest, the black men would have to bury their faces in half a melon and scoop it out. No aprons were provided. Their hands were tied behind their backs.

Footraces were held. Whites were tied at the feet and had to hop. Blacks were tied hands and feet.

The next contest was never engaged in by whites. It took place in the creek. Two blacks would have a boxing match with bare fists in a barrel. They could hardly fit in it together. The barrel would tip over in the water. The two men would have to keep beating each other to a pulp until the whites said it was enough. Then the two bleeding men were rescued.

In Mitchell's Dam, blacks were permitted to walk only on the dirt road, not on the paved sidewalks. They were allowed to cross the sidewalk only to enter a store. The saying went, "The color of their money is the only good thing about them."

But if blacks were in one store and wanted to go to the store next door, they had to go out, cross the sidewalk, walk down the dirt road, and cross the sidewalk again. They were not to walk across the sidewalk.

One Saturday, Solly was standing in the movie line, waiting for the theater to open.

From the line, he watched the black people shopping for groceries. They were jammed into the narrow dirt roadway.

The pressure of the crowd suddenly pushed two black men up onto the sidewalk. By chance, they jostled the sheriff, who was standing by Solly.

"What are you, a couple of smart niggers?" the sheriff said.

They did not say a word.

He took his revolver out, aimed it at each man's head, and pulled the trigger.

Their bodies lay in a red puddle in the ditch.

He aimed his revolver at two black men in the dirt roadway. "You two niggers," he said, "come over here."

The shaking men approached him. He pointed to the two bodies in the ditch. "Drag them over there and leave them there all day. This will show you niggers your place."

The Hermit Smorg

A lonely guy becomes a spy.

—G.L.

Sid Smorg of South Philadelphia kept squares of Swiss chocolate in his mother's refrigerator. They were his luxury, late at night, in his room. He didn't deserve them. Jews were burning.

A bald, virginal, fatting man, at forty-two the chemist remembered what others had long packed away: the girl he shared a seat with in the ninth grade, how she felt at his side, her smell of licorice; eating a sizzling kosher hot dog at twelve on a winter day; his rabbi's words at his bar mitzvah. Once, at eight, he was swimming; a girl appeared beside him in the pool, said "You're handsome," and dove away.

Sid remembered his two years at YMCA summer camp. Frail and sickly, he gained seven pounds each summer. He learned to love spinach (a passion he kept the rest of his life), played soccer, and shivered with delight on the boulders around the campfire while the counselors (strapping college athletes) told ghost stories. Sid developed a sound appetite. Years later, his Soviet friend Alexei would say fondly, "Sid will eat anything that will stand still long enough and that won't eat him first."

Sid read manuals on how to appeal to the opposite sex. He kept a bowl of apples on his kitchen table, because he had read that apples kept the breath sweet.

You could win Sid's gratitude by asking him how things were going. He thanked the bus driver for saying good morning. He waited each week for Fibber McGee to open his closet, and he listened to Jack Benny for eighteen years.

When Sid was in his senior year of high school, his English teacher gave an exam in his class and then asked Sid to remain afterward. He asked Sid to take the exams home and grade them that night.

Some of the other kids saw Sid take the exams. They surrounded him in the hallway pleading with him to pass them. Many of them had not even bothered to speak to him before. Sid saw many new attractive attributes in them.

Sid took the exams home and sat up until 5 A.M., erasing wrong answers and filling in the right ones, even faking the kids' handwriting. When he was through, they had all passed. Sid downgraded his own paper to make things look less suspicious.

Sid handed the exams in to the teacher. In the afternoon Sid met the teacher in the hallway. The teacher said, "The class did very well, did they not, Sid?" turned his back and walked away. This comment burned into Sid. For twenty-four years he thought of it and considered looking up the teacher in the phone book, apologizing, and explaining why he had acted as he did.

Each year when the new phone book arrived, Sid looked at the women's names and wondered what they were like. Stephanie Schnall: a tremulous librarian with suppressed emotions and chestnut hair; Bridget Hart: a vixen who kept a little braided whip in her glove compartment.

Russ Columbo broke Sid's heart, and he had a special shot of Grable's legs in his dresser drawer under his shirts and mismatched socks.

The seasons came and went; Sid sat quietly on the bus on the way to work watching the young lovers, the cycles. People's grief gave him strength—he cheered up.

Later, in Jersey City, when his friend Pete Boston introduced him to the Soviets, Sid was uncertain. He had considered himself a Norman Thomas Socialist. But he saw these were interesting men. The Philadelphia Communists he knew, were weird and shabby losers—libertines, gap-toothed wonders—no way he would join those furry nuts. The Party was their glory. It made them shoot up a few inches, gave them a set of balls. Pete had taken him to their meetings, hoping Sid would join.

The local Party office had walls papered with drawings of brawny, upright workingmen in overalls with upraised, gigantic muscled arms and capitalists with fat cigars and big bellies sitting on piles of coins.

The leaders, with their pipes, tweedy vests, and blank faces, had this "You go out and get your heads cracked, it's only the cops" attitude. He saw a small black woman make a suggestion about a demonstration and the leader coldly respond: "We will decide who we will learn from." She steadied herself by putting her hand on the chair.

One angry Greek exploded at the Marxist dialectics (Does the Party shake the workers or do the workers shake the Party?) and shouted, "The hell with this bullshit—give me five good men and I'll take Rittenhouse Square by storm." The meetings broke up at 4 A.M. They were dominated by what the Swiss called the *ploder sacken*, the endlessly boring talkers.

Sid couldn't take those pig festivals on the Jewish holidays—the Jewish Communists' celebration of the pig. Not just spareribs in Chinese restaurants, mind you—okay, that was odd on Yom Kippur, but they thought they were proving they weren't narrow Zionists. But pictures of pigs on the mantelpiece! Pig recipes! Pig poems! Sex tips! This was excess, Sid thought.

In his parents' house he'd lived in the same room since childhood. Sid had sat in the back row in the living room beside his bachelor uncles in the darkening dusk. Uncle Simon was known for his Republican rage. You never mentioned F.D.R. in his presence. If you did, he turned livid red and screamed, then didn't talk to anyone for days. Whenever Simon sat quietly in his chair, everyone assumed he was thinking about how much he hated F.D.R.

When Sid was introduced to Alexei by Pete, he was touched by Alexei's concern. Also Alexei was dark and handsome, which Sid couldn't help admiring, and had a lock of hair that kept falling over his forehead. "Sid Sid Sid Sid!" (Imagine, hearing his name said over and over again.) "Sid-Sid-Sidney," said Alexei, gazing at Sid fondly, licking a vodka martini, "I don't expect our boys to be social butterflies, but this is ridiculous. What can we do with you? You're so pale. You don't play cards, you have no girl. You think we don't care about these things?"

Sid sat, his head down, eating it up. Come on, Alexei, you guys don't care that much. Blood came to Sid's face. To have such friends—and to help the USSR at the same time, the only country where anti-Semitism was a crime against the state. Anything that strengthened the USSR would help to save the Jews.

Tears came to Sid's eyes when Alexei told him that Stalin had struggled to learn Yiddish, that he *davenned* when he prayed. This was no normal leader.

The Jew thing, who could ignore it? Sid had gone to the library every day as a boy, walking the two miles. The Neckers festered near the city dump amid mosquitoes, raising hogs. They were kids who lived in the marshy wasteland of Stonehouse Lane and did lightning forays on Sid's neighborhood, throwing bricks and smashing windows. When he was fifteen, they beat him. Blood dripping down his face, he watched the legs of his friends skitter away into the bushes.

Sid's father, one of the only Jews at the factory, was baited by the other workers. They stole his chisels; they put glue on his good clothes. Yus Smorg struck a man who grinned and ran together the words "HiJew?" and almost lost his job because the man had a weak heart and fainted.

Yus Smorg's foreman told him, "I'm going to make you quit." He moved him to a quicksilver production line where Yus was the only worker hand-sanding cabinets. He came home at night with the skin rubbed off his fingertips. Sid's mother would bathe Yus's fingers and put ointment on them. Sid's father went back to work the next morning without a word of complaint.

Sid graduated from the university in 1932 and went to work as a laboratory worker at the Richmond Sugar Company. He was now a main support of his family.

One week before Christmas, he was laid off. He searched frantically for a job, walking in a perspiring heat in snow and slush against tides of smiling, happy employed workers with tinsel on their faces, bearing green, gold, and red Christmas boxes with silver bells to their families as carols tinkled from storefronts. This was capitalism. As he approached a factory gate, a bundled laborer walked toward him and asked what he wanted. When Sid told him, the man snarled, "Better go back, boy. Enough people out of work here."

One night a old co-worker of his, Fred Stone, came with the news that a former classmate of Fred's, Pete Boston, was leaving his job at the Terrill Manufacturing Company in Jersey City and might be able to put Sid in his place. A week later a telegram arrived: Sid was told to come to Jersey City that night to see Pete Boston. He anxiously packed a brown cardboard suitcase, borrowed six dollars and a jacket that closely matched his pants, and took a Greyhound to Jersey City. Boston was waiting for Sid in front of his house. Pete Boston's biceps could make a man blush. Plus a huge, friendly, freckled face, pug nose, the grin, the feel of the bearlike grip of his hand.

They sat up until morning talking. Boston briefed Sid on soap chemistry. Then there were "complicating circumstances." The boss, Roger Whitman, would never hire a Jew. Sid would have to say that, despite his name, he was really not Jewish. His grandfather had converted and married a Christian girl.

Then Boston got down to brass tacks. He told Sid he was a Communist Party member, and that he had purposely selected Sid because Fred had told him that Sid was a Socialist. Pete said, "We figure that when you really know the score you'll want to struggle for real change." Boston talked for three more hours about how mankind had advanced to a new level in the Soviet Union.

Sid was hired the next day. Roger Whitman told him what a great man Hitler was, and how the Jews in the United States should be put on ships and the vessels sunk in midocean.

Sid's thirty-dollar-a-week salary kept his family off relief. He repaid Pete by consenting to go to the Communist Party meetings in Jersey City, which he detested. He couldn't hurt Pete's feelings when Pete asked him to join the Party. He said that he felt he "must be adequately prepared" in the tomes of Marxism-Leninism-Stalinism and "steeped in the struggle" before he would be worthy to take such a step. Pete was moved, and tried to assure Sid that there "are years to go to drink from the fountain of wisdom of Marxism-Leninism-Stalinism; the Party will guide you."

In the fall of 1933, Sid was rehired by the Richmond Sugar Company. Pete kept coming to see him in Philadelphia, where they would meet at the Automat and Sid would splurge on his favorites, mashed potatoes and creamed spinach. Pete talked for hours about Soviet justice. Pete was also welcomed by Sid's family at his home, where he was considered their savior for having given Sid a job.

One night Pete began their conversation by telling Sid about yet another incident of discrimination so typical of American society. He had attended the Christmas party of his Jewish girl friend's company. The party was sedate and dignified, with good, rich food. Near the end, a partner in the firm, who did not know his secretary was Jewish, rose and proposed a toast: "A Merry Christmas to all us Christians here. I am so thankful there are no others in this firm."

After a long pause, Pete said, "Sid, the Soviet people eat off rough bare boards. You can help them live a little better, a little more as humans should, by getting this information." He said that he had met a man who worked for Amtorg, the Soviet trading company, in New York City. The man wanted to obtain—"unofficially"—a quantity of specialized information and data on American chemical processes. The information on paper fillers, vitamin D concentrates, and sulphinated oils could greatly benefit the lives of the Soviet people. It could affect education (paper), food (fish-oil concentrates), and clothing (sulphinated oils). Pete said a great deal more information was also needed about products made by the Richmond Sugar Company. It would go a long way toward making the harsh life of Soviet citizens, who were still in the first stage of Socialist humanism, less difficult.

"Will you do this for the Soviet people, Sid?" Pete asked, that wonderful brisk look of love in his eyes, a look no one had ever bestowed on Sid before.

Sid said, "I'll have to think this over." Actually, he had already made up his mind. His pulse was pounding. This was great. Pete was his benefactor. Sid had been living in sin for so long by avoiding the Communist Party membership Pete wanted so badly for him. He felt he had been breaking Pete's heart, and hated himself for it. He had torn clumps of hair out of his head at night in anger at himself. Now he could please Pete, get him off his neck about joining that bunch of furry nuts in the Communist Party, and strengthen the Soviet Union, his people's best friend, as well.

How sweet it was.

During the next seven months, Sid and Pete fumbled about trying to figure out how they could go about copying the data kept in the office of Dr. Bachrach, the director of research at Richmond Sugar.

There were voluminous plant operation reports, blueprints of equipment. The reproduction costs were prohibitive.

Sid worried himself blue about it, wondering what he could hock that would cover it. Could he ever correct his faults? In the meantime he did manage to provide Pete with the process for the manufacture of phosphoric acid. This was a simple matter; Sid drew all the necessary sketches and copied the essential data himself over a period of forty-eight hours on a weekend during which he did not eat or drink.

In the late fall of 1935 Pete came to Philadelphia with exciting news. Amtorg itself would provide excellent facilities for copying the information. Sid just had to bring the material to New York. Best of all, Pete told Sid that Dmitri, the Russian engineer from Amtorg, was very anxious to meet him, having heard so much about the canny Sid Smorg. Pete said the engineer had very warm words of praise for the information Sid had given the Soviet Union on the phosphoric acid process.

Sid dove into the air and chased a fly.

He had entered into history. He was making a difference.

Sid and Pete did some of their secret work together. Like Sid, Pete was no libertine, and he avoided marriage because he had to conserve his energy for his activities on behalf of the Soviets. Pete kept a snake, a crow, and white mice as pets, but this was not, he told Sid, because he was a bohemian. It was calculated to give people the impression he was a bit "off" so that they would not notice his secret work.

Pete was a superb lab man with an uncanny dexterity in those huge paws of his. The two friends worked in the lab together for hours without talking and it seemed to Sid as if each could anticipate the other's thoughts and desires before they were expressed. Sid hoped that at some time in the future, when Nazism had been crushed, he could settle down to working with Pete in aiding the sick. Perhaps nutrition research. He could think of no more glorious project.

With his new friends and engulfing work, Sid pondered the course of his life up to this point. He was embarrassed that he had spent so much time writing to Betty Grable in Hollywood, telling her of his hopes and dreams and what her legs meant to him. He had expressed this feeling to her in so many ways, in so many letters, it must have bored her to tears. He blushed. She must have thought, What a lonely man Sid Smorg must be. And this wasn't really true, at least not any more. He thought up a letter telling her to forget those other letters, but he never sent it. The truth was, he just didn't want to nibble at her toes any more.

Sid's two new Soviet friends, whom he knew only as Dmitri and Alexei, were among the most interesting men he had ever known. Dmitri had a swarthy complexion, black dancing eyes, and a warm smile. He had read widely in English literature, and discussed Browning's "My Last Duchess" with Sid. He called Sandburg "a mediocrity and a bit of a faker," but liked Dickens, Edgar Lee Masters, and Wordsworth. "My life is drudgery, Sid," Dmitri confided. "It's a succession of days of waiting apprehensively on street corners in all sorts of weather; sometimes the people don't show up. Having to cajole and plead and threaten. Eating in cheap, out-of-the-way restaurants." Sid wished he could do something to cheer his friend up. Dmitri often went to the ice hockey games at Madison Square Garden and joined in the free ice skating afterwards. Sid would watch Dmitri and his red-and-gold muffler fly around the rink, happy to see him freeing himself from his everyday cares. Dmitri would wave at Sid. Once, to Sid's delight, he executed a somersault.

One day Dmitri exploded with anger at Sid. Sid had traveled to New York four times in a single week in a fruitless effort to obtain a report that Dmitri wanted on synthetic rubber from a gull named Herman. Dmitri shouted at Sid, his face livid: "Just look at you, my boy. You not only look like a ghost, you are one. You're dead on your feet. What will your mother think? You goddamn fool. You're not coming to New York again for two weeks. Go home. Spend time with your family. That's an order. I'll bet you that asshole Herman hasn't even begun that report. The hell with it for now. Even if Moscow were to fall tomorrow (and it won't—ever) I forbid you to come to New York again for two weeks." After that outburst, Dmitri calmed down. Gently, he said, "Come, Sidney. We'll zip over to the Ferris Wheel Bar, have a few double Canadian Clubs and some sandwiches. Then I'll put you in a cab and personally buy you some Corona Corona cigars and a parlor-car seat for the train."

So it was.

Sid settled down in his parlor-car seat in a haze of holy contentment.

Sid was busy day and night writing reports (grieving over his deficiencies in grammar), stealing blueprints, copying and returning them, seeing Dmitri and Alexei in New York, Cincinnati, or Buffalo, raising money for his trips (since he hated to take it from the Soviet people) by working weekends on his job for time and a half, telling lies at home.

Sid's mother was certain he was carrying on a series of cheap, clandestine love affairs. Sid worried about not living up to her code of ethics. She often said that a thief "could not look God in the eye nor at himself with respect."

Sid had fallen in love once, on Monday, August 30, 1937. A girl in the laboratory. Her unassuming manner, her snub nose captivated him. He courted her for a month and told her he loved her. One day as they walked by the river, she told him she did not believe his love, and cited his "lack of ardor" as the reason.

He drank heavily. He thought of making a clean breast of it. Having seen a lot of Bing Crosby movies, he was tempted to confess to the Jesuit priests in the neighborhood, especially the dazzling Father Mahoo, or the erudite tall parish priest at St. Ambrose's, Father Culligan.

Whenever Sid was down, Dmitri's concern picked him up. Dmitri said over drinks, "I realize it's because of this work that you have no wife and family of your own. But this is not natural. You are a normal man with normal instincts and desires. We must find a solution, Sidney. As soon as possible you must get out of this lousy business. Forget it. Then you can run around with girls every night in the week." Blushing at all this, Sid said he wasn't that kind of guy.

"Secret work won't always be necessary," Dmitri said. "You'll see. After the war we'll give peace a chance. It will be a wonderful era for mankind. There will be open borders; nations will hold hands. You'll come openly to Moscow and you'll meet all your old friends again. Oh, they will be so glad to see you, Sidney. We'll have a great party and we'll paint the town red. Oh, we'll have a marvelous time."

*　　　*　　　*

Sid had begun to tell his American contacts that he was married to a redheaded woman with freckles and that he was the father of twins. Perhaps, he thought, in doing this, he was affirming the fine old family values he believed in.

In October 1943 Sid received a gold medal: "The Order of the Red Star." In December, he was asked if he would accept the most important assignment any agent had ever had.

In January 1944 he met Herman Rolle, and from then on traveled to meet him to transmit stolen documents on a regular basis. Sid liked this tall, thin, somewhat austere man, a noble genius in his estimation. Those huge horn-rimmed glasses!

At their last meeting in the hills between Santa Fe and Los Alamos, Rolle told Sid of his impending transfer back to England. Rolle raised a toast: "I hope that sometime in the not too distant future, we shall be able to meet openly as friends in Great Britain."

"I would love that," Sid said. "I hope you won't think I'm being presumptuous in saying that it would be a thrill for me to visit such famous landmarks as where Walter Scott, Bobby Burns, Wordsworth, and Shakespeare worked, with you by my side, Herman."

"That's certainly a visit I will look forward to," said Rolle.

Sid entered the apartment on Perry Street as if going into a darkened theater and having the stage light up on his fondest dreams and hopes. . . . Josh Moroze sang "This Land Is Your Land," "Ain't Gonna Study War No More," "We Shall Not Be Moved," and the "Starvation Blues." Bobby Metzger had taken out his guitar and Joe Klein his harmonica and paper comb and they accompanied Josh, stomping their feet.

Sid saw men and women with warm Jewish East Side faces, red shawls, moustaches, suspenders, black silk stockings, garter belts, Professor Myron Wooman, the tap-dancing magician, Hershel the horn player leading the musicale, in a corner two microfilm machines blazing away, people scurrying to and fro in a fire of happy activity, Jews stroking, hugging, nipping at each other's faces, nibbling. . . . "Sid, Sid," they called his name; as soon as they heard it, he was one of them, their breaths were his. . . . A fat man on two chairs fluttered his eyelids and said, "Is that the kind of thing you kiss me? A little sick kiss?" Sid gazed upon them, and as his face swept around the room, he spotted a tall, moustached, cigar-smoking young man sprouting a beaver coat, a gift from the Soviets; the young man lifted a wad of documents from the pile on the floor beside the microfilm machines, and gleefully handed them to Sid.

A few hours after F.B.I. agents began to interview Sid, he broke down and said, "Yes, I am the man to whom Herman Rolle gave the information on atomic energy."

He said he wanted a lawyer who was not a "pinko" or a "bleeding heart."

"Punish me and punish me well," Sid said.

As Sid was admitted to prison, he noticed that the admitting sergeant was struggling to spell the word "espionage." The word was strange to the policeman.

The virgin hermit Sid Smorg thought, "Why did I do it?"

Awake and Sing

How to understand everything once and for all.

—G.L.

He knew the score, and he could never go back to what he had been.

Shortly after his bar mitzvah in Alabama, Solly returned to New York with his father. The price of cotton, which had been thirty-six cents a pound, dropped overnight to six cents. Solly's father had paid for his stock with cash. He was wiped out. Solly's mother Sarah and sister Ruth, who had been living with relatives on Pitt Street, rejoined Solly and his father at a flat on Delancey Street.

When he was in his junior year of high school, Solly's father wanted him to return to yeshiva study afternoons after school. He told his father he could not go back. Society was collapsing all around him, and at the yeshiva they discussed what happened when you cut open a pregnant cow: was the baby a dairy or a meat product?

He could not consider the 613 laws of the *Halakhah* while capitalism was reaching its final stage: fascism. One day on Rivington Street, a man in a red beret had handed him a Communist Party pamphlet. Solly stayed up all night reading and rereading it. So this was why there was so much suffering all around him in the face of so much plenty. He had always been moved by the idea of the prophet Elijah coming and the hearts of the fathers returning to the sons and the sons' hearts returning to the fathers: the time when there would be love in the world, when people would be compassionate and their hearts would turn toward one another. And here was the way to reach that reality.

He would help to smash the legacy of endless wars, racism, and white chauvinism. He understood, he understood everything; he shouted down his father at the dinner table as a Jew who buried his head in the sand.

In Harlan, Kentucky, the coal miners were shot down in cold blood by the capitalist pirates because they struck for a few more pennies. When his father cursed the Communists, Solly told him, "Look what's happening in Kentucky. All the miners want is to live, Papa. What happens? They're shot down by the ruling class in cold blood. Do you really think the workers can take over the means of production without a violent revolution when even for pennies they're dropping blood?"

Solly could quote a certain pamphlet, a transcription of one of Stalin's speeches, *The Soviet and the Individual*, by heart: "Of all the valuable capital the world possesses, the most valuable and most decisive is people," and the intriguing passage: "We pushed forward still more vigorously on the Leninist road, brushing aside every obstacle from our path. It is true that in our course we were obliged to handle some of these comrades roughly. But you cannot help that. I must confess that I too took a hand in this business. . . ."

He learned about deviationists and social fascists and Trotskyite vermin. He stood up and shouted, "Comrades, let's not be bashful about the trials of the Trotskyite and Bukharinite wreckers and spies. Let's hail the death of the twenty-one traitors and the findings of Soviet workers' justice with gusto and joy. Hurrah! Hurrah! Let's eradicate this scum and smooth the grid for the coming advance of peace and solidarity." Standing on a soapbox at City College, it was Solly who answered a Jewish heckler by declaring, "Stalin brought Russia into the twentieth century. He is the new Moses of the Jews."

Solly's face was aglow, sitting in Madison Square Garden, watching Earl Browder, the quiet man from Kansas, mumble, "We're living in the rapids of history and a lot of folks are afraid of being dashed on the rocks. But not us, comrades!" After the cheering, Browder mumbled, "Our ideological struggle has to be conducted as a concrete struggle arising from unfolding events. We demand that it be carried out in a fresh language. We will defeat those who spread pessimism and despair, confusionism and obscurantism, adventurism and recklessness, and thus establish unshakable ideological ties with the workers and the peasants. As the great, the wondrous Stalin says, 'We will abolish underripe fruit and overripe fruit and quench our spirits with fresh fruit forever!' All hail to the Union of Soviet Socialist Republics, the first land of Socialism! All hail! May Stalin's example be a fresh banana forever!"

Since revolution should be fun too, Comrade Stalin had designated a little laugh that the comrades could insert into their daily speech. It went like this: "Hey *huh!* Hey *huh!*" and it could be correctly expressed with a snicker or a snort.

And so as Comrade Browder spoke, he was interrupted after each lofty phrase with the audience of twenty thousand snorting, "Hey *huh!* Hey *huh!*"

"We will root out petit bourgeois influences, eliminating the final vestiges of right-opportunism and left-adventurism, never adopting a middle-of-the-road policy, steering a firm course at this critical crossroads. At this juncture we must particularly stress the next immediate stage of progress for the people, which is inseparably bound up with, and requires the crystallization of, a broad democratic front coalition."

Browder drew a breath, smiled, and finished reading: "Comrades, it's no accident that we are here today. It is no accident, furthermore, that ours is the party that combats left-sectarianism, right-opportunism, and philistinism of all sorts. We shall continue to develop correct tactics adopted to the concrete situation."

The crowd stood and shouted, "Hey *huh!*"

29 Perry Street

Combining espionage and rich cultural evenings.

—G.L.

In the late fall of 1954, three months after Solly and Dolly Rubell had been executed for espionage, some of the gang assembled for a musicale at 29 Perry Street.

It wasn't easy to talk: walls had ears. They confined their conversation to certain topics and what might be inferred between the lines, and they played the radio loudly. Josh Moroze, the People's Songbird, tuned his guitar in a corner.

Sophie Rich, Dolly's best friend, said, "This happened in Florida a year before the arrest. It was a family vacation. Dolly's father, Sammy, was getting senile. His wife Ruth would treat him like shit. He came out of the cabana with his penis hanging out of his pants. Dolly went up to him and told him very gently so he shouldn't be embarrassed, and he put it back in. She loved her father to the very end."

Hermie, Sophie's husband, said, "And how that witch Ruth tormented Dolly." Dolly's mother Ruth had come to the death house only to put pressure on Dolly to confess, was buddy-buddy with the F.B.I., and didn't even go to the funeral. "I don't go to political rallies," she said.

They were the children of Seward Park High School, CCNY's engineering school, the Y.C.L. and the Steinmetz Society, old pals. Who says children cannot kill?

They had escaped the net. They didn't know whether to laugh or cry: Solly, Dolly burned to death, unimaginable suffering; Maury

95

Ballinzweig caught in Toronto after fleeing from New York; Bobby Metzger in jail for five years on a perjury conviction (only Wilfred Fuller and Joe Klein escaped to the Soviet Union)—and here they were, guffawing with relief, sucking candies, afraid to speak out loud, but free: "Ain't this an amazing bitch?" said Max Finger in a half-whisper. He'd been in it up to his eyeballs.

"Look, I don't know what they got," Renée Finger said, "but I do know what they could have had when they went through my stuff."

"Darling," whispered Sophie Rich, "I had a camera that was no bigger than my garter."

They had done the microfilming in this room. Once they had spent seventeen hours in a row photographing classified aerodynamics stuff Bobby Metzger had filched overnight from his Columbia University physics prof—he'd been entrusted with the combination to his personal safe. Then they'd collapsed in nine sleeping bags on the floor.

There had been drama in this room, soirées, good fucking, lectures on child rearing and string quartets that Solly had hired. Bobby Metzger had learned to play the guitar here. Dolly had sung arias here; they had celebrated Rosh Hashanah here by singing Christmas carols and roasting delicious suckling pigs and candied apples, rinsing them down with Riesling wines and Soviet vodka. Then they had watched porno movies, a thing they did only on Jewish holidays. There were glory days to reflect on; nobody could take them away from them.

The great Negro tenor Radford had been flown in from Holland one beautiful night; that booming voice, those eyes that were worldwide: "THE LIGHTS OF WALL STREET BURN BRIGHT ALL NIGHT LONG, COMRADES: WE MUST KEEP OUR LIGHTS BURNING TOO."

Josh Moroze began softly strumming "The Peat Bog Soldiers." Sure enough, Hermie's lips moved and he was singing not the original words to the concentration camp song, but the words that Dolly had penned in her cell:

> "We're on our way, death house defiers
> To remove you from their midst, those fascist liars.

RED LOVE

"Up and down we hear them marching
Millions, millions by our side—
Those who live and those they buried
Shall no longer be denied.

"Until at last the death house defiers
Wait not in terror for that dark and lonely chair."

Renée Finger ran from the room, weeping.

Do We Ever Really Know Anything?

Define "ever."

—G.L.

I

Six days after Solomon Rubell's arrest in 1950, Sophie Rich had been sent by Solly's friends from Manhattan to Bobby Metzger in Pittsburgh, where he was working for NACA. To Bobby's amazement, Sophie had knocked at his door, walked in (her finger to her lips), sat down on the couch, took out $3,000 in bills, and wrote out a message in longhand on a pad of ruled paper. The message from Solly gave Bobby instructions on how to flee the country through Mexico. Declaring aloud, "Begone, stranger, I know not what thou seeketh, you must be nuts," Bobby slammed the door on his old friend and flushed the message down the toilet.

Only a few days before Sophie's visit, the F.B.I. had called Bobby in for a chat about the Perry Street apartment, and he was now sure they knew of Sophie's visit. He panicked, and went to the Pittsburgh F.B.I. office and told them of the strange visitation. He said he thought he was being set up, although he did not know "by whom or what for."

The following day, F.B.I. agents knocked on Sophie's apartment door on the Lower East Side of Manhattan and told her what Bobby had told them. Bobby was no stool pigeon, so this was very strange news indeed. Sophie pulled herself together.

"Yes, indeed, gentlemen, Bobby is correct. Except that the message was not from Mr. Rubell, whoever that is."

"Who was it from?" the beefy Irish F.B.I. lad inquired.

"Well, I really don't know," Sophie answered. "Why don't you come in?" Beckoning the two agents into the apartment, she explained what had occurred.

"This may sound funny," she said. "A stranger knocked on my door. I was on the phone with my boy friend at the time. The stranger was carrying an apple in his hand. I was uncertain about him, but told him to come in. Just to make certain, I left the phone off the hook so no one could disturb us."

The agents sat down on the chairs Sophie provided for them and gazed up at her. "Well, sirs, the man came in and asked me if I knew Prescott. I said no, and he said, okay, that didn't matter. He wanted me to go see Bobby in Pittsburgh. He took out $3,000 in small bills wrapped between pieces of black cardboard and held together with a purple rubber band. I hope you're writing this all down.

"I immediately made plane reservations for Pittsburgh using the name Mrs. Harry Salsberg, and flew there the next day. When I saw Bobby he was very negative about this whole thing. He said I was 'nuts to get involved with such people.' He was absolutely right. Sometimes I don't think I have a brain in my head. I went back to New York with the $3,000. Two nights later, the same stranger turns up here, asks me what goes, and took back the money. That was it."

Summoned to appear before the grand jury the following week, Sophie sat in the waiting room across from Solly Rubell. The two sat facing each other for two and a half hours without showing any sign of recognition. Solly, whom Sophie had known for fifteen years, who had given her the greatest break you could ask for in this life.

When Sophie was called in to talk with the prosecutors, of course she told them she had been advised by her lawyers of her right to avoid self-incrimination. She would answer no questions without a grant of immunity.

Dolly Rubell was arrested three days later.

Sophie was given summonses four more times. Each time she refused to answer any questions, although they threatened to jail her for contempt. Agents followed her wherever she went and inspected her garbage.

Then she was called in and asked to look at pictures of men who might have been the stranger with the apple who sent her to Pittsburgh.

She gazed at pictures of her dearest friends, all the group from Perry Street: Maury Ballinzweig, Wilfred Fuller, Joe Klein, Max Finger, everybody she knew from the neighborhood. None of them, she said, was the stranger who sent her to Pittsburgh.

When Bobby Metzger was summoned before the grand jury, he was asked if he knew Solly and Dolly Rubell, Maury Ballinzweig, Jed Levine, and the rest of the old gang. He said he did not know Solly at all and could not identify a photograph of him, and that he'd seen some of the others around but knew them only casually when he was at City College. He said he had not stayed in the apartment on Perry Street since June 1948 (when he had dropped in sometimes) and that there was never any photographic equipment there.

Bobby went on trial for perjury in February of 1953. The prosecutor recalled his answers to questions from the grand jury about Sophie's visit to him in Pittsburgh.

QUESTION: What did you say to her, "Hello, Soph"?

METZGER: I may have said, "Hello, Sophie," and "What are you doing here?"

QUESTION: What did she say after you said, "Hello, Sophie. What are you doing here?" You probably added, "To what do I owe the pleasure of this call?"

METZGER: She must have said something to the effect of, oh, she would like to talk to me.

QUESTION: What did she talk about?

METZGER: Well, I don't think she said anything about her mission to me aloud. She may have mumbled something else.

QUESTION: "Do you have a piece of paper," or something?

METZGER: I think she just peered about, saw some paper, and took it.

QUESTION: Did she beckon you to come over and sit beside her?

METZGER: Did she beckon?

QUESTION: Yes.

METZGER: I do not recall specific beckoning.

QUESTION: And she wrote that she was told to come out and see an aeronautical engineer.

METZGER: Yes.

QUESTION: Did you ask her why she picked you out of all the aeronautical engineers in Pittsburgh?

METZGER: Gee, I didn't.

QUESTION: Didn't you think it was rather strange that she chose you?

METZGER: I did think it was strange.

QUESTION: Did she explain to you why she picked you out?

METZGER: No, she didn't.

QUESTION: Didn't you ask her?

METZGER: I think I did.

QUESTION: What did she say?

METZGER: She?

QUESTION: Sophie.

METZGER: It may not have been her.

QUESTION: It may not have been who?

METZGER: Sophie. It looked like a man.

QUESTION: Now, hold it. Fun is fun, but let's not get ridiculous.

METZGER: What must you mean?

QUESTION: You must remember something she said. Where was your mind?

METZGER: I was real upset at the time.

QUESTION: What did she say after she started to write on that pad?

METZGER: She or he had memorized instructions as to how this engineer and his friend were to leave the country.

QUESTION: Yes, but what were they? What were the instructions?

METZGER: I didn't let her get that far. I told her I wasn't interested in what she had to say, that I hoped she wasn't getting in trouble or doing anything naughty.

QUESTION: You've said you thought her visit was a trap. What sort of a trap?

METZGER: Of course I had been reading about the spy cases in the paper. She did mention in writing that she knew Solomon Rubell. Well, here I was being asked to flee the country for some reason. So I wondered if somebody was trying to trap me into something, since I had no reason to leave.

QUESTION: You knew exactly that Rubell had been arrested?

METZGER: Yes.

QUESTION: So that when his name appeared on that paper of hers, you weren't completely ignorant of the fact, were you?

METZGER: Oh, no.

QUESTION: Didn't you immediately connect that arrest up with her visit, in your mind?

METZGER: Yes, I think I did.

QUESTION: Of course you did. You are a doctor, with a Ph.D. The Rubells and the arrests and the F.B.I. visit—that is one, two; and when she is there, asking you to flee the country, you immediately have to associate yourself with the Rubells in your own mind, and her visit—is that correct?

METZGER: Yes.

QUESTION: Then you must have said something to her. You must have not only been confused, but you might have been shocked. Look, I know that if I was in that situation, and I was completely innocent, and somebody knocked at the door and said, "Look, get out of the country. The Rubells—" I would resent it; I tell you, the air would be blue by the time I got through with someone like that. I think that's what any normal, innocent person would do. Now Mr. Metzger, what *did* you do? Hmmmm?

METZGER: I don't think I lost my temper. I thought she should leave.

QUESTION: You mean you were practically accused of espionage, and you didn't lose your temper?

METZGER: Not in the conventional sense.

QUESTION: Don't you ever get mad at anybody?

METZGER: Not very often.

QUESTION: If someone came up and slapped you in the face, wouldn't that make you mad?

METZGER: Yes, but I don't recall when that has ever occurred.

QUESTION: Generally speaking, what did Sophie Rich say to you when she came to your apartment?

METZGER: I don't know. It may not have been her.

QUESTION: Oh, please, please. Here is a woman that practically accuses you of being a spy. She puts a finger on you. She selects you out of hundreds of millions—she picks you as the one to flee the country. And you don't even recall what was said. You are painting yourself almost as a person who is committing perjury, my friend. Are you telling me you can't even recall what happened at that time?

METZGER: It certainly seems incredible, I know.

QUESTION: If I told you the same story, you would think there was something wrong with me, wouldn't you?

METZGER: I couldn't answer that. I don't know.

QUESTION: Tell us everything that Sophie Rich wrote down that day when she dropped in on you in Pittsburgh.

METZGER: She wrote that she had instructions from a stranger in New York, and money which she was to transmit to an aeronautical engineer in Pittsburgh. She made some mention of a second friend in along there. The instructions were how this person, and presumably this friend, were to flee the country.

QUESTION: Go on. That isn't all?

METZGER: I believe I interrupted her on occasion, with questions as to why she had visited me, and why she thought that I had anything to do with this, whatever it was; that I hoped she wasn't doing anything naughty, although I realize this all sounds kind of trivial now. At this point I think she mentioned she knew Solomon Rubell.

QUESTION: Did you ask her why she happened to pick you out?

METZGER: Yes, I asked her about that.

QUESTION: What did she say?

METZGER: I don't know.

QUESTION: You don't know what she said when you asked her why she picked you out?

METZGER: That's right. She said something like, I might judge this for myself. I recall that phrase.

QUESTION: What did you do with the paper on which she wrote out her message to you?

METZGER: I destroyed it.

QUESTION: Why?

METZGER: I don't know why.

QUESTION: Well, you must have had some reason?

METZGER: It was . . . I was really rather upset and I presume I acted in response to an impulse to deface the memory of this visit.

QUESTION: Why, for what reason, if you were innocent?

METZGER: I can't give you a logical reason.

QUESTION: You have seen the pictures of the Rubells, haven't you?

METZGER: Yes.

QUESTION: You still cannot identify them?

METZGER: That's right, sir.

QUESTION: You graduated from CCNY in 1938?

METZGER: Yes.

QUESTION: Well, wasn't Maury Ballinzweig one of your classmates?

METZGER: Well, I understand that he was.

QUESTION: You know he was.

METZGER: I am sorry. I cannot recall Ballinzweig being in my class.

QUESTION: Perhaps this will help you: When Maury Ballinzweig applied for a position with the General Electric Company, your name was given as one of his references, as a man whom he knew for more than eight years. Why did he pick you out?

METZGER: This is news. I don't know.

QUESTION: It may be bad news.

METZGER: I certainly must have known him in City College.

QUESTION: You certainly must have; and you certainly must have known him afterwards, and you certainly must have met him almost every day at the meetings of the Steinmetz Society.

METZGER: I can't recall anything like that.

QUESTION: Were you ever present in the apartment of Solomon Rubell?

METZGER: Well, I would say no definitely, but it has to be to the best of my recollection.

QUESTION: Were you ever present in the apartment at 29 Perry Street rented by Solomon Rubell?

METZGER: I would say not.

QUESTION: How well did you know Ballinzweig after college days?

METZGER: Well, I don't know.

QUESTION: You don't know how well you knew him? What was your relationship, just a friend?

METZGER: Well, it certainly couldn't have been more than a friend.

QUESTION: Well, what was it? Tell us. I don't know. I'm just asking.

METZGER: Well, at school, he was a classmate, and to some extent I kept in touch with him afterward.

QUESTION: Well, in what manner did you keep in touch with him?

METZGER: Well, either by correspondence or occasional personal contact, or both.

QUESTION: In other words, you were quite friendly with him?

METZGER: Well, I wouldn't say I was quite friendly with him.

QUESTION: What was the correspondence about?

METZGER: It may not have been direct correspondence.

QUESTION: What would the personal conversations be about, the oral conversations, what would you talk to him about, what would the meetings be about?

METZGER: Oh, just general, social stuff.

QUESTION: I thought you said you weren't friendly with him.

METZGER: Well, I don't know. I can't recall specific meetings. I don't recall coming to New York for the purpose of seeing Ballinzweig.

QUESTION: And you said you never saw Rubell after City College days.

METZGER: Yes.

QUESTION: And you were not with him on any occasion after you graduated from City College; you never spoke with him.

METZGER: Yes. I can't recall any such occasion.

II

The third day of Bobby Metzger's trial began.

Maury Ballinzweig's best friend, Jed Levine, was called as a witness for the prosecution.

QUESTION: Did you ever see the defendant Robert Metzger with either Rubell or Ballinzweig or in the company of both of them at any time while you were at City College?

LEVINE: Yes.

QUESTION: How often?

LEVINE: Well, Metzger and Ballinzweig, I would say three or four times a week, at least.

QUESTION: Where?

LEVINE: In class, the hallway, we had lunch together, just around the school.

QUESTION: Did Rubell and Ballinzweig talk to Metzger?

LEVINE: Yes.

QUESTION: Did he talk to them?

LEVINE: Yes.

QUESTION: When you were in City College, did you see Metzger with Rubell at any time?

LEVINE: Yes.

QUESTION: How often?

LEVINE: Maybe once or twice a week.

QUESTION: Where did you see them talking together?

LEVINE: In the hallways, again in classrooms, in the alcoves at lunchtime.

QUESTION: Do you recall what Maury Ballinzweig was studying at City College?

LEVINE: Electrical engineering.

QUESTION: And do you recall what Solomon Rubell was studing there?

LEVINE: Electrical engineering.

QUESTION: And do you recall what Robert Metzger was studying at City College?

LEVINE: Electrical engineering.

QUESTION: Now, do you recall any other occasion when you saw Bobby Metzger in the company of either Rubell or Ballinzweig?

LEVINE: I attended two Young Communist League meetings in the East Bronx near Westchester Avenue between 1936 and 1938 in the company of Bobby Metzger, and at these meetings we saw Maury Ballinzweig, Solomon Rubell, and Joe Klein, and we went over to say hello to them.

QUESTION: Did you ever have any conversation with Metzger with reference to the Young Communist League?

LEVINE: Yes.

QUESTION: Would you state what that conversation was?

LEVINE: He told me that he was active in Y.C.L. and pointed out as examples of members Maury Ballinzweig, Joe Klein, and Solomon Rubell.

QUESTION: Were there other occasions when you saw the defendant in the company of either Ballinzweig or Rubell?

LEVINE: On several occasions we went downtown to rallies at Union Square and on these occasions Bobby Metzger, Max Finger, Joe Klein, Maury Ballinzweig, and Solomon Rubell were there together.

QUESTION: What was the Steinmetz Club?

LEVINE: It was associated with the Young Communist League at City College.

QUESTION: How many meetings did you attend?

LEVINE: I would estimate from ten to twelve.

QUESTION: What period did these meetings cover?

LEVINE: Approximately from the fall of 1937 through the spring of 1938.

QUESTION: Do you recall the people who were regularly present at those meetings?

LEVINE: Solomon Rubell was present; Robert Metzger; Ballinzweig; Klein; Finger; Rich; Bernstein; Fuller; Roth; Stone; Goldberg. That is about all the names I can recall right now.

QUESTION: Do you recall anything about Solomon Rubell's role at these meetings?

LEVINE: Solomon was the leader.

QUESTION: And Bobby Metzger's?

LEVINE: I recall Bobby Metzger as being a man of guarded opinions, a man of great reserve. But when he spoke, he spoke very fittingly, very aptly, sometimes with a touch of irony, sometimes a touch of wit.

QUESTION: Did you ever live with Maury Ballinzweig?

LEVINE: Yes, in Washington from 1939 to 1941.

QUESTION: Did Ballinzweig make any trips out of Washington while he was living with you?

LEVINE: Yes, he did.

QUESTION: Where did he go?

LEVINE: He went to visit Metzger when Metzger was working in Virginia.

QUESTION: Did you ever attend musicales at Perry Street?

LEVINE: I did. In 1944.

QUESTION: Who was present?

LEVINE: My wife, myself, Solomon and Dolly Rubell, and Joe Klein. There was a little dancing, and we had sandwiches later on. A string quartet arrived from the Jefferson School, and a folk singer named Josh Moroze. Joe Klein played guitar music, and he also had some records of guitar music by Segovia. He also had a book on music composition and harmony that we all looked at. Bobby Metzger took out his guitar and played duets with Joe Klein.

QUESTION: Was Solomon Rubell there during all of that time?

LEVINE: Yes.

QUESTION: Do you recall where the apartment was located in the building on Perry Street?

LEVINE: Well, it was the top floor, either the fifth or the sixth floor. It was a walk-up apartment.

QUESTION: Did you ever see Bobby Metzger again?

LEVINE: Yes.

QUESTION: Where?

LEVINE: In New York.

QUESTION: When?

LEVINE: In 1946.

QUESTION: How did this come about?

LEVINE: I came in from Washington and called Solomon and arranged to meet.

QUESTION: Where?

LEVINE: We went to a restaurant a few blocks away from the Perry Street apartment, the Blue Mill. Bobby Metzger was there, Joe Klein, Max and Renée Finger, they were waiting for us, and Solly Rubell. Maury Ballinzweig and his wife soon joined us. We had dinner.

QUESTION: What did you do after dinner?

LEVINE: Sol Rubell asked us all to go down to his other apartment on Catherine Street.

QUESTION: What time of year was this?

LEVINE: It was Christmas. We took a trolley there. There was a Christmas tree and a Chanukah menorah in their apartment. Also a picture of Porky Pig.

QUESTION: Do you remember what was discussed that night?

LEVINE: We talked about the problem of how to handle these holidays in terms of small Jewish children.

III

QUESTION: Well, now, you heard Mr. Jed Levine testify, did you not?

METZGER: Yes, I did.

QUESTION: And he testified, in general, to the times when he saw you and Rubell together, or you and Ballinzweig together. Do you recall that testimony?

METZGER: Sure I do.

QUESTION: Well, now, can you say as you sit on the witness stand whether you recall the incidents that he described?

METZGER: No, I do not.

QUESTION: Even now, after you have heard Levine testify, can you today recall definitely one instance where you were with Rubell? Or Ballinzweig?

METZGER: No, I cannot. No specific occasion.

QUESTION: Well, let's come to the general situation. Do you recall generally that you met them in college?

METZGER: Not that I met them. I presume I met them. One doesn't sort of meet people. I recall them from City College.

QUESTION: Do you recall ever talking to either one of them?

METZGER: Specifically, no.

QUESTION: Can't think of one conversation you had with either of them?

METZGER: Nope. That's right.

QUESTION: Do you know Sophie Rich?

METZGER: At the present time I do not know her. I know who she is, and I knew her, but I cannot say that I know her at the present time. I know the person you are referring to.

QUESTION: Did you know her in July 1950 when she visited you in Pittsburgh?

METZGER: In a sense. I knew who she was, probably, yes, and I would say in the sense in which you probably think you mean it I "knew" her as you put it, then, yes.

QUESTION: One more time. Now, I would like to have the answer again to this question: Do you know Sophie Rich?

METZGER: I can't answer that in the way you ask it.

QUESTION: Now, tell me why you cannot answer it.

METZGER: There wasn't enough of a contact to tell you about her. I think I explained this before. I know who she is. If you brought her in here I think I would recognize her, say "Hi, Soph," and if I had anything personally to do with her, if I saw her socially, I would, of course, say that I know her and regard myself as knowing her, but I haven't seen her for some time. Lots of strange things, strange to me that is, have happened since then, and I cannot say that I know the person at the present time.

QUESTION: Just what is the concept conveyed to you in your mind by the word "know" when you are asked, Do you know an individual?

METZGER: My answer would simply depend on the individual and the circumstances.

QUESTION: Without the individual being named, just generally—if you were asked, Do you know an individual, what concept is conveyed to your mind by the word?

METZGER: When you put it that way, the only way I could answer your question would be to go and look it up in the dictionary and tell you. Look, I don't think I have an unusual reaction to being asked whether I know somebody or not. My point here was simply that whenever you pinpoint a word, at that moment you become very scientific about it, and at that moment the ordinary standards of social contact and the meanings we attach to words in talking with each other cease to apply.

QUESTION: Now when Sophie Rich came to see you in Pittsburgh in 1950, she was no stranger to you, was she?

METZGER: No, she was not.

QUESTION: And when she mentioned Solomon Rubell to you, you knew that that was the Solomon Rubell from City College whom you had seen during those years since, didn't you?

METZGER: Well, with all this characterization, I would say no to that question.

QUESTION: Did she mention the name Solomon Rubell?

METZGER: I don't think she did.

QUESTION: Do you recall whether she did or didn't?

METZGER: No. What I recall is that she wrote it down. I don't think she mentioned it at all.

QUESTION: When she wrote the name down, did it awaken memories or recollections in your mind as to a certain individual by that name?

METZGER: Well, in a sense, yes. I had just been reading about his arrest in the papers.

QUESTION: Did you realize whom she was referring to with relation to your own past experience or contacts?

METZGER: No, I didn't recall Rubell from school. She didn't refresh my recollection in that respect at all.

QUESTION: Mr. Metzger, hadn't the F.B.I. questioned you about Rubell in the week preceding Sophie Rich's visit to your apartment in Pittsburgh?

METZGER: I am not sure.

QUESTION: Do you deny that they did?

METZGER: No, I can't deny it.

QUESTION: When Sophie Rich offered you money to flee the country and identified herself by using Solomon Rubell's name, didn't you stop to ask yourself where you had met Solomon Rubell?

METZGER: Perhaps I did have some such reaction. I mean that is a peculiar question, but I believe I may have had some such reaction, yes.

QUESTION: When Sophie Rich mentioned Solomon Rubell's name, what did you say to her?

METZGER: I don't recall.

QUESTION: Mr. Metzger, isn't it a fact that you knew exactly what she was talking about, and that is why you did not ask her anything about Solomon Rubell?

METZGER: No, on the contrary, I didn't know at all what she was talking about.

QUESTION: Did you want to cooperate with the government at that time?

METZGER: That is right.

QUESTION: And you say that Sophie Rich wrote down all these instructions and information on a piece of paper which she left in your apartment. Is that correct?

METZGER: Yes.

QUESTION: You didn't call the F.B.I. that day, did you, Mr. Metzger, and tell them about this visit?

METZGER: No, I didn't.

QUESTION: Did you call them the next day?

METZGER: I don't think I did.

QUESTION: Isn't it a fact that you didn't tell the FBI about Sophie Rich's visit until they called you into the office three days later?

METZGER: They called me?

QUESTION: Yes.

METZGER: Oh. I was just about to.

QUESTION: You realized the importance of this piece of paper, didn't you, Mr. Metzger?

METZGER: Well, to what extent?

QUESTION: In connection with this F.B.I. investigation of Rubell, about which you had been interviewed just before.

METZGER: I can't answer that. I don't understand your concept of "important" there.

QUESTION: Isn't it a fact that at the time Sophie Rich visited you, you knew the F.B.I. had you under surveillance?

METZGER: Yes, I knew that.

QUESTION: Isn't it a fact, Mr. Metzger, that the only reason you told the F.B.I. anything at all about Sophie Rich's visit was that you believed they knew about it?

METZGER: Not at all.

QUESTION: What did you do with the paper that Sophie Rich wrote those notes on?

METZGER: I destroyed it.

QUESTION: Is that your idea of cooperation with the government?

METZGER: I was under emotional strain at the time. Sorry.

QUESTION: Mr. Metzger, what connection of yours with Rubell were you hiding when you destroyed that paper?

METZGER: None whatsoever.

QUESTION: Now, Mr. Metzger, isn't it a fact that you paid rent over a two-year period and gave your address as 29 Perry Street in the years 1947 and 1948 for the purpose of voting?

METZGER: Yes.

QUESTION: Didn't you give Columbia University 29 Perry Street as your permanent home address?

METZGER: I may have.

QUESTION: Mr. Metzger, were you living at 29 Perry Street?

METZGER: No, I don't think I was.

QUESTION: Mr. Metzger, why did you deliberately conceal that address in filling out government forms and the questionnaire that you filled out for the Atomic Energy Commission?

METZGER: There was no attempt at concealment.

QUESTION: Mr. Metzger, did you have good reason to lie about living at 29 Perry Street?

METZGER: No.

QUESTION: Do you mean to tell me that you didn't know Solomon Rubell was the tenant of the apartment you lived in and that you were subletting the apartment from him?

METZGER: Certainly not.

QUESTION: Do you deny that Rubell, yourself, Ballinzweig, and many others engaged in the microfilming of stolen documents in the Perry Street apartment?

METZGER: It never happened to the best of my memory.

QUESTION: Didn't you meet Solomon Rubell regularly there while you were living there?

METZGER: No, sir, I did not.

QUESTION: Once again, did you ever live at 29 Perry Street?

METZGER: Oh, I stayed there a while, yes. I don't believe I regarded myself as living there, but I stayed there off and on for a certain period.

QUESTION: You didn't regard that as your residence?

METZGER: Well, in what sense?

QUESTION: A place where you resided.

METZGER: Yes, I resided there occasionally.

QUESTION: And did you live in a continuous fashion at 29 Perry Street?

METZGER: Well, no. This is a question of attitude.

QUESTION: How long did you live there?

METZGER: Well, I stayed there on various occasions between 1946 and 1948.

QUESTION: For how long a period of time were you there?

METZGER: Oh, days, weeks, months, years. That sort of thing.

QUESTION: Mr. Metzger, you have stated many times that you did not know Solomon Rubell.

METZGER: That is certainly correct as I recall. I believe I said that.

QUESTION: Mr. Metzger, I show you Government Exhibit 32-C for identification, and ask you if that is your signature?

METZGER: Yes.

QUESTION: What address do you give on that money order?

METZGER: 29 Perry Street.

QUESTION: What month is that?

METZGER: March 24, 1948.

QUESTION: And where do you send the money?

METZGER: To S. Rubell at 110 Catherine Street, New York City.

QUESTION: I show you Government Exhibit 32-D for identification, and ask you if that has your signature?

METZGER: This is a similar money order with my signature from 29 Perry Street, dated April 26, 1948.

QUESTION: To whom is it addressed?

METZGER: S. Rubell, at the same address.

QUESTION: I show you Government Exhibit 22-F for identification; is that your signature?

METZGER: Yes, this is a similar money order dated May 22, 1948. The other facts are the same.

QUESTION: Same address, 29 Perry Street?

METZGER: Yes.

QUESTION: Addressed to Solomon Rubell, New York City?

METZGER: Yes.

QUESTION: I show you Government Exhibit 22-G for identification, and ask you if that is your signature?

METZGER: Yes, it is.

QUESTION: What address do you give there, Mr. Metzger?

METZGER: 29 Perry Street.

QUESTION: Where do you send it?

METZGER: To Solomon Rubell, 110 Catherine Street, New York.

QUESTION: And what is the date of that?

METZGER: June 23, 1948.

QUESTION: I show you Government Exhibit 22-H for identification; does that have your signature?

METZGER: Yes, it does. The address is 29 Perry Street. I send this to S. Rubell at 110 Catherine Street, New York, and the date is October 26, 1947.

QUESTION: I show you Government Exhibit 22-I, Mr. Metzger; is that your signature?

METZGER: Yes, it is.

QUESTION: What address do you give there?

METZGER: 29 Perry Street.

QUESTION: To whom did you send it?

METZGER: To Solomon Rubell.

QUESTION: To what address?

METZGER: At the same address, 110 Catherine Street, New York City.

QUESTION: What is the date of that?

METZGER: November 28, 1947.

THE COURT: I think at this time we will adjourn.

Dolly, 1934

Miss Smarty-Pants.

—G.L.

Dolly Stern would walk from Seward Park High School with her friend Sylvia Packman to the Jefferson Street Library, across from the Educational Alliance and near the *Daily Forward* building. The two girls often saw the old black woman seated on the bench by the library. She was in her forties, wrecked. Straining forward on the bench toward the sky, crying out, "Hurry, sundown . . . hurry, now . . . oh, *hurry*, sundown . . ." with different inflections and emphases, louder and softer, cutting through the afternoon dusk.

How differently such a woman would be treated in the Soviet Union, Dolly would say, and her friend would nod her head in agreement.

They hurried up the library staircase to the third floor, where their club, Pindar's Children, was located. There they read and wrote poetry.

Afterward they slowly edged their way home. They walked along dark and cluttered Delancey Street, the elevated subway roaring by above them. Men sold apples at the corner. At the market, a *schochet* stood by as a truck unloaded crates of chickens. Feathers landed in the girls' hair, and Dolly tried to pick the feathers out.

At Rivington Street, peddlers passed them, returning from their day's work, their pushcarts smelling of rotting fish and vegetables. The girls looked up and saw quilts, mattresses, and featherbeds made of goose feathers hanging out of windows.

Dolly wore a steel brace because of a recurrent back problem. She stood erect. She would cock her head when she spoke and held it up high. Sylvia thought it made her look stiff and stuffy, but couldn't tell her so. With her pale, small face, her black curly hair, her frailness, her silence, Dolly was almost like an invisible person.

But she was really pretty, too, she loved poetry and singing, and was really a good Joe when you got to know her. She had a beautiful singing voice and was a member of the music club.

The kids called her "Dictionary."

Sylvia and Dolly did not go to Hebrew school afternoons like the other kids. They studied together, at the East River Pier on Houston Street when it was hot, other times at the Jefferson Library or the Hamilton Fish Library on Houston Street.

They sang together, walking across the Williamsburg Bridge. The girls in front of them giggled as the boys, waiting on the bridge, pounced on them. But no one bothered Sylvia and Dolly. And they pretended it was the last thing that mattered to them.

They would go camping with other friends in the Palisades. Dolly's pancake, that's what they called it. They would lie under the blanket and try to sleep. If someone wanted to turn over, she would signal, and they all turned. The blanket just wasn't long enough otherwise.

Friendship for the two girls meant they could sit for hours, reading separately, not speaking. Staring through the windows of the dazzling Paramount Cafeteria on Delancey Street, where the vaudevillians and musicians from Loew's Delancey gathered. Dolly confided to Sylvia that she was afraid to go inside, that she might not use her knife and fork the right way.

It was something to be the star of the school assembly. After rehearsals, the girls would stroll down Rivington Street in the soft spring night. The tugboats' whistles sounded from the river. Dolly was radiant. She recited a poem by the people's poet, Sol Funaroff:

> *"The poet, in his nightcap,*
> *descends the stairs of the dark,*
> *and holds a flickering candle.*
>
> *"There are always bugaboos and drafts.*
>
> *"His magic cap makes him invisible.*

*"But the flame he carries reveals him.
Here in the streets of life,
His bright body walks."*

They didn't want the night to end. Sylvia would walk Dolly home. Then Dolly walked Sylvia. Back and forth.

"I'm not getting married," Dolly said. "Spending my life shopping, cooking, and cleaning.

"I'm going to be different," she said.

She got the part in the school play, *The Valiant*: the sister of a man facing execution. She recited the lines from *Julius Caesar*, her fist clenched, sweat appearing on her brow: "Cowards die many times before their death. The valiant never taste of death but once."

Dolly refused to take a typing course. She dreamed of and waited for college.

In winter Dolly's parents sat in the cold kitchen with their feet in the oven. A tub on high legs with an enamel top stood beside them. The front of the unheated flat was a store and workshop for Dolly's father, a dental technician. The flat was long and narrow. There was a toilet in the hall shared by three apartments.

In a windowless bedroom slept Dolly, her brother Hershie, two single aunts, and a bachelor uncle, Moshe. Moshe was a survivor of a famous lost battalion of World War I.

The backyard had a wooden fence around it. Dolly's brother and his friends played handball against the fence, punchball and stickball, ring o'leaveo, kick-the-can, Johnny-on-a-pony, and running bases. They swam in the East River at Jackson Street, opposite the Brooklyn Navy Yard. On very hot days the boys opened the fire hydrant and placed a barrel over the pump to get a shower of spray.

The boys hung out on the street in winter, building fires to keep warm. To earn money they collected scrap or stole large milk containers from Ratner's restaurant. They built a fire around the container and lid, and melted off the lead used to solder the joints. A can and lid contained a pound of lead, which they sold for seven cents.

When Hershie celebrated his bar mitzvah, Dolly's mother, Ruth, treated his friends to the movies at the Cannon Theater. It cost three cents to enter, or two admissions for five cents. Kids would go in the mornings, bring their lunch, and stay until evening. Mothers were allowed to come in and search for their children.

Ruth called her daughter Dolly "Miss Smarty-Pants." She smiled when she told Dolly she could not go to college. "You want to do something? Make slipcovers, like I do."

Dolly slammed the door. In the backyard, she whispered to herself. Here in the streets of life, his bright body walks. Her pounding heart gradually quieted. A pigeon hopped along the pavement.

Jerry Burns

A sensitive dog.
—G.L.

I remember blazing klieg lights, armed guards escorting me down aisles of reporters and photographers to the waiting arms of red-faced, beaming senators and congressmen with shining shoes. I always saw "Jewboy" on their rich lips, but it never came out. I would be wearing a very nice suit. (Joe would often toss me a hundred bucks and tell me how important appearance was after I went out to get him some Jim Beam). The microphones would be adjusted.

The Rubells had just been executed. I remember a truck going by on the street with streamers that said, "Two hot Rubellburgers coming up."

There I'd be on one side of the aisle with the oily and the powerful. Facing me would be some progressive, some fish wriggling on the hook. Someone who'd befriended me, most likely. My mouth would open, and I would speak.

I knew what was expected of me. Ever since I'd announced that the Communists used sex to ensnare teenagers; the next chance I got, I said the Reds were deep into the Boy Scouts.

That's how I became an expert.

It was a long climb from the Labor Youth League sessions at the Brighton Beach Community Center. I guess I saw a golden opportunity and I plugged into it. I was always an impatient person. When I got out of the army, I missed the camaraderie of group life. I thought I found it in the Party. Probably the high point was when

I sold 236 subscriptions to the *Daily Worker* and won myself a free trip to Pago Pago.

That was the stage at which I really thought I was progressive. But when I got back from my trip, I found myself still treated as a political beginner. I was twenty-six. I had considerable acting skills, a poetic sensibility. This really meant nothing to the Party. I came to realize this. You were a number to them; they looked right through you. The thing they hated most was the F.B.I. I looked up the F.B.I. in the phone book. I couldn't believe I was doing this. "I have information for you," I said curtly, my voice deepening with authority.

Basically it was like leaving a sinking ship. I see that now.

They gave me some assignments at that point.

Later they asked me: "At any point, did you hear anyone advocating the violent overthrow of the government?"

I had read the newspapers: Winchell, Pegler, Jack Lait, Lee Mortimer. I explained how the Reds used sex with young people to exploit them, "to undermine everything we hold dear."

Glances were exchanged, phones lifted, reporters arrived swiftly.

The title of the series in the *Echo* was: JERRY BURNS—I WAS A CHILD COMMUNIST. I received a hundred dollars for each article, which I dictated to an attractive secretary who admired my courage. That was the beginning.

You fall into these things. I didn't lie most of the time—I just added a key detail here and there.

When I first faced the comrades across the aisle, it was very embarrassing. But the rewards outweighed the drawbacks.

Many of the progressives had treated me like a son. Now this new rich world I had entered reacted in much the same way to me. We would all stand around with drinks in our hands discussing the next world war. They would ask my opinion. But they also regarded me as green, a boy to treat gently, to instruct.

Joe McCarthy drank a lot; he was into a very good thing; he had a real affection for me. This is how I knew him. I did little errands for him. A very attractive supporter of his who had contributed money to his campaign had to be shipped out of the country for a while. Joe slipped his arm around me and explained that someone would have to take care of her for a few months. That's how I got to go on a cruise to Tijuana, and how I met my beautiful and rich wife, Pippy Paris. The marriage was a sad, disjointed affair, but an experience I do not regret.

At first Joe had liked me, but he was a little squeamish with a Jewish boy on the make from Brooklyn. One night in West Virginia, I blazed into town with the usual drama. I was hurried into a police car by soldiers who stood at attention and was taken to the courthouse. Armed guards stood by me as I testified against a left-wing labor official, and some union members were expected to get rough. The guards took me back to my hotel and told me to be careful.

Then they left, and I proceeded to go ahead with my usual routine in these towns where I testified. I lit a candle, took my notebooks out of my briefcase, and for several hours I wrote poetry. Near midnight, I had a snack, popped into a taxi and rode out to the next town, where my agent had booked me as a burlesque comic and harmonica player.

Sherry Britton was the headliner (they still used pasties in those bygone days). I will never forget that night. Halfway into my act, Joe walked into the club. When he saw me, his mouth popped open. Then the broadest smile I'd ever seen came over his face. We understood one another truly. "You dog," he said. From that night, he was my greatest benefactor.

That was the night he showed me his war wound, a scar that sliced his back in half.

For a year or so, things went well. This, at least, was what I told myself. Yet deep down inside, I was not so sure. My marriage faltered almost from the beginning. Pippy was not happy about my place in the limelight. It was looked upon at her level of society as "gross." In fact, some of her friends nicknamed me "Gross" and called me that behind my back. It seemed a contradiction that my wife should take such an attitude (being such a supporter of Joe) but that's the way things stood.

I began to take quick flights to New York, where I haunted my old progressive hangouts. I would disguise myself: sport a moustache, color my hair, and attend a few Party functions, nibbling at the home-cooked delicacies like knishes and latkes that the little old Jewish women baked. They loved to see a young person among them again, and as in a time warp, once again I was being given socks, milk, delightful rooms filled with flowerpots on windowsills in sunny apartments on the Grand Concourse. After all, young progressives needed support. They invited me in, gave me their food, their hearts. I made notes of my conversations with them for the F.B.I., but my heart wasn't in it and sometimes I burned them. Sometimes I didn't. I would rush back to my wife's mansion in Arlington, guilty and confused.

I also began to deal in a little pornography at this point, but I soon found this was a dead-end street and abandoned it.

I guess the point is that I began to notice (and this is an indication of maturity) that my deeds had consequences. I hadn't meant any harm in putting myself forward, and yet now I realized that innocent people were losing their jobs or even going to jail. My acting career was at an impasse; my poetry seemed lackluster.

On a midnight flight back to Arlington one night, I could not eat or drink. I was in a profound state of crisis. What had I done?

On the plane I tried to set down my confused thoughts to Joe in a poem. The next day I mailed it to him. I waited anxiously for his response.

Steve Tabackin

Solly lowers his head.
—G.L.

I

Sid Smorg had led us to Hershie, Dolly Rubell's brother. That night Hershie told us that Solly had recruited him into the ring.

At this point I was formally assigned to the Rubell case. It was one o'clock in the morning in the U.S. courthouse, 26th floor.

There was, oh, a little bravado about Hershie. A bit. And a smile. I know his smile. But not fresh or anything like that at all. We were very careful with him. Very careful with him. Then he started talking about Solly, how Solly told him he had to get away to Mexico, the F.B.I. would take him next.

When we finished with Hershie we all slept on cots in the nurses' room. At eight o'clock we woke. We didn't even have a car with us. We walked to Catherine Street; it wasn't too far away.

We knocked on the door. Solly answered it. We told him who we were. Can we come in. Dolly was there and so were the kids. The apartment was a shambles. We didn't have a search warrant. We asked if we could search the house. Solly said no. But would he come down to the office with us? Oh yes, he'd come down to the office.

Did you ever see anyone transfixed? They were in complete shock. I don't think Dolly had any change of expression whatsoever. Joseph said, "What's the matter? What are you doing here?" I said, "I want to talk to your father."

I didn't know Solly Rubell from a hole in the wall. None of us did. How could we? We didn't know who he was. We had no case on him. We were going from that hermit Sid Smorg to Hershie to Solly. That was the whole thing at the beginning.

And you know, I knew in my heart, my head, and everyplace else what was going to happen. And we walked him down to the office. And Solly was scared to death. We got him to the office. Solly could hardly talk, he was so frightened. He had phlegm on his mouth. We said, "Solly, you've read about Herman Rolle, you've read about the hermit Smorg, now you've heard about Dolly's brother Hershie, it's all over the papers." I can't say he did know. I think he was so—stunned—and so down, there was no real reaction from him at the beginning.

And we started to talk to him. Now the extent of that conversation was an hour, maybe an hour and a half on the outside, if it was that long.

I said, We have Hershie, we have the hermit, we have Rolle and everybody else who was involved in this thing. Remember, we're just starting, Solly. We just heard about you a few days ago. And by the time we get finished with you, we're going to know everything about you. So if there's anything that's bothering you, that's troubling you, why don't you tell us about it now? Or whatever you want to do.

And Solly put his head down like this. When people do that, they're thinking, well, should I, should I not, and they raise their head and say, Okay, fine, or they say, I have nothing to say. That happened with Solomon. Because he put his head up.

There was no yelling, no threats of any kind. Why should I threaten the guy? I didn't know anything about him. Except I knew by that time he had been thrown out of the Signal Corps. (They had found out about his membership in the Party.) But other than that, and that he went to CCNY, I knew nothing about him. So I said, We're going to have to check everything, Sol, all about you, whatever Sid and Hershie said, we're going to go through the whole thing. Where it ends I don't know. But if it ends where I think it might, all this happened, all we're talking about, during the war.

Sol said, "May I speak to my lawyer?" I said, "Sure." I think it was Luke Rogers of FAECT. They were all members of that union. So he picked up the phone. Turned to me and said, "Mr. Tabackin, he wants to know if I am under arrest." I said, "Tell him, no, you are not under arrest." Sol put the phone down and said, "Mr. Tabackin, he told me to leave the office right away." I said, "Okay, I'll walk you out." I walked him out. Solly said goodbye to the other agent sitting there, and I walked him to the elevator.

After Solomon left, I went to my boss and said about Solly putting his head down: "Bill, this guy is not going to go anyplace with us at all. No place at all." I knew it. Because he put his head up. He never put it down again. He was, like, ready to go, and I thought he would go, he would talk, and I think he was in turmoil in his mind. As soon as he sat up and sort of got hold of himself and said, I'd like to speak to my lawyer, that was the end of it. If he was going to go, that was the time to go. I knew then it was a waste of time to even think of this guy as cooperating at all, saving himself, saving his wife, saving his kids. His mind was made up long before he came into the office.

II

Solly knew. He was just waiting for someody to come. He told Hershie that Rolle was the one, and Sid Smorg, the man who came to you in Albuquerque, would be next, and you'll be after that. And that was the way it went.

What their problem was was that we had informants all over the place. All over the Party and in the Party. And we found out afterward through them that after we took Solly down to the office, Dolly took the camera in her bag and six or seven thousand dollars and went to New Jersey someplace. Now I don't know where that Jersey place was. We never did find it and I didn't waste any time looking for it.

Anyway, that was it. Solomon went home. Or to the lawyer.

When we sat down and put everything together, we knew we had something. We also knew that Hershie would be a linchpin in this whole thing. We knew he was going to talk.

He didn't say everything at once. It doesn't happen that way. He's a human being. You want him to jump out a window or go nuts or whatever? And he can't remember all at once: his whole mind is a turmoil. You won't know this unless you interrogate people and arrest them for killing, robbing, or whatever. And I had a lot of experience with that. You go ahead, Joe—whatever you want to tell me, go ahead. Talk and talk and talk and talk and talk and talk. "All right, all right, I'll tell ya." At their due time. You try to force them, they'll balk on you. You're not trapping them; he's either going to come around or he's not.

Well, that was Solomon. After that I'd go and look at his house. I didn't have enough men; I didn't have enough time. We opened up a surveillance on them and I said, Hershie and Solly aren't going to go anyplace.

And so I'd drop by the machine shop once or twice a week. I'd wait out there. I told Solomon, I'll be outside waiting. I'll be there. I said, If you want to see me, come my way and we'll walk across the park. Or I'll go your way. The guys in the shop saw me and came out; they're all looking.

And then Solomon came out. I said, If you want to come over and say hello? He didn't. But I thought, give him a chance. They don't want to come down, I'll come up. I don't stand on any formalities. That was the last I heard of Solomon—until I arrested him. And that was that.

Maury Ballinzweig: here's the picture. That's the smug face he had on the first day he came into the office. Solomon was so much more tense: no expression. Just looking straight ahead. Mouth closed. Not a word.

Maury's wife was a dish. The Committee to Resurrect the Rubells had a meeting. My informants went. A rabbi stood up and asked Mrs. Ballinzweig about the finances of the committee. She fainted. There was pandemonium all over the place.

This was no isolated case. This was just one of many. We had so many things bouncing at the time.

For instance, a man born in Scotland of good Protestant parents who came to this country and spent his youth in the Midwest. Went to college, then Fort Hamilton, Texas, U.S. Army Air Force. Graduated, became a second lieutenant, 1923. He met this girl, a Party member, and she recruited him. They were married. I had the marriage certificate, the whole bit. And he became a courier all through the U.S.

In 1937 he picked up a beautiful blonde, she had a baby, he left his wife and they went to Moscow. He was a courier through central

Europe. Also an instructor at the espionage school in Moscow. He was there during the Yerhoz purge.

Later he came back to New York City. On a day in January 1953, I and another agent went up to see him in Mosholu Parkway, cold as hell. He wouldn't let us in. He had sneakers on, on this cold day. He came out, we walked around the parkway. I showed him pictures of his wife. I said, What are you going to do? He cursed me, got a little violent. I told the other agent to stay out of it. I said, Let him alone, Jim. He's not going to go anyplace, Jim. He's going to go right back to me. He had no place else to go.

So he came back in ten minutes and apologized. Now this was a cultured gentleman. So I said to him: "Listen, I have no objection whatsoever. If I were you, I'd feel the same way. I'll tell you why. You've been active for a long, long time—thirty odd years? And you never thought that someone like me would come up here and talk to you about it on a cold, cold day in January. Correct?" He said, "That's right, Mr. Tabackin." "If I were you, maybe I'd get even more upset than you've gotten," I said. "Your whole life is going to unravel in front of you. Don't worry about the cursing. It doesn't bother me. You're cold now; why don't you go back home?" So it ended pleasantly. And I really wanted this guy. I concluded: "If you want me, I'm in the office."

This was Tuesday. He called me Friday afternoon. He said he'd like to see me. He said, "You'll have to have a lot of time for me." He didn't want to come to my office or for me to go to his house. I said, Okay, you pick a place. He couldn't make up his mind; finally he said he'd see me Tuesday at eleven at my office.

I spent all weekend in the office. I reviewed that file. I knew every word in there. On Sunday around ten-thirty I got a call: that he had jumped under a subway car at 42nd Street and Sixth Avenue. His remains were at the police department.

I was really sick about that.

I hate to see someone die unnecessarily, not as in war or to defend your wife, but for some silly thing. Like Solly and Dolly did.

There's a guy who knew more than Rubell. A damn sight more.

So you see, all these cases taken together sharpen you and cut the edges off your square head.

You get tempered after a while; you know what to say and how to say it and what to look for. You get a sense of what's going on.

And never be mad at these people. I was never mad at anybody. I call it opposite thinking: putting myself in their place. Give me a problem 12 and 13, and give me 8, 9, and 10, and I will fill them all in for you. "I'm you." You're dealing with a human being. I have never forgotten that. Agents don't go around whacking people with clubs, throwing them into a patrol car. No. With these cases, we were dealing with a different kind of person.

Ruth Stern, the mother of Dolly and Hershie, became my friend. I first met her when I went to her house to speak to Hershie. Ruth was so nervous she wasn't able to hold the baby, and her daughter was in the hospital. I told her to make a bottle and I'd feed the baby for her. She just didn't know what to do. She knew this was coming. Absolutely she did. It was always Mr. Tabackin and Mrs. Stern. Later on it was Steve and Ruth. She said, "You realize how badly I feel about this situation. This whole time Solomon had been after Hershie. And he had my daughter in there with him. How I feel about it. I'm glad my husband is dead. We came from Russia to escape persecution. This country I love; it was our salvation. If my husband was alive today this would kill him. Or he'd kill somebody. That's the way he felt about this country. So to have my own son and daughter do this—for the Russians!"

As I said, at the beginning you just want something. Don't try and disembowel a person. Wait for him to come back. And then of course by looking at Solomon, by looking into him. We went to City College and found out about every classmate he had. One was Jed Levine. We brought Jed down. And I remember Jed saying one day, "What are you bothering with me for? The guy you want lived in back of me." Who was that? "Maury Ballinzweig. I'll tell you all about him." We went to Ballinzweig's house. The old newspapers were all outside on the step, the milk bottles were there, the mail was there, and Ballinzweig was gone. Didn't cancel anything. He just left. So when the fellows took a look at that, they said, Hey, what the hell is going on here anyway? Who is this guy?

So Jed told us about Maury. Other fellows checked the airline terminals and found his flight to Toronto. Then of course we found him. Not at first, because of his aliases, but we had agents there with legal attachés. There were fliers about Ballinzweig all over the place—on trains, all the buses.

Now I knew nothing about Ballinzweig at this point. I didn't even know who he was. I had enough problems of my own. Now the Canadians decided they wanted no part of this thing at all. They realized what it was and got rid of him. They put him in a car and drove him to the border. Some place along the line, driving home, Maury grabbed, or tried to grab, a gun from the officer. They got him and they whacked him a couple of times. Now he was a tough guy—absolutely. You play games like that in a foreign country with a guy like that driving eighty miles an hour. . . .

Maury was stocky. Not a pleasant man at all. When he was brought back by the marshals, the U.S. attorney had Maury brought over to his office to talk to him, and he asked me to sit in on the conversation. Maury was five foot nine, big head on him, and how do you do, I'm Mr. Tabackin . . . and so on. Maury sneered. He said something fresh to me and to the attorney—he got really fresh. Without any necessity, since we hadn't said anything to him. Something about he didn't like us, didn't like the government. It was something absolutely uncalled for, arrogant and fresh. I said, "Now listen, Mr. Ballinzweig, don't you get fresh with me. If you want to try something, go ahead. But you're going to get hurt. You can bet your ass on that, mister. And this conversation will end right now." He said nothing more. It was, go ahead, you guys, prove what you can.

He was absolutely nothing like Solomon. In the first place, he wasn't involved on the level that Solomon was. He was working for Solomon, but he wasn't running things. And there was a difference of personality. Maury was a very surly fellow.

Solomon was scared to death. With Maury, there was almost like a threat from him. At the time, I would have knocked him on his ass and thrown him out a window.

With Solomon, I saw the fright. I knew immediately when I smelled him, that odor. I'll go to my grave with it. It's noisome—wretched and terrible.

When we arrested Dolly's brother Hershie, I wanted to have a person who was qualified to ask questions. A man of authority, of position. We brought Hershie down, and this man questioned him at some length. When it was all over with and Hershie was gone, we sat there and said, "Well, how did it go?" He said, "Mr. Tabackin, let me tell you something. You're very lucky. We're lucky that that man Stern did not have a college education. It would have been worse than it already is."

One other thing about Maury Ballinzweig: he got fresh with one of the guards on two occasions in the city prison. He had a fight with one of the guards and the guard decked him—twice. So he wasn't a softie, this guy. I was surprised when I heard that. Because you don't deck a guy in prison. You can have all kinds of things happen to you. That was the end of him. I heard nothing about him after he went out to Alcatraz.

The Rubells' lawyer, Henky Rubin, was a very nice guy, a little gutteral, his voice, but a nice guy. The only thing I said to him later was, Henky, you know I've thought a lot of you, but I don't think you give me enough credit, buddy. That I'm as smart as I am! Because I'm smarter than you are, Henky. Now you wanted to take this goddamn Committee to Resurrect the Rubells and raise money on behalf of the kids. I beat your ass, buddy.

The Committee raised fifty thousand dollars for the kids. I was determined to see that the Party didn't get this money.

For those crazy kids. I got that money for them. I did a lot of work on that. I knew where that money was. I knew how much was in the pot. Informants advised us that when it reached fifty thousand dollars, that was as high as it was going to go, that the Party was gonna grab it. They were not going to give it to the kids. And I said, Screw you, buddy, if you think that a lot of good innocent people are going to give money for these kids and you're gonna take it and give it to the Party. When Henky, who had control of the cash, died, I got Sarah Rubell to become administrator of the estate of the Rubells and coguardian with Dean Smyth of the person and property of the children, which included the bank accounts. That's what happened. Before that, Henky's name had to be on every check.

To this day I have no case against the children at all. When I locked Solomon up, I said, "Now Solomon, tell Joseph to sit down or I'll slap his ass for him. He's kicking me." You see the kid was crying. He kicked me: "Leave my father alone."

I did get the money for them. It was cinched for Joseph, let's put it that way. Maybe some day I'll see to it that they know that I did that for them.

In the last minutes of the trial, that passport photographer showed up and said that Solomon and Dolly had come to him and asked for ninety-six passport shots. People thought it looked suspicious that the guy's office was right behind the courthouse. The thing is, I had known all along about the passport photos. I just didn't have the time or the man power to do anything about it. I looked at the yellow pages; there were scores of passport photographers.

I got a call from the warden one day: "Come over tomorrow morning first thing before the trial." Our informant in the House of Detention, Davey, wanted to see me right away. Davey told me, "Solomon came back from the trial last night all shook up. I said to him, 'What's the matter with you, Solly?' He said he was afraid that son of a bitch Tabackin was going to find the passport photographer, and he didn't want him to."

I said, "Really, Davey? Is that what he said? Forget it, Davey, thanks." Oh shit, the guy knows I'm looking. *But I had forgotten all about it.* When I heard that, I got about three hundred guys together and I said, "Get those yellow pages, get out and check every damn photographer in the city of New York." That was the next-to-the-last day of the trial.

Later in the day, a couple of agents came to see me. One said, "Steve, I think I found the passport photographer." I said, "Where?" He said, "On Park Row! Back of the courthouse." I said, "Why do you think so?" He said, "Well, he thinks he recognizes the prints, and he recognizes her, Dolly. What got him were those damn kids." I said, "Really? What happened?"

The photographer said it was Saturday, he was orthodox, the store was closed. He was making up his chemicals for the next day. But he let Solomon in when he banged at the door. The kids were kicking his cameras; he said, "Mr. Rubell, get those kids out of here." Then he did ninety-six copies of photos, which was one hundred and three dollars.

Well, I told you Joseph started kicking me when I started to arrest Solomon. I remembered those kids. They could pull a house down, it was perfectly all right. I said, "Get him over here right away." The photographer came over: Joe Epstein. A nice simple soul. I said,

"Come in here." I said to the attendant, "Get a seat for me and my friend right down in the front row."

We walked down the middle aisle of the courtroom. I said to Joe, "Look around and see if you can spot anybody you know." He said, "Oh, that's the guy; that's the woman over there."

So I came back and said, "I got the photographer. He just identified Solomon and Dolly."

That is the story.

A Soviet America

Get those hookers out of here.

—G.L.

In Solly's favorite pamphlet, *Happy Days for American Youth in a Soviet America*, by Max Weiss (the cover a smiling young worker in beret holding a sledgehammer over his shoulder), he read of the death of the spirit in the United States: "How many Shakespeares and Miltons are buried together with their talents beneath a sea of poverty! . . . Not so the youth of Soviet America! For them, the world would for the first time open itself wide, to be rebuilt, to be changed, to be written about. . . . There would be no mute, inglorious Miltons in Soviet America! . . . Undoubtedly a workers' and farmers' government in America would be of a Soviet form."

It was the Soviet Union that informed his hopes and his dreams. There was the concrete reality, where civilization had progressed to the stage of human brotherhood. The Soviet Union, whose constitution declared anti-Semitism a crime punishable by death. Small wonder that the workers' fatherland was bearing the brunt of the war against Nazism while the West practiced appeasement. And that antifascists from every country in the world were finding sanctuary there.

And as soon as that final battle against fascism was won, the police, jails, and army would be abolished, for no soldiers were needed to keep down a liberated mankind. Time would no longer be wasted on military drills and tactics; soldiers would lead rich cultural lives.

Even at this early stage, there was free education, free medical care, tree houses for honeymooners, the elimination of prostitution

and crime and homosexuality and venereal disease and mental illness; so soon the elderly were living to a hundred and one hundred
and twenty even more because they (and children, of course) came
first in the society. Yiddish was spoken everywhere by many workers and by many soldiers in the Red Army as well—but, in the spirit
of proletarian internationalism, Yiddish was only one choice; all the
nationalities were free to practice their customs as they saw fit. Yet
he was acutely aware of how the Yiddish theater and Yiddish books
were flourishing.

Tears would come to Solly's eyes as he contemplated the reality,
and he grew lyrical talking about it at meetings and on soapboxes.

He repeated all the information he'd received in his unit; the end
of racism and exploitation; the vitamin-filled food the workers received on the job; the poetry they wrote in their spare time in the
club rooms and libraries attached to their factories, mines, and mills;
how they played chess and checkers, sang, danced, played. The
factories themselves, so sunny and spacious, all the machinery made
safe and reliable. The infant stations at each factory where mothers
happily left their children for glorious days.

This was the end of the Dark Ages; this was where history was
tending. A new age—he would live to see it, he would live to see the
end of sharecropping and peonage and sweatshops and Jim Crow
and limbless soldiers returning from wars of capitalist conquest. He
was a red-hot; he wanted to implement his beliefs with action. He
wanted to fight with all his heart for the day when his own country
would reach that level, and he felt ennobled with the joy and the
hope and the humanity of it. Every child he saw in the street, so
innocent, so trusting—so soon to be trampled on by capitalism's
uncertainties and insecurities, mortalities, and endless cycles of war
and depression—made Solly vow to fight even harder to bring the
day sooner when a Soviet America would end the needless suffering
of all children. And he thought always of his people, herded off in
freight cars to deaths in gas chambers all across the Nazi continent,
deaths that were slow and filled with the newest, most ingenious
tortures ever devised by man. Practiced by creatures who prided
themselves on their anti-Communism. Yes, Solly knew where he
stood and why. Brecht: *In Praise of Communism*. They say that it is
evil. *But we know it is the end of evil.*

Solly was the first to arrive at his unit's headquarters every day, and he was almost always there when the others had left. He seemed to the others never to go home. Sometimes he acknowledged to himself his loneliness, but it was always with the realization that his feelings were unimportant compared with the objective situation.

Of course it was true he yearned to be holding "a dear one" (as he put it to himself) when he watched the Almanac Singers at hootenannies or the Jewish People's Philharmonic Chorus at Lewisohn Stadium in summer or the Freiheit Gesangverein, a Yiddish choral group that sang workers' songs at Webster Hall, or Soviet films at the Stanley Theater. Of course he wanted to share the struggle with someone who had a correct perspective. Among his subjective feelings were questions about what it felt like to hold a girl in his arms, what a breast felt like (he often stroked his pillow and thought the softness must be a little like that), and what a kiss felt like, how you did it, how much pressure you applied, what you did with your tongue, and with hers.

In the deserted unit, at night, he suddenly heard his pounding heart.

Vomit You Fascist Despoilers into the Sea

Speak English, for Christ sake.

—G.L.

A play by the famous Soviet playwright Yuri Yevbrashsky had been hastily translated into English on behalf of the executed Rubells. *Vomit You Fascist Despoilers into the Sea* had a cast of four: Dolly and Solly Rubell, Lash, a dour government agent dressed in black and wearing an eye patch, and Wilhelm, a cynical but sentimental prison guard. It was set in the Rubells' death cell.

The play began with Wilhelm holding a camera and waving a hundred-dollar bill before the Rubells. He was pleading with them to kiss so he could sell the photograph to a Hearst reporter waiting outside. "For upon executing this embrace of love a lot of money I can totally receive!" he declared.

"Sweet guy, never will us, designated progressive lovers, crazy with commitment, befoul our nest to Trotskyite plotters of capitalist press," the Rubells said in unison.

At this point, Solly fell asleep and talked aloud about the destiny of an apple sitting on the table and about the inspiration he had derived from Beethoven, Michelangelo, and Sacco and Vanzetti.

Lash entered and handed Solly a confession. "Glorious life of bourgeois trash will enhance your pleasures withal," he said, "and freedom for you and your helpmate on a big horse down Wall Street and plenty of bucks, if you sign on the line that is dotted."

Solly tore the paper into shreds. "Never will us, designated progressive lovers, crazy with commitment, blow up our honor forever for termites of McCarthyism."

At this point Solly recited the Gettysburg Address. Concluding, he turned to Lash and said, "Please to inform the Attorney General and the President, in their hands our livelihoods are perched, yet the truth it is amazing, but their mercy we throw into the garbage!" Dolly raised her fist and shouted, "For to confess to save our livelihoods, all the American workers and peasants to be dishonored they would be!"

The second and third acts consisted of further discussion and argument between the Rubells and Lash about confessing. Lash began whispering that he was on their side, but that the government held him in its clutches because he too had a progressive background. Still the Rubells would not confess, and the annoyed Lash ordered Wilhelm to escort Solly and Dolly to the death chambers. The Rubells held their heads high throughout this, murmuring "Brotherhood" and "Jackie Robinson" to the audience and applauding back Soviet-style when the audience cheered them. "Okay!" Solly called out.

Suddenly the lights went out, and the frightened Lash wondered aloud if the peace forces of the country had arisen in fury and were hurrying to the defense of the Rubells. But the lights went on again, and the Rubells walked quietly to their execution while the angry Lash stormed out of the cell.

The lonely prison guard, Wilhelm, stood alone in the empty cell. "What, pray, is this?" he said, and discovered on the wall a message in Solly's handwriting. "To our children," he read aloud: "Do not forget us. Remain faithful to the future. Peace, lead, and roses."

The curtain fell.

The Prince of
Progressive Humanity

Sensitivity rewarded.

—G.L.

When Maury Ballinzweig came out of prison in 1966 after sixteen years under lock and key, the balance of forces in the world had shifted to his side, to the side of rationality, peace, progress, and human problem solving.

Yet curiously, cancer now seemed to be riddling almost everyone.

These were the exhilarating contradictions.

"Are you having an affair, Linda?" he had asked his wife when she visited him in prison near the beginning of his stretch.

"I am." She had paused. "But with X, not Y."

She was glowing, in a black gown. She was on the way to meet Sartre on Maury's behalf and could not conceal her excitement.

He had looked at the ground, unable to raise his head.

Although in time he had come to realize how glad he was that she was not sacrificing herself for him, and how good it was that it was X, not Y.

A steel rod, that's how they designated the Lincoln Battalion members in Spain who had been honored with Party membership. Those who could be trusted to maintain the purity of the Party line. Who could not be broken.

Maury Ballinzweig had no use for Susan Sontag. Or the likes of Susan Sontag. He didn't care what she had said, and wondered why all the hoo-ha. Berlinger of the Italian C.P. had said worse about Poland, and that didn't bother him. Maury snorted at the sentimentality.

Look, after they arrested him, the Party demanded that Maury's mother give up her Party card and not come to Party club meetings ever again. He understood that was necessary. He often said, "I don't go by the heart. I know that by the heart you can get a Nazi as easily as a Communist." He waited for his visitor, and sat snuggled into himself, clasping his hands between his knees in the barren room crowded with wall posters for Vietnam and Chile and Nicaragua and American political prisoners and *Guardians* and revolutionary papers strewn across the floor.

The reporter stood in the doorway shaking hands with the man in green work shirt, brown pants, and slippers, who looked like his coat had many buttons in need of sewing. Maury's long white hair was held in a ponytail by a white rubber band. He fidgeted and jumped.

He looked much older than in the black-and-red posters of the reporter's youth. The posters had been everywhere. There were large pictures of Solomon and Dolly Rubell with Maury looking from a distance over their shoulders. It was logical: the Rubells had been executed. Maury only was sentenced to twenty years.

After talking about his Social Security and about the weather, they sat down. "Whoo!" Maury yelped. "I've got two girl friends. The first one was very sweet and never surprised me. I found her boring. The new one is full of levels and she drives me crazy." He laughed buoyantly and munched pumpkin seeds.

The reporter sat in a chair wearing the Japanese slippers Maury had handed him—an aid to contemplation. Maury sat on the floor gazing up at him.

The wall posters proclaimed CHILE: FREE ALL POLITICAL PRISONERS. WHO KILLED LETELIER? The battered book-shelf contained books about the Case from all viewpoints.

Maury whistled and said, "God . . . of course you know that epilepsy is loaded with ideology coming from the ruling class!"

"Oh . . . sure. . . ."

"I might like to leave New York," he said. "I could live on my Social Security. Should I move to Oregon?"

"I like the passion of New York," the reporter said.

"The passion. Yes. True. Interesting. I don't know. What I really want to do is to help Vietnam and Grenada. What is their optimum trajectory for technical development?"

The reporter stroked his beard and muttered, "Mmmm. . . ."

They sat in silence except for the cracking of Maury's knuckles.

Maury looked at the floor and said, "So? Begin."

"About Solomon Rubell—"

"So you're going to write the twenty-fifth book about Solly."

"Tell me about him."

"As a scientist, Solly was a fish out of water. He should have been a Greek scholar. He wasn't a natural."

"Solly and Dolly went to Coney Island one day. People left their clothes in the lockers. But Solly brought all of his things out to the beach with him." Maury put up his arms and waved them. "Legend has it that all the lockers were robbed that afternoon. They always told afterward how wise Solly was."

The reporter stared.

As a boy, the reporter had pondered the posters of the Rubells with Maury Ballinzweig looking over their shoulders. At the rallies before and after the execution, the people around him had wept and moaned, they collapsed in a frenzy in the aisle, the elderly had strokes.

On the stage, Linda Ballinzweig pounded her breast. Rubell's mother wept. Maury's mother screamed—and then there was the collection. Actresses dressed in Lincoln Battalion uniforms came down the aisle, while the band played "Beyond the Blue Horizon."

The children, the children, someone screamed. The music stopped. Red and black klieg lights swept across the huge auditorium, criss-crossing the stage. An organ softly played. A drawing lit up of Solomon and Dolly in the electric chair with Maury waving good-bye, and in front of it the huddled figures of the Rubell children, in their little white stockings and caps, who held each other by the hand and walked slowly onto the stage.

People gasped. "Harry, oh my God," a woman said to her husband, "this society is killing us. We've got to stop the killing before it's too late." And she bent his nose with a kiss. The second collection began. "My daddy is innocent—" began one of the children. Screams resounded across the auditorium and klieg lights crisscrossed, the organ ripped into the shrill light and the natural voice of the people was heard:

"INNOCENT . . . INNOCENT . . . INNOCENT . . . TOSS THE WRETCHED MONOLITHS INTO THE SEA . . . RIP THE MARBLES OF STEEL OFF BY THEIR HINGES . . . ISSUE FORTH THE DAWN."

A speaker added, "And don't forget Maury Ballinzweig."

Maury fidgeted as they talked.

"I've read a lot about you," the reporter said.

"Yes. What?"

He hesitated. "Well, that your wife told you of her relationship with another man while you were in prison."

Maury stared at the toe of his slipper. He glanced up and looked down quickly, hiding what the reporter thought was a flush.

"The way the warden and the prisoners baited you about your wife. Your lousy lawyers, your best friend's betrayal. The death of your father."

Maury remained immobile.

"How did you survive?"

"Historical and political perspective," Maury answered. "I didn't look at it in personal terms. Solly was an ordinary person. I can't consider myself heroic either. 'Ordinary' doesn't mean you can't become a hero."

"About Solomon—" the reporter said.

There was a long silence.

"I never had a good hold on him."

"Did you like him?"

Maury didn't answer for a long time. They looked at each other. Maury lifted his arms behind his head and breathed from the belly. Then he looked down. "He was a comrade. This to me is saying a good deal. To understand what this meant is a whole story in itself.

"At that time I couldn't relate to people. I was an atheist at five. I got into people much more in prison."

"But did you like him?"

"He was wonderful with his kids."

"Whenever people mention Solomon, they mention you."

Maury shrugged. "It was a long time ago." He paused.

"You said that to understand what Solomon's being a comrade meant is a story in itself. What's the story?"

Maury shifted.

"My friend," he said, "beyond that, you'll have to use your imagination."

Later, the reporter said: "I thought it was Solomon I was most interested in." He added, "Now I think it's you."

"Well, I'm here," Maury said immediately. "Solomon isn't."

At the door, they said goodbye. They would meet again soon, Maury said. They shook hands, and Maury held the reporter's hand for a moment longer.

Such buoyancy! Such sweetness! Such willingness! Such trust toward a stranger! Such civilized jargon! The reporter was astonished.

What had preserved Maury?

"I want to help you," Maury had said to him.

The reporter went in search of Solomon Rubell's sister. He found her living in Lefrak City with her second husband. Color TVs flashed in the living room, where her husband sat, and in the kitchen, where she talked to the reporter. She turned off the sound, but left the picture on.

"When I went to visit Solly for the last time, I was waiting outside. I heard the guards talking in the enclosure. One of them said, 'When the spy is put on the slab.' I wanted to run in there and say, 'He'll never die.' I held myself back. I didn't want them to know I was Solomon Rubell's sister.

"A little boy, I remember him. He was the youngest of all the kids we played with. And such a beautiful baby. Little gold curls. And blue eyes.

"He sold lollipops on Shabbat, he wouldn't take the money for them. He would come back the next day to collect the penny for the lollies.

"I loved his character. Nothing but pride. He was a wonderful person. Knowledgeable, very well educated, well read. To me he was like a king. If you look at me you'll see Solly, but you'll see a much handsomer man. Before you knew it he went to

159

Hebrew school, took a keen interest in Hebrew. Put his whole heart into it.

"When he walked, he may have sloped a little. I don't remember. He entered school speaking Yiddish and didn't know English. But he learned so fast.

"Stanton Street and Pitt Street where we used to live are torn down. All gone. It was a *shtetl.* You were happy, you walked out, you were among friends and relatives. It was just a *haimish* atmosphere. In later years we had hot water and steam too. Jewish girls went with Jewish girls and Jewish boys went with Jewish boys.

"We used to walk by the river and throw our sins away . . . on *Tashlikh* on the first day of Rosh Hashanah . . . like crumbs or something. You say a prayer.

"Mama would cook and bake for every occasion. I loved Fridays but I hated Sunday when the laundry had to be done. Everything had to be stripped. And that tub in the kitchen. Mama used to stand with the board and wash the clothes. The tub would have curtains around it that she made.

"When my father got up to talk, everybody listened. And this is Solly, he inherited his intelligence, ability to talk; he was a born leader, a brilliant boy. He made sense. He wasn't as fiery in later life as he was in youth. He changed. He married and had a family. Responsibility. You look toward prospering.

"The lawyer Rubin kept saying, '*They won't dare kill them.*' When my husband opened the door at eight o'clock, the first thing he said to me was, 'I didn't think they'd do it.' He repeated that several times. And he embraced me. And we both cried. A half hour before, my little son who was twelve years old got up on the chair. He turned the clock back a half hour. He had the sense to get up on the stool, a little fella, to turn the clock back.

"Maury Ballinzweig? He wasn't cut from the same cloth. Even his mother, I heard her say in court before he testified, she said, 'I hope he'll have some of Solly's courage.' She wasn't sure."

As a boy of fifteen in the fifties, the reporter learned about the Case. The Party took it up only after the Rubells had been safely executed.

He had stood in the thin crowd, the blinding sun on the podium at Union Square in 1954. They toiled onto the stage, the released

Smith Act prisoners, blinking into the sun, thin, waving at the barricades behind which no one stood. Telegrams from Moscow, China, people's republics of Eastern Europe were read. Fists clenched. Anna Louise Strong took a bow. Johnny "Apple Seed" Beaver sang. Reverend Jilly Morris Rogers blessed the Red Army. Molly Leash read martyr poems. Solomon's sister spoke in a trembling voice: "To think he didn't live to experience the joys of television"—and wept.

Henry Winston, blinded in prison, stood with his stick. Robert Thompson, his skull bashed in by a Yugoslavian fascist in prison, sat on a chair with a pillow. Benjamin J. Davis, dying of cancer, stood tall. He shouted, "I'd rather be a lamppost in Moscow than president here." He dropped the rest of his speech and went right into his crowd pleaser: "They can call me red, they can call me black, *but they can't call me yellow.* They can call me red, they can call me black, *but they can't call me yellow.* They can call me red, they can call me black, *but they can't call me yellow.*"

They bared their throats for slitting.

This was what they knew.

Their pale complexions and gabardine suits.

They knew their lines.

Eugene Dennis read and squeaked his proclamations. No one listened. There were no human sounds. In the dry listless day, on the hot earth across from Klein's, the people's martyrs stood silently.

The problem was that two days before Solomon Rubell was arrested, Maury Ballinzweig fled to Toronto with Linda. Within three weeks they were located by the Canadian police and Maury was handed across the border to a United States agent.

Maury had locked up his house in Flatbush, left his new Chevrolet in the garage, and had not told his employers of his plans.

When he reached Toronto, Maury cashed in his return trip airline tickets and wrote to a friend in Manhattan, using such aliases as "M. Ballbearing" and "Myron Ballast." Enclosed in his letters to his friend, Maury included notes for his parents and aunts and asked his friend to forward them.

Maury left Linda in Toronto and traveled to Vancouver by himself, using five other false names, to try to find a boat that would take them abroad. Traveling around the west coast of Canada, he inquired about passage to Europe or South America. He wrote later of those lonely days:

> I spent a lot of time at the docks, walking around, hoping to find someone to talk to, someone who could give me a lead. Frankly, a lot of the time I just stood around, observing the local customs, or went "slumming." The music in the pubs was mainly starkly conventional; Doris Day and Guy Lombardo, and at first it was a novelty to observe another culture. Then it got on my nerves. I hope the music did not adequately reflect the cultural outreach of the habitués. I might have enjoyed a dance or two, but this seemed to me like impermissible self-indulgence. For these forays, I purchased prescription sunglasses, fearing slip-ons would mark me as a tourist.

After he returned in despair to Toronto, Maury and Linda were sitting peacefully in their room sipping wine and reading the Bill of Rights and the Constitution when the door was broken open. Four men surrounded Maury with guns. "Don't shoot," he pleaded. They picked him up and carried him to a car, where they beat him over the head with truncheons.

They drove around with him for hours, questioning him and slapping him in the face when he refused to answer. At the Canadian border he was handed over to a U.S. agent, handcuffed, placed in jail, then returned to Manhattan. This kidnapping became the basis of Maury's unsuccessful appeal of his conviction.

His flight had occurred at the height of McCarthyism.

But it just didn't look right.

At the Rubell-Ballinzweig rallies, there were endless explanations of Maury's "flight from the fascists." They said that what had happened "would never be allowed to occur in the Soviet Union." Progressive historians and dialecticians explained it over and over, and Maury himself called it "the most traumatic event of my life" and said that he had acted irrationally because of the atmosphere of "intimidation and repression" against opponents of the Korean War.

The explanation that stuck came from the historian of the Case, Jim Bailer. Only he had read all the intelligence sources, he said. Only he had discovered the wonderful news that the Soviet Union had never once conducted espionage against the United States. The

Soviets had told him personally that espionage was forbidden by the Soviet constitution. Then he presented the obvious parallel between Nazi Germany and America.

"Why did Maury flee from the truncheoned fascists, you ask? Should he have just stood there and waited for the knock at the door?

"I had the special privilege after I was wounded in World War II to visit Dachau with the fabulous people's singer, Paul Robeson, in 1945. In traveling from Munich to Dachau, we asked lots of people where the concentration camp was. Not one of them admitted they knew. This should tell us something about our fellow Americans who pretend not to know what is going on all about us here in America. When we got to the camp, the most significant experience for me was this: seeing the 'shower rooms' at the death chambers, where they put so many innocent victims, both politicals and Jews, to their death. There were nozzles on the ceilings. They thought they were going to be given normal showers. Instead gas came from hidden pipes on the ceiling. *Let us not be like those victims in Germany who went to their death not knowing what was happening. Let us be like Maury Ballinzweig.*"

In a public letter to Linda, Maury later wrote:

I am trying to conjure up memories of that time, yet I can remember the most trifling incidents of my life more easily. Whence the disparity?

The vacation—or "flight"—had many motivations. To see the land, to search out others—these too contributed a taste to the feast.

History entered, as it must: the Korean War, the witch-hunts, fascism's imminence. Perhaps I was frightened of something, or thought I was.

Why did I apparently decide to opt for the experience of an "assumed" name? Why did I crave this particular experience more than once? Was I trying to hide something, and what could it have been?

Clearly there was some movement on my part toward anonymity. Was I on some level running away, or perhaps toward myself? Perhaps you, my wife, could contribute some wisdom to our understanding of these events.

Was I sympathetically projecting onto Solly's experience and did I fear the concept of execution?

Put brutally, was there a cause for my behavior? What was it? Can one isolate in the maelstrom of being one simple cause in any case? This reduces life to simplistic levels, and is not my style at all.

The reporter called Maury every Sunday night, trying to get him to agree to a second meeting.

One Sunday in January, Maury told him that his mother had been mugged and that he was proud of her for not identifying the mugger. Then he said perhaps he could see him again in the springtime.

"I haven't been sleeping well since I saw you," Maury said.

"Maury, look, I want to see you again. I don't want to push you—"

"Pal, you don't have to—you don't have to! Really! I understand. Let's put it this way: the only chance I won't see you—" Maury paused, and out came a stream of laughter, "is if I go down to El Salvador!"

"Oh God."

"Look, going to these places is my idea of having fun!"

"But—"

"*I know, but I'm trying to have fun!*"

Linda Ballinzweig had been impressed by Jack Henry Abbott. "These jailers who destroy people: they're the ones who are guilty for any murders that happen afterward," she said. "Look at the black people. They're robbed of everything before they are even born. They don't even get necessary nourishment in their mothers' bellies. They're justified in whatever they do."

Maury's early attempt to join the antifascist struggle on a politically mature level took him to Cats Paw, Georgia, on a dusty hot August day in 1941. Dressed in old khakis, sweatshirt, and sneakers, driving his beat-up old Ford, he planned to melt into the local population. He carried two expensive cameras with him.

Several things bothered Maury immediately about the town: the accent of the people, which grated on him, bringing to mind reactionary viewpoints of the worst racists; and the curiosity of the townspeople toward him, which he didn't understand. Why did they stare at him? They were especially interested in his "German accent." He told them with a snort of contempt that he did not have one, and "obviously could not have one, since I was born in Brooklyn."

The young man checked into the Loveheart Tourist Home on Route 5. Then he walked into the Pevear Flour Mill and asked to see Mr. Pevear. He asked Pevear for permission to take pictures of the mill. He photographed the outside and inside of the mill and took close-ups of each piece of machinery. Then he headed for the Harris Lumber Mill and asked the foreman where and how much of the lumber was being shipped. The foreman didn't reply. Maury asked if he could take pictures. The foreman told him to get permission from the owner. Within a few minutes, the foreman saw Maury snapping away and assumed Maury had gotten permission. When Mr. Harris, the owner, saw Maury taking pictures, he did not know that Maury had been told to ask his permission.

Crowds gathered.

Maury tried to relax them by chatting about matters of general interest on a level they could understand. He asked one worker if there was a shortwave radio set in the town, and the man stammered he didn't know. "Well, can't you find out?" Maury said and turned away. He asked a man who looked more enlightened, but the man walked away without replying and called the police. Maury said to a group who were looking at him, "Can you believe those English? Such incredible arrogance? In this day and age, with all those outmoded customs and mores?"

"What do you want here, mister?" one of the men asked.

"Basically, I have a deep interest in studying Tobacco Road country," Maury replied.

When the town was getting ready to arrest Maury, Pevear took him aside and told him that he was acting in a very peculiar way. Maury took out his navy shipyard card and explained that he was on vacation.

"But what does that have to do with your taking pictures of the mills?" Pevear said.

"I'm sorry I can't seem to satisfy you," Maury said. "Nobody seems to know anything," he continued. "The English go on acting like they own the world, and in my estimation they can't do anything right. Would you want to place your destiny in their hands?"

Maury walked off and entered a radio shop. He again asked about a shortwave radio, explaining he wanted to send a message.

Maury disappeared the next morning. When the F.B.I. arrived, the landlady told them, raising her eyebrows, that the young stranger had received two special delivery letters and that he was carrying *one small bag*.

Before meeting Maury, the reporter had spoken to anyone who was close to him: old Communists, a progressive historian, Sylvia Pollack, and Sophie Siskind. He traveled to Washington for the Freedom of Information files. He'd gone to a rally for Nicaragua on a steaming hot Sunday in Tompkins Square Park. Linda had mentioned the rally, and he thought Maury might be there and he could see what he looked like now. And there he was: an old man with a long white ponytail bobbing along with quick little steps, bringing a Coke to the tall young blonde who towered over him.

The progressive historian who knew Maury well had a cheery face. Yet when she spoke agitatedly in the dark room about the Hitler-Stalin pact, the reporter could swear a change took place—her face became redder and redder. Sweat poured down her; her cheeks hollowed out. He saw horns, and smoke.

"Maury was raised in a family of Party people," she said. "His aunts were in positions of leadership: on the National Committee, chairmen of the Disciplinary Committee. From childhood on, as soon as he walked, as soon as he remembered, he was surrounded by the Party. He still resents to this day the domination of his mother. When he got his first job in Chicago, she brought the dishes and the linen to his new apartment.

"She had a great contempt for her husband. Her family was important in the Party. Her husband didn't have time, although he was a member, to be active. He ran the pharmacy, and he was there practically twenty hours a day. She played a strong activist role, and felt he wasn't active enough—that he was a *yeshiva bocher* type, that he allowed himself to be pushed around. She thought Maury was from her side of the family, and that he identified with her.

"She was wrong. He loved his father, he treasured the memories of his father. When his father became ill, his mother put him in a home. Maury never forgave her for letting his father die there while he was in prison."

*   *   *

Maury was too busy to see the reporter again. He phoned Maury every week. Maury had six, ten projects: to help improve the medical equipment in Vietnam, to attend the farewell dinner for the Vietnamese ambassador, rallies, demonstrations. "I met Abbie Hoffman for the first time at an affair for Nicaragua!" Peals of laughter. Why was this man laughing?

The months passed. On a spring day, a spy was arrested. When the reporter called him that night, he could barely recognize Maury's voice. It was minute, strangled, terrified. He did not understand why. Had the arrest brought back memories? Was Maury afraid of *him?*

Yet that was the night Maury finally agreed to see him again. They agreed on "next Wednesday night." Maury called back. He was suddenly effervescent again. Was it to be that Wednesday or the following? Maury was delighted with "the ambiguity in the language." He rocked with laughter, and hung up howling.

On Wednesday night, the reporter walked through Harlem to Maury's apartment.

He removed his shoes and put on Maury's slippers.

Maury said he felt upset that night. He looked much older, his hair frazzled. He sat scrunched up, his hands between his legs, peering downward. The reporter suddenly saw him in prison.

Maury talked again about his Social Security; he was afraid he would be getting less than he had expected.

"You said you became a much more social person in prison."

"There's a real camaraderie," Maury said. "There was an escape attempt. Half the joint knew what was going on for months. That's how tight the thing is . . . But even if I felt close to someone, for their own sake I kept aloof. It hurt me, especially with black people. One guy wanted to get even with a guy who fired me. But I said no. . . .

"I had the outside to keep me going. That was a stress inducer and a stress reducer. You go insane digging a ditch in your mind deeper and deeper into events that happened, going over and over them, with no way of breaking out. If it were analysis, okay; but it wasn't."

"You seem to be a happy person," the reporter said.

"I have to make up for those years. That's why I'm happy. In prison, you develop humanity. You see all these unfortunate people.

You feel for them. My confrères opened up to me. We walked the yard and talked. I developed a radar. There's either an open loop when you speak with somebody or there's a servo loop—engineering terms—and you really listen to what they're saying. In college I was an open-loop person. I didn't listen. In prison I listened."

"But you call yourself primarily a political person."

"Yes. People unfortunately react with their hearts rather than their heads. The heart betrays. I strictly avoid self-sacrifice. In Argentina the bastards are getting the people's support. In England they support the bitch. We wouldn't have wars if people didn't respond that way."

Maury stretched his legs out before him. "Before prison I never really had a world view, a long view. It was through the heart, not the head. Linda was very political, even when I met her in 1940. So was Solly.

"In prison the government was testing me, trying to make me a witness. Why did I resist? I didn't feel pressure. It isn't in yourself to turn somebody in to save yourself."

He suddenly said, "You know, I can't get deeply involved with a 'personal' person."

"I guess that's me," the reporter said.

"I once wrote to the Metropolitan Opera radio host asking him to compare Tosca with Leonora: two women trying to help free their men from prison. Tosca uses womanly wiles to try to help her man. Leonora turns into a boy, Fidelio, and succeeds in freeing hers.

"Apropos culture," Maury said. "I can't believe you hated *Reds*."

"Did I say that?"

"You said it. On the phone. You're an effete aesthete," he snapped. "I'm the radical, you're the liberal."

"But you couldn't tell what John Reed was motivated by."

"All right!" Maury shouted. "So you couldn't tell. Maybe Reed didn't know himself why he was doing what he was doing! So what?"

Maury sprang up and ran water into a glass. He paced around the room. He picked up a book. "Ever see this?" He showed the reporter Linda's book of poetry: *To My Beloved Prisoner*.

"No, I haven't."

"Two of the poems were to me. The others were to other people. This wasn't generally known at the time."

"It must have hurt you, about Linda," the reporter said softly. Maury stiffened.

"That was our relationship. I was powerless. Under the circumstances any other way would have seemed more painful."

"When did she tell you?"

"About a year into it. Haven't you had extramarital affairs?"

"No."

Maury was striking his hand against the chair. "Look, I don't believe in self-sacrifice. I was caught in a situation. I did not choose. They came to me with all these deals. They were not viable alternatives. She had alternatives, which would in no way take away from me. If I had faith in her, it would not take anything from me. If it hurt me, it was my own fault. It's because I'm too damn bourgeois."

"Did it hurt you?"

"Of course it hurt me." Maury stood up and moved to a table. He took a framed picture from it and silently handed it to the reporter. It was Maury as a boy in Brooklyn, sitting on his father's lap. His father was smiling. Maury took the picture back and placed it on the table.

"You don't know where I'm coming from," he said after a silence. "You're too full of feeling—that's what I get from you. Feeling just works off guilt," he said with contempt.

"No one's more full of feeling than you."

"But I control it." Maury stood up. "I think that's it for today." The reporter put on his shoes and coat.

Maury ripped the reporter's name off his bulletin board.

"*Farfallen*," he said.

"What does that mean?"

"The opportunity is lost."

Put Down Your Forks, Comrades

I'll have a bite.

—G.L.

Solly was squashed into his seat at the Paramount Cafeteria on a Saturday night at eight-thirty beside the other comrades from his unit.

Leon Pepstein, who always wore a tweed scarf draped over his shoulder, was talking about the coming abolition of the army in the USSR: "Why waste time on military drills when you have close ties with the workers?" he shouted. No one disputed him. "None of this blind obedience to bullshit orders! No class distinction! As the masses become social beings, as the economic basis for crime and other antisocial acts is removed, police won't even be necessary."

Leon suddenly pounded on the table and they all sang out the City College song against President Robinson. Robinson had welcomed the fascist students from Italy and suspended student protesters who had objected, calling them "guttersnipes," pointing his umbrella at them.

> "We're all fed up with Robinson's rule
> We're sick of high-priced knowledge
> To get the nineteen back in the school
> Strike City College!"

Solly, in a mischievous mood, took his knife and fork and the silverware of the other comrades and stuck them in his jacket. "This place is already rich from the workers it exploits," he declared.

173

"No, Comrade Solly," a little voice piped up. It was the pretty new comrade who had recently joined the unit. The only girl at the table, she had been eating her food very carefully, her eyes glued to her plate. Solly couldn't bring himself to look much at girls anyway. She had looked at her plate, and he had looked at his.

Now he gazed directly at her.

"Remember," she said, "what Lenin wrote: to steal less than the state is petty thievery. When the Bolsheviks took the Soviet Union, comrade, they took a state. If you fight, you fight for a country, for important things. For principles." She took a deep breath. Everyone was silent.

Solly grinned. He dropped the silverware back on the table with a little crash and leaned toward her.

"My name, in case you're wondering, comrade, is Dolly, Dolly Stern."

The Komsomol Badge

Dreaming of Soviet justice.

—G.L.

Antonio Carelli's father stood out in the Italian community in Buffalo. The other men were immigrants who spoke little English and dressed up only on Sundays when they went to church. Arturo Carelli had an accent, but he spoke English better than anyone in the neighborhood. He always carried books with him.

On Saturdays, father and son would put on their Sunday clothes and go to the movies—usually westerns starring William S. Hart, Tom Mix, Buck Jones, or Hoot Gibson. Antonio was a small boy. When his father held his hand and they walked down the street, he was in heaven. He would cuddle up to his father while they watched the movie. Afterwards, they would go to the five-and-dime store, and his father would treat Antonio to a glass of milk and pie.

His father forbade him to salute the American flag in school or to pray with the other kids in the morning. They already knew that he didn't go to church on Sunday. But they didn't know his family was Communist.

At the beginning he didn't know the words to the prayer, but he clasped his hands and bowed his head. He didn't want to be different. And he saluted the flag with everyone else.

He was afraid that his father might find out.

At first Antonio Carelli had been ashamed of his father's politics. When he was three, his father, who was active in the hod-carriers union, was arrested in the Palmer raids. He called it his "revolutionary baptism." When he was four, his father took Antonio to a silent movie about the Bolshevik revolution. There were scenes of trenches filled with dead Russian soldiers and the Women's Death Battalion marching with rifles slung over their shoulders. His father and the whole audience cheered and shouted when Lenin and Trotsky stood beside a flag with the hammer and sickle.

His family celebrated May Day and attended meetings each year in November celebrating the revolution and marking the assassinations of Karl Liebknecht and Rosa Luxemburg. His father once won a portrait of Lenin at a raffle and hung it in the parlor.

Arturo Carelli worked during the day as a laborer. But after work, he came home, washed, ate dinner, and left to carry on his Party assignments. Many comrades visited the house on the weekends. Antonio understood little of the conversation, but he was aware that his home was very different from his friends' homes.

Antonio joined the Buffalo branch of the Young Pioneers. Wearing a white blouse and red kerchief tied under his chin, he sang with the other boys and girls, "Give a yell! Give a yell! Give a good substantial yell! And when we yell, we yell like hell and this is what we yell: Pioneers! Pioneers! Rah! Rah! Rah!" And "Two, four, six, eight: Who do we hate? Capitalists! Capitalists! Rah! Rah! Rah!" He read the Young Comrade page of the *Daily Worker*:

> *Y* is for Youth who leaders shall be
> *O* is for Oil which capitalists own
> *U* is for Union with which we agree
> *N* is for Nonsense which into our minds is thrown
> *G* is for Groups which we organize
>
> *R* is for Russia, that country of ours
> *E* is for Ended which capitalism will be
> *B* is for Bunk which teachers tell for hours
> *E* is for Endeavor a workers' world to create
> *L* is for Lenin whose ideas we follow
> *S* is for bosses' Stuff which we will not swallow

Antonio attended a meeting at which Mush Snitkin, district organizer of the Young Communist League, spoke about the "treacherous role organized religion plays in the lives of the workers from the cradle to the grave." At this meeting, held to replace bourgeois christenings, five newborn babies of Party members received their names and were enrolled in the Young Pioneers. There was a lot of howling and crying, but afterward there was a dance and what the Party called "general jollifications."

Antonio Carelli's father wanted him to learn how to speak to crowds the way he did. When Antonio was eleven, his father picked him up and put him on a soapbox at the park where the workers gathered on weekends. Antonio began his memorized speech, but in the middle he became confused and forgot his lines. To save the situation, he shouted, "In conclusion, comrades and fellow workers, don't forget Patrick Henry's words: 'Give me liberty or give me death!' "

He noticed the smiles on the faces of the workers, and then he jumped off the soapbox into his father's outstretched arms.

At the Young Pioneer school Antonio observed Lincoln's and Washington's birthday by learning what frauds they really were. The teacher was Mush Snitkin. The Y.C.L.'s district organizer, Mush was from New York City. Antonio worshiped Mush, who was handsome and wore bell-bottoms like the sailors wore. Mush's sister Clara was a legendary leader of the Gastonia textile workers' strike in North Carolina.

Mush spoke under a banner that said SMASH THE BOY SCOUTS. "Washington was not the popular idol bourgeois historians now paint him to be," Mush declared. "Not at all. Let's look at the record, comrades. He commanded the revolutionary armies, spilling the blood of artisans and poor farmers so that his own class in the colonies could rule. Before, the British landowners and capitalists in America could exploit the workers, farmers, toilers, and Negroes. Now the rich merchants and planters could do it on their own. This bastard Washington was the richest land- and slave-owner in America. Can you compare such a bourgeois lackey with such working-class leaders as Stalin, Lenin, and Marx? Come on now!"

The kids laughed and applauded. They all wore the same flaming red mufflers. Antonio fingered his proudly.

"As president," Mush said, "his policies were consistently for the benefit of the ruling class. The heavy taxes for the profits of the rich produced revolt among the masses, including the Whiskey Rebellion by the farmers in Pennsylvania against the whiskey tax. Washington sent troops against the farmers, just like Roosevelt is doing today.

"And Lincoln," Mush continued, "he wasn't even opposed to slavery, comrades. His aim was to save the capitalist union, not to free Negroes. The bastard used the slaves as a pawn to weaken the Southern landowners and strengthen the Northern capitalists."

Mush then talked about how Stalin and Lenin led the fight for workers' democratic rights, including the fight for land and the full equality of Negroes.

"The very fact," Mush said, "that the children have to struggle in school for food and against discrimination proves that the American Revolution did not benefit the workers and that Lincoln didn't free the Negroes."

When he was twelve, Antonio traveled by train with his father to New York City to celebrate Revolutionary Christmas Day at Madison Square Garden. The Young Pioneers, Young Communist League, and the Communist Party were sponsoring the event.

Before the festivities began, the secretary of the Young Pioneers, George Winfield, walked out to a standing ovation. "Before the constructive fun begins, comrades, we must take note of that organization for capitalist war, the Boy Scouts. The Scouts glorify the wars of the bosses! Their real aim is to prepare the workers' children to be good soldiers in the armies of the capitalists.

"Just what are the differences between the Boy Scouts and the Young Pioneers? Study them and you will clearly see your duty as workers' children. We must smash the Boy Scouts, the organization of our class enemies, the capitalists."

The audience chanted "Smash the Boy Scouts! Defend the Soviet Union!"

"And the Boy Scouts attack Workers' Russia," Winfield said. "The Soviet government is a government of and for the workers and toilers. The Soviet Union is the worst enemy of all the bosses the world over. So the bosses hate it and are plotting war against it. The workers and their children all over the world have only one fatherland—the Soviet Fatherland, Workers' Russia! We know that in the Soviet Union there is no child labor. Workers' children go to the best schools there are and have free vacations."

Winfield concluded, "Comrades, we want a workers' and farmers' government where the workers will rule like they do in the Soviet Union!"

Winfield held his fist clenched while the chants continued:

"BURY THE BOY SCOUTS!"
"SIX FEET UNDER!"
"SOVIET JUSTICE FOR THE BOY SCOUTS!"

The chants were interrupted by a shouting voice. "Ooh, don't you just hate the little fuckers?" a lone, screechy male voice called. "Smash the little cocksuckers," it called again.

Heads turned. Winfield screened his eyes to get a better look. Adults in the crowd muttered, "Who approved those slogans? They seem a trifle much."

"Shut up, fuckface," the same voice called. A disheveled man in sneakers and an apron was laughing and pedaling his legs in the aisle. Two bodyguards reached him and rapidly carried him upside down to the back as he called, "Bury the little cunt-sniffers."

Winfield held up his hand. "Your attention please, boys and girls. Now let's get on with the fun part of our day: let the parade begin!"

From the back of the garden the musicians came down the aisle playing kazoos, paper and comb instruments, and drums. Winfield shouted, "And now, some of the products of the system!"

Young Pioneers dressed up as caricatures—with cigars and daisies in their mouths and roses and lilies in their ears—of priests, rabbis, soldiers, policemen, politicians, and Italian gangsters danced down the aisles, rubbing their private parts and farting at the delighted audience.

The curtains opened. A Revolutionary Christmas tree stood there on which was a cartoon likeness of Herbert Hoover with an apple instead of a head and placards against war, the police, and capitalism. A large dollar sign took the place of the star at the top of the tree.

A boxing match took place between Science and Religion. The referee was dressed in purple polka-dot tights. After seven rounds, during which the contestants punched the referee as well as each other, Science knocked out both Religion and the referee.

A poster showed a crystal gazer watching a large fire in her crystal ball. The fire singed and burned up an insect that fell in its way. Many other insects were also being consumed. The fire was labeled The Soviet Union and the insects were labeled The Capitalist Nations.

An animal trainer whipped beasts into submission. The beasts included a lion ("High Society"), tiger ("Capitalist Parties"), elephant ("The Boy Scouts and Militarism"), mongrel dog ("The Socialist Party and Social Democrats") and a bear ("Religion").

The Revolutionary Christmas tree was wheeled onto the center of the stage. God, dressed in a business suit flecked with cigar ashes and dripping blood, danced around the tree with a Harem of Angels, including priests, rabbis, capitalists, and other Dope Peddlers.

George Winfield grabbed the microphone and said, "Boys and girls, this is our answer to the bunk called religion and the capitalist Christmas. I wish you all a very revolutionary Christmas. We must all be in constant readiness to meet the opposition of our enemies. *Are you ready*?" Antonio and hundreds of other children in his section arose instantly and with raised, clenched fists shouted in perfect union, *"Always ready."*

As the Depression deepened, the Party's slogan, Work or Wages, made headway. The Unemployed Council was organized in Buffalo, with Arturo Carelli as district organizer. The Party rented a large hall above a Chinese restaurant. Unemployed men, sitting on benches or gathered around the potbellied stove, talked and spat into spittoons. Antonio listened to the World War I vets, Great Lakes sailors, and longshoremen talk for hours.

In the afternoons after school, Antonio went directly to the Party hall. He cut stencils for leaflets, painted signs, worked the mimeograph, and distributed Party literature house to house.

The Party was in motion. There was the Italian-American Workers' Club on Seneca Street and the Russian Workers' Club on the East Side. The Ukrainian, Hungarian, Polish-Lithuanian, and Latvian clubs were located in the Black Rock and Riverside sections.

Organizers came from New York and Chicago: the field Y.C.L. women, the Agitprop, the Marine Workers Industrial Union comrade, the Negro field organizer from Harlem, one of the Gastonia prisoners out on bail. On Sunday nights, Antonio's father invited them for spaghetti dinners with homemade Italian wine and espresso. They discussed tactics, strategy, and theory. It was time to raise the level of the struggle.

The Party and the Unemployed Council called on the unemployed to congregate on the streets on March 6, 1930, and march on government buildings. Antonio distributed leaflets to the workers at the plants and factories: "Drop Your Tools! Solidarity With Your Unemployed Brothers!"

The organizers instructed the rank and file to fight the police. The comrades stuffed their hats with newspapers to soften the blows of billy clubs and blackjacks. Women were told to scream and claw at the police.

On March 6th, placards nailed to wooden sticks were handed out. A long column, four abreast, was formed and marched up Broadway chanting, "Starve or Fight."

When they reached City Hall, the mounted police and riot squad charged. The police swung their clubs. The workers fought back, screaming and shouting, trying to keep from being trampled.

The demonstration made headlines. Arturo Carelli was arrested as a leader of the demonstration. At school, the kids stared at Antonio and whispered about him. He was no longer ashamed.

Arturo Carelli was released in two days. He was now a full-time functionary for the Party. Antonio proudly watched his father in his red velvet vest standing on a frail wooden platform near the steel factory. "Look at my hand!" Arturo boomed, holding his hand high above his head. "When a hand is like this, all five fingers separated, each finger can easily be broken by snapping it backward. All five fingers can be smashed, just like that. Why, fellow workers? Because they are alone, separated! Now—look—look—what happens when I make a fist? The fingers are united. You would need a sledgehammer to break them.

"Just look at yourselves. Is it your fault you're unemployed? You're out of work because you produced too much and the result is overproduction. Who suffers? The bosses? No, the working class! *You* suffer."

The crowd nodded and applauded.

"In Great Britain, when a worker is laid off, he gets unemployment relief. How come the British workers get help, and here in America the workers get nothing? Is it because the English bosses are overflowing with the milk of human kindness? Heck no! Over there the workers organized themselves into a fist and demanded relief! They demonstrated, fought, got their heads broken, but they made themselves into a fist and they won.

"So fellow workers, join us—join the Unemployed Council. Join the fight for unemployment insurance. If the British could do it, so can we!"

The first summer vacation Antonio and his sister ever had was spent at the Spellman cottage. He was fourteen. The Spellmans were affluent Communists. Millard Spellman was a radio technician. His wife had a horse face and a beautiful body. Antonio noticed comrades going into Anna Spellman's room at night: sailors, Dutchmen from South Africa, Comintern reps, Mush Snitkin, longshoremen, lumberjacks. Millard seemed to have no objection, even when drunken fights broke out between the men over Anna.

Antonio slept on the porch. One night a car drove up in the middle of the night and seven men got out. There was a lot of noise. Anna Spellman made Antonio go upstairs to sleep in his sister's room. Antonio listened. It sounded like she had sex with every one of them.

On the following two nights, he listened to the conversations of these men for hours. They were especially interested in visiting Niagara Falls because of the chemical plants along the river. In case of war, these plants could be converted into weapons factories within twenty-four hours. Two of the men were chemists planning to apply for jobs in the plants.

He learned what a hit squad was. The five other men traveled all over the U.S. "The Flying Squad," Anna called them proudly.

After the March 6th demonstration, Antonio saw less and less of his father. Arturo Carelli was sent to Jamestown, Binghamton, Syracuse, and Rochester on Party work. He served short jail terms in many cities.

Several of the comrades were sent to Moscow to study at the Lenin School, although this was supposed to be a secret. Almost all of the functionaries had at least two names. Antonio liked the romance of it.

Antonio had also joined the Workers' Shortwave Club. Every second Thursday, lessons were given in Morse code for comrades who were building small shortwave receivers. Party organs carried notices about Moscow programming on short wave broadcast from 8:00 to 11:15 P.M. every night. Antonio knew what was going on in Moscow every day of the week and could vicariously take part in the building of socialism. One day it was announced that tree houses were being built for honeymooners; another that in their spare hours Red Army soldiers were studying Yiddish, Italian, and Greek.

Antonio became a constant speaker on soapboxes. Some people said he would someday be the Lenin of America. One day while on the soapbox, he was asked by a young worker about forced conscription in the Soviet Union. "How do you explain that?" the boy asked. "People come to the United States to avoid being drafted."

Antonio didn't know how to answer this truthfully and went to see the new district organizer, A. W. Weber. Weber explained: "Even though sometimes you will be asked questions by proletarians, you must keep in mind that they are not yet class conscious. They don't understand. We understand." Antonio looked at Weber through the haze of smoke from Weber's pipe. "Therefore," Weber said, "in such a situation, objectivism is a danger. As Lenin said, 'Marxism is a solid block of steel.' Hence, comrade, you must put it this way: there is no one in the Soviet Union who does *not* want to join the Red Army. It's a great privilege, and there are no deserters."

Antonio's next role in the struggle came on May 30th—Memorial Day—in Youngstown, Ohio. The Young Communist League called it National Youth Day. Memorial Day was capitalist demagoguery— honoring the heroes of imperialist war and those who were preparing to attack the Soviet Union. Y.C.L.ers and Young Pioneers came to Youngstown from all over the country for the demonstration against war, poverty, and unemployment. It was a great ride on the truck for Antonio, staying up all night with the other kids, talking, and singing "Solidarity Forever."

They were denied a permit to march. The American Legion was scheduled to march on the same route at the same time. The Buffalo contingent was surrounded by cordons of police and the mounties of the riot squad. Antonio held hands with the other kids. Someone brought a soapbox and a Y.C.L. banner. The police chief walked over to them and told them not to disobey the law. The Pioneers booed and jeered him. A Party organizer from New York, Damien Petitt, jumped up on the soapbox and screamed, "Down with police brutality!"

The police charged, swinging their clubs on the heads of adult demonstrators. The comrades threw rocks and empty bottles. The police ordered the adult comrades to take the children away from the scene. Antonio ran, clutching the hand of a pretty comrade, Suzie Abersoll. They sat down on a bench, exhausted and excited.

Suzie wore a shiny brass badge on her blouse. Antonio had never seen one like it. "A Komsomol badge from the Soviet Union!" she said.

"Wow! Let me hold it," he said, looking at the badge, her bosom.

He placed it carefully on his fingertips: the red star in the center, the rays extending from it, and the three letters, KCM. It shone in the sunlight.

There was a mass meeting that night in Youngstown. They sang:

> *"I'm spending my nights in the flophouse*
> *I'm spending my days on the street*
> *I'm looking for work but I find none*
> *I wish I had something to eat."*

After the meeting, policemen and detectives stood outside with searchlights, looking for the leaders of the demonstration. They grabbed them and pushed them to the side, where they were clubbed and blackjacked. Antonio heard their screams.

He was taken to a comrade's home, where he fell asleep on the floor. Deep in the night, a boy beside him tugged at his arm. He whispered, "Look. Look over there. That boy and girl are making love." Instantly alert, Antonio looked over in that direction, and heard the sounds of love.

In the morning, walking toward him from that corner, her blouse very ruffled looking, was Suzie.

They were all put on the truck and driven back to Buffalo, where they ate a hot breakfast and were greeted by the comrades at the Unemployed Council headquarters.

When he was fourteen, Antonio moved from the Young Pioneers to the Young Communist League. The minimum age was sixteen, but an exception was made in his case. He had been arrested twice, he was a public speaker, and he worked at Party headquarters until midnight after school. If someone was being evicted, he would take the lead among the youths in helping to push the furniture back into the house.

In 1932 Arturo Carelli led a delegation to City Hall. The City Council was about to pass an ordinance preventing meetings and demonstrations that "disturbed the peace."

Antonio joined a group of Y.C.L.ers on the steps of City Hall. He carried in his pocket a razzer—a small wooden mouthpiece with a rubber tube attached to it.

Arturo Carelli was refused permission to address the council. The comrades shouted, "Free speech! Free speech! Let him speak!" Antonio blew his razzer. A comrade slugged a policeman. The police ran toward the crowd and pounced. Antonio's father was beaten, and the police would not let the boy near him.

Antonio and the others screamed and shouted.

Arturo Carelli was sentenced to a year in prison followed by deportation to Italy.

His father would be imprisoned or executed by Mussolini. The Party, working through the International Labor Defense, obtained a court procedure for Carelli's asylum in the Soviet Union.

The family waited while Arturo Carelli served his prison sentence. When it was completed, he was deported to the Soviet Union.

In August 1935, Antonio, his mother, and sister boarded the SS *Bremen*. They left New York City on a silver midnight.

He looked up at the stars and lights of the city and bade them goodbye.

Antonio climbed down a steep embankment into an oblong excavation pit. A drainage ditch ran through the center. Mounds of soil fifty feet high lined both sides of the pit. He was standing with the other prisoners of the Yurkov work brigade on gold-bearing sands. It was raining.

Only the highest officials at the site wore rubber boots and raincoats.

He had arrived the previous night at the Razvedchik camp. The searchlights had shone on the prisoners' faces. Below the gates of Kolyma's gold mines was a poster that said: Labor in the USSR Is a Matter of Honor, Valor, and Heroism!

He was on the night shift.

They were divided into groups of three. Their heads and shoulders were covered with mosquito nets. The two other men picked and shoveled the soil into a wooden wheelbarrow that Antonio pushed on wooden rails to a bunker.

Horses worked eight-hour days. Prisoners had twelve-hour workdays.

At 5:00 A.M. the inspector measured the work site with a tape measure to determine how many cubic meters of gold sand the prisoners had dug and carried away. Twelve hours had passed.

When Antonio saw the inspector, he thought it was over at last. The overseer shouted to them, "Grab a shovel," and led the men to the drainage ditches. They bent down, dipped their shovels in the water, and scooped wet soil onto the banks of the ditch. They worked for two more hours. Then they were marched back to the camp, where they were given a bowl of hot soup with three grains of cereal floating in it.

A guard laughed. "By the way, one of your party has already left us. Slashed his wrists with a razor blade. An American named Brenner."

Antonio knew him. George Brenner. He'd known his brother Sidney in Buffalo. When he'd first arrived in Moscow, Antonio heard Brenner sing at the Foreign Workers Club. Brenner sang American progressive songs. Antonio remembered him singing, "Got the blues, got the blues, got the starvation, no ration blue-hoo-hooss . . ." with a captivated smile on his face. The comrades sang along, "Woo . . . woo . . . woos. . . ."

On the second night, Antonio had just fallen asleep when the guards stomped in and woke the men up and told them to stand at attention. They called out the names of those who had fulfilled less than forty percent of their work quota. Antonio's name was called. He and two others were led back to the gold fields for ten more hours of work.

Ravzedchik was a clearing about one hundred yards long and seventy-five yards wide, enclosed by a tall split-rail fence entwined with barbed wire. Two watchtowers stood diagonally opposite each other at the corners of the camp.

There were worse camps, prisoners said. Camps where they slept in tents instead of barracks, without electricity, where they received their portions of gruel in their caps.

His hands ached. A throbbing pain hammered down his arms. He could not open his swollen fingers when he woke. He could think of nothing but eating a large piece of black bread.

On the third day, an old man, one of the group, fell on the ground from exhaustion during a march. A guard hit him with his whip, but the man did not move. The guard said, "We'll finish you off quick, you old fart." The group was told to move on. Antonio heard the snarls of the wolfhounds, their frenzied breathing; he heard them tearing at the old man's rags, the sound of bone cracking. He heard screams.

The guard's Komsomol badge shone in the sun. Antonio thought of Suzie Abersoll's white blouse.

In October, the nights became longer and colder. Snow fell. Antonio was transferred to the day shift. He was sent in his summer clothes to drag timber down the slopes. He pushed the logs down the slope and carried them on his shoulders to the construction site.

Eight more men died.

They were divided into groups of three. They picked up a long heavy log and placed it on their shoulders. They carried it half a mile to a precipice which dropped about fifty feet. Below were holes in the side of the cliff, entrances to the gold mines. They shoved the log off their shoulders.

Antonio was transferred to another brigade working at the gold-washing barracks. They pushed the wheelbarrows full of already washed, heavy, wet sand covered with a quilted rag through a doorway outside into the chilly frost.

When he returned to the barracks, he could not sleep. He was too hungry.

The gold-washing season came to an end. Razvedchik had fulfilled its annual gold output quota. A prisoners' brass band played "Happy Days Are Here Again."

The temperature reached seventy degrees below zero. The officials boasted that Kolyma had the coldest climate in the world.

Antonio was becoming a *fitil*, a *dokhodyaga*. The *fitil* is the wick of the candle. The *dokhodyaga* is taken from the verb *"dokhodit"*: to arrive or to reach. *Dokhodyagas* had arrived at the state of socialism. They were the perfect citizens of Socialist society.

Dokhodyagas and *fitils* no longer washed. They did not kill the lice that sucked their blood. They no longer wiped the dribble off the ends of their noses with their sleeves.

They had frostbitten noses, cheeks, and chins. Huge black blood clots covered their faces.

They were oblivious to blows. When attacked, they covered their heads and fell to the floor. When the attack was over, they got up and walked away whimpering.

They hung around the kitchen begging for scraps. The cook would get a laugh by throwing a spoonful of soup in their faces. The *dokhodyagas* would respond by running their fingers over their wet whiskers and licking them.

Behind the mess barracks stood the refuse pile. The cooks threw slop and dishwater which instantly froze over it. *Dokhodyagas* gathered around the pile. They chopped off a frozen barley kernel or a herring skeleton with a stick and stuffed it into their mouths. Some of them wiped off frozen urine. Some did not bother to.

They stood around tables, waiting for someone to leave some food behind. When someone stood up to leave, they lunged at the plate. As they fought each other, the soup would spill. On hands and knees, they fought for the liquid and food dribbling away on the floor.

The nonpoliticals, the thieves, amused themselves with the *dokhodyagas*. They pushed their plates away. As *dokhodyagas* leaped toward them, the thieves took the plates and hurled them at the faces of the *dokhodyagas*.

Each day now a member of his brigade died.

*   *   *

The frozen mist hung over them. There was a burning sensation in his nose when he breathed. His urine froze instantly in the snow when he relieved himself. His fingers were constantly freezing. He jumped up and down and did the Lindy Hop, the dance that was popular in Moscow during the months before he was arrested.

The *dokhodyagas* were drawn to the spell of the bonfire. They placed a log close to it and sat. The heat burned their faces and their backs froze. They sat in their burnt clothing and frostbitten faces. The sparks often flew on their clothes. They would doze off and be awakened by the smell of burning cotton.

It was hard to pull away from the fire. When it began to die out, they bent closer. Their backs freezing, they held their hands above the coals. The trickle from their noses fell and hissed on the embers.

Antonio became friendly with a young prisoner, a doctor from Leningrad named Boris. He had a gouged eye from his interrogations. Antonio had become so thin that the winds would constantly knock him down and he would fall into the snow. Boris would unwrap the scarf that was protecting his own head, tie it around Antonio's waist, and walk forward so that Antonio could be kept upright.

Boris suddenly got a prized job: dishwasher. Antonio saw him in the kitchen, grinning and weeping, his mouth full of food.

When he came to bed, Boris brought two packages of burnt buckwheat mush crusts, wrapped in rags, and kept them beneath his boots. During the night, Boris got up five times and went to the outhouse. Each time he returned, he ate more crusts and lay down again.

In the morning, the buckwheat crusts were gone. Boris was sick. He couldn't breathe.

He was found lying in the snow, buckwheat mush seeping out of his mouth and nose.

In the spring, Antonio felt a numb sensation in his leg. He lowered his trousers. One leg was purple and swollen to twice the size of the other. There were blotches all over it. In two days they turned into huge boils. Blood and pus trickled from them. The entire brigade had scurvy.

*   *   *

One day Lev, one of the *blatinye*, the thieves, asked him, "What did you do before your arrest?"

"In America, I drew a lot. I was a painter." He did not mention that he drew signs and posters for the Party. The thieves hated the Communists.

"No kidding? Maybe you can draw me?"

Lev took him to his barracks, where a circle of the thieves gathered around Antonio. They were curious about the American.

"Did you ever see Al Capone?" someone asked him.

"No—"

"Tell us, tell us about him!"

He told them about the St. Valentine's Day massacre. Their faces were rapt with interest.

Lev handed him paper and pencil. "Here, you'll do a drawing of my exceptionally handsome face."

When Antonio finished, he handed it to Lev. Lev slapped him on the back and showed it to the others. He took bread, butter, and sugar out of a cloth bag and gave them to Antonio. They watched him eat, and then they gave him gruel and a can of hot tea.

They told him, "You'll come back tomorrow and tell us more about Capone."

"How did you hear of him?" he asked.

"There isn't a thief in all of Russia who doesn't know of Capone," Lev said.

On his way out, Lev called to him. "I have a piece of advice that is more important than the food, Antonio. Whatever happens, remember the saying: 'Be lower than the grass and quieter than the water.' " He patted Antonio on the shoulder and closed the door.

They liked his stories of America, his drawings and tattoos. One man asked for a tattoo of a nude woman surrounded by a bottle of vodka, a dagger, the ace of spades, and the words, "Our Undoing." They asked for "I'll Never Forget Old Mom" and drawings of nudes and mermaids.

They sat around him in the hut. They asked: "How come they don't arrest Capone? Are there really moving sidewalks in America? What's a skyscraper like?"

He told them about John Dillinger and sang popular American songs to them.

His face filled out with the food. He no longer looked like a *dokhodyaga*.

In 1944, Henry Wallace, vice-president of the United States, Owen Lattimore, professor at Johns Hopkins University, and a group of others visited Kolyma.

The wooden watchtowers and barbed wire were razed in one night in honor of the Americans' visit. Prisoners were kept inside for the entire three days of their stay and treated to movies from morning to night. They were warned of instant execution for one false move or word.

Lovely and elegant girls and boys took the place of the prisoners, who were inside watching the movies. They were put to work on the model pig farm. Wallace asked them some questions about pigs and couldn't get a straight answer, but he thought they were shy.

Wallace would later write that "the Kolyma gold miners are big, husky young men." He noted that the political police "were treated . . . with great respect."

Wallace and Lattimore were moved by the chief of Kolyma, General Nikshisov. Lattimore wrote that "Mr. Nikshisov . . . had just been decorated with the Order of Hero of the Soviet Union for his extraordinary achievements. Both he and his wife have a trained and sensitive interest in art and music and also a deep sense of civic responsibility." Wallace wrote that Nikshisov "gamboled about, enjoying the wonderful air immensely."

Lattimore loved the "first-class orchestra and good light-opera company" and wrote: "high-grade entertainment just naturally seems to go with gold, and so does high-powered executive ability."

General Nikshisov and his wife, Major Gridassova, commandant of the camps, took off their uniforms for the visit and put on civilian clothes. Gridassova was introduced to Mr. Wallace as a grammar school principal.

A choir was organized in a hurry for the Americans' visit. Prisoners rehearsed all night. Before they sang their opening number, they saluted the visitors in English by shouting: "Okay—America! Okay—

Soviet Union!" After the performance the prisoners were loaded into trucks and shipped back to camp.

A box was reserved for the general and his wife at the Gorky Theater. Ordinarily, at the start of performances, at intermissions, and at the finale, the performers, who were all prisoners, would bow endlessly to the haughty couple on their cushioned seats. For fun, the drunken general would shout "cocksuckers" and "assholes" at the bowing actors and actresses on the stage with such zest that the spray from his spittle was visible. He would clap his wife on the back to make sure she was enjoying it. On this occasion, the general was moved to tears by the performance.

Among the members of the American party was Clara Gale, a young progressive New York lawyer who represented a Soviet travel agency in Manhattan. An obese woman with a truck driver's voice and large floppy hats, she prided herself on her belches and her knack for grabbing men publicly by their private parts. But the visit to Kolyma brought out her femininity, her vision of the future. "So much sharing!" she told her associates. "So much caring! We Americans have so much to learn from them: I'm so ashamed of our emphasis on superficial values, on *things*, on getting ahead and competing with the next guy. It makes me want to vomit all over again!"

One day Clara chanced upon a surprising scene. The U.S.-USSR Friendship Society had sent over tuxedos and silk gowns for the workers to share on their days off from their productive labors. The clothes were kept in the sewing room. When the wives of the officials got wind of their whereabouts, they hurled themselves toward the room, broke down the door, and grabbed for the goods. They rolled on the floor, scratching and biting each other for the gowns. Clara didn't know what caused the scene, but she loved it.

On many occasions there were tears of joy in the eyes of many in the delegation.

Two years later Antonio was moved to Chai-Urya in Kolyma. It was known as the valley of death.

In the red cattle car, a man beside him named Levin, whose gray face was covered with white stubble, asked him, "Is your father also in Russia?" Levin was a "former person," an intellectual who had written several works of philosophy.

"Yes," Antonio said. "But I don't know what happened to him."

"There was an Italian in my cell in 1937. His last name was Carelli. He was deported from the United States and arrested in Moscow. Could it be this was your father?"

Antonio could not speak.

A kaleidoscope of childhood scenes flashed before his eyes, his father in all of them. His first flubbed revolutionary speech—"Give me liberty or give me death"—and the jump off the soapbox into his father's outstretched arms.

He grasped Levin's hand. "Do you know when my father was arrested?"

"The autumn of 1937. He wore white pants and sneakers. They picked him up on the street. That's all I know, my boy."

The bitterness he had felt at his father for doing this to him, for wrecking his life and that of his family, was gone. He felt only love and deep forgiveness for him.

The barracks of Chkalov Satellite Camp No. 7 of Chai-Urya were in darkness. There was no electricity.

Antonio worked the night shift. Layers of frozen empty soil were blown up beforehand. Then he climbed down with the other men into the smoldering excavation. Rocks, frozen lumps of clay, and large chunks of earth were piled all over. The men broke up the segments and piled them into wooden boxes on sledges. Two men harnessed themselves to either side of the sledge. The third man in the rear pushed with his hands, slipping and falling until they reached the foot of the dumping hill.

Antonio danced to keep his feet from freezing, shuffling to the memory of "The Darktown Strutters Ball."

By mid-December, half of his group had died. By February almost all were dead.

Those who were not breathing each morning were stuffed under the floor planks for days. The living took their rags and bread portions.

The food suddenly improved. The soup had large chunks of fresh meat and bones in it. For two weeks they ate well.

Then the cooks were arrested. They had stolen the regular food and substituted the flesh of corpses.

The prisoners chopped off their own body parts to escape the work. They blew off their fingers with stolen detonators. It was better to lose a hand or foot than to die.

Shirkers were dragged from their hiding places, pleading and whimpering, and thrown at the feet of the guards. If they could not move from exhaustion, the wolfhounds were ordered to chew them up.

A brigade of *dokhodyagas*, the ideal Soviet men, carried naked, frozen corpses up the slope every day to the burial site. The bodies were piled like logs. Holes were bored and the blasting began. The corpses were thrown into the mass grave and covered.

He did not think he would make it. There was no flesh on his bones, only gray, scaly skin. His buttocks were almost gone.

Then the brigadier, Prokhorov, called him in. "The men tell me you're an artist. The bread distributor has made us an offer. He'd like drawings of nude beauties. We can get notebooks and pencils. Can you do it? You'll get all the bread you want, and you won't have to go to work. You can draw in the barracks."

Prokhorov paused, and the expression on his face was different from any Antonio had ever seen before. "You'll make it. You can draw. It's saved you before and it will now. I have nothing."

Each day he drew a girl in different poses and hairdos, standing, reclining, sitting, smiling, pouting, flirting.

He began tattooing again as well. They gave him bread, sugar, gruel, and tobacco. His body began to take shape again. The frostbite crusts started to fall off his nose, cheeks, and chin. His right leg was still bloated from scurvy and full of boils.

In the spring, the prisoners picked berries and carried them in pailfuls back to camp for the officials and guards. They were not allowed to eat them. The bushes drooped under the weight of the fruit. The streams and rivers were full of fish. At night, eating their oatmeal gruel, they smelled the fish frying for the guards.

Antonio ran off with two other prisoners into the forest to eat the berries.

Shots crisscrossed around him, bouncing off the ground. He crawled on his hands and knees, his heart pounding.

He was led by the guards, hands behind his back to the isolator, a hole in the ground. His head protruded above the ground. The guards covered the hole with heavy logs and securely fastened them to stakes. He fell on his knees in the hole.

He had to keep moving to survive. He wrapped his arms around his body. He lifted one foot and kicked the wall, then the other foot. He moved his neck and banged his head against the logs.

To warm himself, he thought of his mother and father, his sister, his school days, thought of anything but time. His imagination bounded everywhere.

He thought of America. And that warmed him.

In the morning he managed to climb out of the hole.

A guard came up to him and, without saying a word, lifted his walking stick and beat him. Antonio fell on his hands and knees, covering his head with his arms. The stick broke on Antonio's back. The guard was very fond of that stick; he thought it gave him a certain cachet. Enraged, he kicked Antonio, picked up the scythe and flayed him with it. Antonio rolled himself into a ball.

The months passed.

The first snows came.

In 1948 Antonio was released and issued a wolf's passport—a Soviet internal passport "without the right to live in large cities." He was thirty years old.

He had to see his mother and sister in Moscow. He sent a telegram telling them he was coming.

The train pulled into Yaroslavsky Station on a sunny morning in February. His sister stood on the platform, her head turning, looking for him. Knapsack in hand, he ran to her. For a moment they looked at each other. They cried and held each other.

As they walked, he asked her about his mother and father. She clutched his arm. "Tony, Papa died—last November. Three months ago you would have seen him."

On Stryeletskaia Street they entered a corner building and walked up five flights. His sister unlocked the door and pulled him into a small corridor. Damp laundered clothes hanging on ropes almost hid his mother. He dropped the knapsack and kissed her sobbing face. "My Tony, my Tony," she said.

Soon they were eating the meal his mother had prepared for him: macaroni and tomato sauce. And they told him about his father.

When Antonio came to Moscow in 1935 with his mother and sister, their father greeted them at the station. Soon after Antonio's arrest, Arturo disappeared. His mother and sister did not hear from him again until a year before. Lucia, Antonio's sister, was shaking a rug on the staircase landing just outside the apartment. She noticed a bearded old man in rags walking up the stairs. She had just closed the door when she heard a knock. When she opened it, the old man stood there. He wore a peaked Red Army helmet and held a sack slung over his shoulder. Lucia was frightened. There were so many beggars in Moscow. She asked him what he wanted. He kept trying to move into the doorway, looking steadily into her eyes. He did not speak, although she kept asking: "What do you want?" Suddenly he stretched out his hand and said, "Lucia! Lucia!"

She screamed. Her mother rushed out into the hall.

Arturo Carelli had also been released with a wolf's passport. He had served almost ten years in the camps. For ten years he did not know what had happened to the family. He was told that he must live in Uzbekistan.

He wanted only to return to Italy. Lucia accompanied him to the Italian Consulate, but he was afraid to enter the building for fear of being arrested again. She went in while he waited outside. The consulate told her they would look into his case, but it would take at least a year. When she came out, he was shaking with fear.

He left for the railroad station that night to go to Uzbekistan. They gave him all the money and clothes they had. Within half an hour of his departure, the NKVD turned up at the apartment looking for him.

Arturo found a job on a collective farm in Uzbekistan after months of unemployment. He worked in a cabbage patch and pushed wheelbarrows. He fell and injured himself, and was fired. Lucia and her mother sent him money regularly. He could not find another job. He was a wolf, a foreigner. He hung around the marketplace during the day and slept at night in the empty stalls. He fell ill with malaria.

After several months the Italian Consulate sent an Italian passport for himself and his wife. Arturo stood in line for two days for a train ticket to Moscow, sleeping on the station floor at night. On the third day he fainted in line. He was taken to the hospital in Tashkent, where his supplies and money were stolen. Lying in the hospital bed, Arturo heard the doctor say that there was no hope either for him or for the man lying in the next bed. When the other man died, Arturo ran away from the hospital and climbed on a train to Moscow without a ticket.

It had been warm in Tashkent. Arturo arrived in Moscow on a cold November day. A thick heavy snowfall covered the streets. There was ankle-deep slush that turned to ice. Arturo arrived at their door dressed in white canvas trousers, a jacket, and a cap. His feet were almost frozen to the thin, cloth hospital slippers he had walked away in. It had taken him an hour to walk up the five flights.

He entered the apartment and said to his wife, "Well, Maria, we are going to Italy!"

They bathed and fed him and tried to keep him warm. It was difficult to wash him. His thin layer of skin peeled off at the touch. He could not sit in a chair. They placed two cushions beneath him so that the bones would not pierce the skin. They wanted to call a doctor but he cried out at the suggestion. He was afraid the doctor would turn him in and he would never see Italy.

A few days later, he complained of a pain in the upper part of his back. It was painful for him to breathe. They consulted a clinic doctor who promised to make an unofficial visit. The doctor examined Arturo and told them that he was suffering from dysentery, malaria, pellagra, pneumonia, and tuberculosis. He was spitting blood now. The doctor doubted he would survive the coming night.

That night Arturo asked Lucia to bathe him. She gave him a sponge bath, changed the linen, and carried his weightless body to the bed. He asked for a cup of Ovaltine. Then he beckoned with his finger to her and her mother. He asked for forgiveness for bringing them to Russia and asked them not to forget his last wishes. If they ever got out, they must tell the world the truth so that others would not be misled.

He squeezed their hands and whispered, "Forgive me . . . goodbye."

They buried him on Thanksgiving Day.

Antonio was imprisoned again. It began with the arrest of eighty wolves, and was called the Purge of the Repeaters. But torture and slave labor become boring, except for connoisseurs of the subject, and the narrative of this repetition in his life will be limited to a few notes.

He was placed in a freight car. The prison at Vladimir. More interrogations and beatings. A month in solitary. The bathhouse, delousings. Five minutes a day outside in the kennels. Four hundred grams of bread and a cup of water. Paul Robeson records on the loudspeaker. Sentenced to eternal exile for suspicion of espionage.

The city of Gorky. Elderly men unloaded from the truck, not running fast enough . . . trousers falling . . . wolfhounds tearing at them. Screams.

March at dusk to Kirov transit prison. Armed convoy guards, through fields and ditches. Long lines of cattle cars, seventy men per car . . . Krassnoyarsk prison . . . two hundred men in each cell.

They gathered at the wharf by the Yenisei River. Representatives from Krassdrev, the lumber trust, inspected the slaves. Up the Yenisei by boat, north to Kazachinsky, farther north to Stryelka, three hundred men and women in barges . . . to Artugan, a logging settlement.

Stalin's death five years later. Amnesty. Riverboat to Krasnoyarsk. Antonio's tiny mother at the station with a bunch of flowers, and his sister beside her.

In January 1960, he visited his father for the last time at the Minaevskii cemetery. He was silent for a few minutes. Then he said, "Goodbye, Pa. I wish you could have lived to come with us. . . . I won't forget your dying wishes." In the morning, he flew with his sister and mother to Rome. In a week he was in America.

He walked the streets of Buffalo again, the West Side streets of his boyhood.

In his mixed-up dreams, he was always going back to America, to the West Side, to Trenton Avenue where he was raised, to see the old comrades. They would have a big reunion and he would tell them the truth. Yet also in his dreams, just as he was about to reach America, he would wake up. He never reached its shores.

A few days after his return, he called Sidney Brenner, the brother of George Brenner, who'd slashed his wrists at Razvedchik.

He asked Brenner, "Did you have a brother in Moscow?"

"Yeah, I did."

"Do you know what happened to him?"

"No. It's been years."

"Do you remember that in 1935 you came to my house with your mother and your father, and that you gave me a message for George?"

There was a pause. "It's coming back."

They were meeting in a downtown restaurant. "You came to see me on the day before I left for Moscow," he told Sidney. "Your father was blind. You took me aside in the living room and said, 'Please, please tell George that he's got to do everything in his power to get Ma and Pa out of here to live in the workers' fatherland. There they can be happy.'"

He told Sidney of the fate of his brother. Sidney cried. "And I often said, me, I said it, You can't make an omelet without cracking a few eggs," he said, looking at Antonio, crying, wiping his face and smiling, then burying his face.

Antonio asked him about the other Young Pioneers and what had become of them. Sidney told him to see Harry Rogers, who had a secondhand furniture store on the main street. Antonio remembered Harry's daughter Sally. He'd always held hands with her. Once Harry's son Larry had talked him into running away with him. They bought railroad tickets for California, where they were going to break into the movies. They got as far as Erie, Pennsylvania. When they came back, Harry was so glad to see them he took them both in his arms and fed them vanilla ice cream.

"Go see Harry," Sidney said. "He might help you find a job."

When he saw Harry, Antonio wanted to grab him, kiss him and hug him.

Harry stared at him.

"It's me—Tony Carelli."

"Yeah, I know."

There was a long silence.

"How ya been?" Harry said.

"Harry, I want to tell you what happened. You remember I went to Russia?" he said in a rush. "They killed my father, they killed George—"

"Oh yeah?" Harry said. "Is that a fact? Why did they do that? Curious."

Harry said he had to get back to work.

The others did not return his calls. Not one of them called him, not even Sidney.

One day in August of 1972 Antonio set up an exhibit of his drawings near a store whose sign read Rosenbaum's Furs. An hour later an old white-haired man with wide-rimmed glasses opened the door of the store, looked out, and spotted Antonio's drawings. He closed the door behind him and walked toward Antonio. He looked at the drawings without speaking. He gazed oddly at Antonio, and walked away. Two hours later he returned, came up to him and said, "So you're Tony Carelli."

"Yes. Do you know me?"

"Yeah. You don't remember me, do you? Charlie Rosenbaum."

"No."

"Well, I heard you were back. So you had a rough time in Russia?"

Antonio stared at him. "I really don't remember you."

"Let's say I was involved," Rosenbaum said. "I was a sympathizer. Never a member of the Party. I remember you. You used to dance with my daughter Bella a lot."

"Are you still involved?" Antonio said. "After everything that's happened, you still believe in that crap?"

The old man blinked and smiled. "Well, at one time, I have to admit, I believed. The reason I believed and gave a lot of money to the Party was the Jewish question. I believed in a Jewish homeland, and that the Soviet Union was providing a solution with Birobidzhan. I thought the USSR was the answer to all our problems. There was no discrimination, Jews would be free, da da da da."

"And now?"

"Well, it was all a dream. But now there is no more dream, because we found out about the Soviet Union." He stared at Antonio's drawings. "But at least now we have Cuba. My granddaughter Prim just came back from there. She was with the Venceremos Brigade. She has wonderful stories. Perhaps there they'll make the dream come true. In fact, Prim is giving a poetry performance at a rally tonight about her experiences there. Why don't you come with me?"

They entered a brown-and-gold school auditorium. The sound system played "Twinkle Twinkle, Little Star."

Prim Rosenbaum was a pretty woman in her early twenties with green earrings. She sat at a table at the front of the darkened auditorium, holding a red rose. She began by saying that she had just returned from Cuba. "I've been out of the country," she said. "Life after Cuba is hard, especially if the playback is the U.S. . . . In Cuba you move safely . . . listen to the birds sing . . . so many voices telling me it's going to be all right . . . it's safe to walk and dream . . . earth is at peace there . . . without fear, without greed, even the ants. . . ."

She punched out a cheer: "Booma Cheeia! Booma Cheeia! Cuba Cuba! *Rah rah rah!*

"In Cuba," Prim went on, "in Lenin Park . . . allowed to feel so much . . . we worked the land again . . . blessed it with our sweat . . . a pure life . . . I smoked the pipe with our Native American sisters . . . we prayed in the sun in front of the healthiest cows I'd ever seen . . . at the Pioneer Palace the children were making radical discoveries, testing mosquitoes and sugarcane. Discovering how to survive." Prim whirled around in a circle and said, "Did I tell you how the children smiled and waved goodbye in Lenin Park . . . how their skirts were red and gold . . . their eyes were worldwide? . . . To eat in Lenin Park! . . . The last day in the fields, we cried, I will be back, red earth of Cuba! I will be back. . . ."

Prim's mood shifted from ecstasy to anger. She was back in the

U.S.A. She saw people on cheese lines. "We need peace, y'all . . .
not a flash in the pan, not a one-night stand. We're talking more than
cheese—more hospitals, books, schools, teachers, theaters, museums.
. . . We're talkin' *world*, y'all. *Call it*. A people organized, galvanized,
solarized, socialized, sanctified, computerized, dignified, never again
horrified. . . . *Stand on line for that, Jack.*

"Nagasaki is a Birmingham church, *call it*. . . . Nagasaki is a
Manhattan welfare hotel, *call it*. . . . Nagasaki is a drunken man in
the street, call it . . . *call it*, you better call it, you better call
it, you better push it, pull it, grab it, you better call it, call it, *peace,*
y'all." Her fist was now clenched high in the air. "Call it, call it, call
it, b-b-b-better call it, you b-b-b-better push it, pull it, grab it,
Venceremos, we will win!" Her voice rose to a howl.

Charlie Rosenbaum howled beside Antonio. The crowd had risen
to its feet and howled with Prim.

Now Antonio looked around him. He saw Harry Rogers howling,
Sidney Brenner howling, he saw dozens of old faces he recognized,
the old gang, in their aged bitter faces he saw the guys and girls of
his youth. They howled.

The Last Stalinist

A stronger rope.

—G.L.

Sylvia Pollack would only meet the reporter at Nutburger or at Communist Party headquarters on 23rd Street. A few months before, she had cracked her head at Nutburger. It was three years after her son's death. She had stood up to put her coat on and fallen backward. The table and chair were on elevated platforms. She hit the back of her head against a stone corner and cracked her skull. Her face went over to one side. Sylvia lost her hearing in the right ear and her speech became slurred. She was eighty-eight years old.

The reporter came to her from Sophie Siskind, ninety-two years old, who lived on Montgomery Street on the Lower East Side and had a photograph of Paul Robeson on the wall and a little bust of Lenin on her bookshelf. "Sylvia is the only one still alive from my I.L.G. Local 50 from 1922," Sophie told him. "She is just a few years younger than myself. I called her 'the youngster from Brownsville.' She still is active all over."

When he called her in January 1985, Sylvia said, "I'd like to meet you. I have no objection whatsoever. But I'm busy. You ought to see my calendar. I have about forty meetings. We can't meet in my house because it's a mess. I had a tragedy in my life three years ago. So I lost interest in the whole thing. I won't let anybody in anymore.

"The thing is, Sophie is not what she was. She's so bitter. There is only one Soviet Union in the whole world. These so-called defectors. They get a wonderful education. I used to go to every concert in the city since I was eighteen. When the dissidents started coming here, I wouldn't give them the satisfaction of spending my money. During the Hitler-Stalin pact, they introduced me as 'Sylvia, the Rock of Gibraltar.' But I have faith in you, although I don't know you very well.

"Now let me tell you something about the Russians. Our country didn't have a war on its own land since the Civil War. In the Soviet Union they lost twenty million people. I lost a son three years ago, and I'm dying inside of me. My heart is aching every minute. Multiply that by twenty million families. Then you'll know how it feels to lose so many people."

When they first met at Nutburger, she came down the street with her cane, lobbing along, and kissed the reporter on the mouth. "It's like a blind date when you're young," she said, "and you don't know what's gonna be.

"My neighborhood in East New York was like a prairie in 1917," Sylvia said. "My father took a pail and got milk from a cow on a farm. Right from the cow. There were gas lamps on the streets that Dickens talks about. They had lamplighters. We used to run in the lots where the Gypsies would camp. There were no cars. We had four rooms, no bathtub. The kids were bathed in the washtub. We had a landlord with a car. Once a week he came and took the kids for a ride. A great thing for us.

"I graduated from junior high school in 1912 and got my first job in a lady's house. She made tassels and colored buttons; we called it 'pasimentary.' I got two dollars a week. My mother was the janitor of the house. My parents couldn't make a living. Then I went to work in a pocketbook factory. They made pocketbook frames on foot-press machines. And so I shuttled from one shop to another. Then I worked in a white-goods factory: cotton nightgowns. I sewed up the sides of the nightgowns and sewed up the sleeves.

"I loved to read in those days. In the drawer of my machine in the shop I always had poetry and while I was turning the sleeves, I used to secretly read. And I learned. Oscar Wilde. I learned the *Rubáiyát* by heart, I learned Shelley.

"I would buy records with my last penny, taking from food, and come home at night from a concert. I wanted to play the record. I used to take a toothpick, sharpen it off, stick my head in that great big horn and play the record so I didn't awaken my family. I'd listen to whatever I'd get out of the toothpick.

"My father would read to my mother the *Forward* when he came home from work. When I was twelve, I heard my father read an article aloud where a father seduced a daughter. My father didn't think I heard. He didn't finish reading the story. I knew I'd never hear the end of that story, 'cause I didn't dare to ask him. I remember my father reading the part where they took the daughter into court. She wore a black cape to hide her pregnancy. I had to know what happened. So I told my father that I wanted to learn Yiddish. And that's how I learned."

The reporter met her next at the large Communist Party headquarters on 23rd Street, seven stories of a former courthouse. Young blacks wearing beanies and holding giant radios greeted Sylvia at the door. Little old ladies sat quietly beside pale white young men and women who looked as if they'd come to New York from the prairie. The atmosphere was exactly as the reporter remembered it from thirty years before: cold and antiseptic, like a hospital corridor. Strangers plunked together in the dust, a cold wind seeming to blow between them. "Isn't it beautiful?" Sylvia said to him, peering up at the barred windows and around the empty shells of rooms. "I love this place. It does my heart good."

They sat down in a private room across from each other. "My mother would tell stories about how much people hated the czar," Sylvia said. "She used to say: 'He should have been buried before I ever heard of him.' She always resented the fact she had no education. She'd see these little children go off to school in the morning and she'd be jealous. She'd watch from the window and I'd watch her.

"When I was seven, we lived in one room in Russia. A young man came to my house and my father covered the windows with blankets and locked the door. My father made an incision in the boy's leg so he could call himself crippled instead of going to the army. My grandmother told me many times they'd helped these young people to escape. So I come from a revolutionary family but I'm the only one who retained it.

"When I was on 'The Merv Griffin Show' my family saw me. Merv had seen me when the six o'clock news had me on. The news wanted to show how old people were starving, so they put me in front of a Shopwell supermarket. I looked through the window, see, and developed a hungry look. Anyway, Merv saw me and asked me to do his show. I accepted with pleasure. When I was on, he mentioned that my son was killed and I said I had to use my own money to cremate him. Then I said plenty: that all the money we use for wars and nuclear weapons we should use for housing and college and libraries and food and all kinds of wonderful things. I let Griffin know how I felt about things, believe me, although I didn't say I was in the Movement. After the show he came over to me and said, 'I'll bet you do a lot of reading. Do you read the *New York Times?*' I said no, I couldn't afford it." Sylvia cackled.

The reporter called Sylvia for three days after that meeting and got a busy signal. She finally answered the phone on the afternoon of the third day. She had accidentally left it off the hook.

"My head bothers me," she said. "I feel . . . badly . . . over my son. I don't go around telling people because each one has his own troubles. But . . . I was looking over a bunch of pictures. . . . I can't accept it. Somebody walks out of the house and that's it. It's more than three years now. As I get older, it grows on me more and more. Things quiet down and you live with yourself."

For the third meeting they went back to Nutburger. Sylvia was wearing three buttons: Outlaw White Violence, Ban Nuclear Weapons, and People Before Profits.

"One of the first musicians I ever heard was Percy Grainger from Australia," she said. "Then I saw Yehudi Menuhin make his debut playing the Beethoven Violin Concerto. He came out in short pants with one of those big collars. I got acquainted with symphonies and soloists. I heard Caruso twice. I would go from the shop to the Met and stand on line. I heard Rostropovich many times. Now if he hanged himself I wouldn't go to hear him anymore. Not since he had the nerve to shelter Solzhenitsyn from the Soviet authorities!"

"Have you ever read Solzhenitsyn?" he asked her.

"I wouldn't think of it. I've heard about him *plenty*. There was a program at Carnegie Hall the other night made up of refugees from the Soviet Union. I might have gone because it was a holiday and there were some very special singers and musicians. But I can't stand them. Most of them are Jewish, otherwise they wouldn't have come here. To hell with them. In the last generation they wouldn't have had a goddamn thing in all their lives. And now they get to the point of being great artists. I'm very much in favor of what the Soviet Union is doing. The fact that people don't have to sleep on the sidewalks is enough for me.

"Michael was born in June 1937. I had met Earl at Camp Nitgedaiget ('Don't Worry') in 1936. Maury Ballinzweig was a lifeguard there, you know. Earl and I married the next year. He was a salesman for a paste-and-glue factory. Very bright, an advanced thinker. But he ran around a lot. There was a great deal of fighting. For a while I took Michael to California and we lived in a bungalow. Pepper trees, eucalyptus, lemon trees. In the middle of the summer you could see the snow on the mountain. I had an orange tree right in my kitchen window. But we came home, and Earl got a divorce. Michael felt terrible. He missed his father.

"We had a lot of trouble together because Michael was not well. He was disturbed, and I feel very guilty about it. I think it was my fault. From the time he was eight or nine years old, they said he was schizophrenic. I took him to Rockland State Hospital, to Bellevue. He didn't want to go. He was screaming blue murder and the nurse said, 'Look, I'm in the hospital. I stay here too.' Angry as he was, Michael turned around to her and said, 'Yeah, but you're getting paid for it.' You see, he was so brilliant. He knew the derivation of words. I don't know how he learned it. The thing was, I trusted the doctors and I didn't know how to handle him myself. He did something bad once in the apartment. I said, 'What should I do with you?' He said, 'Love me. Just love me.'

"He had a wonderful sense of humor. When he was twelve, I took him to a TV preview studio. They showed an ad for a life insurance company which advertised insurance for the husband so the family would have something when he died. They lived in a slum, but when the husband died, they fixed up the house, they got new furniture. So Michael stood up, raised his hand, and said, 'It seems to me from your commercial that the wife is better off with her husband dead.' Everyone roared."

Sylvia paused, and said, "The thing is, he often said: 'I love you, but I don't like you.' As he got older, he seemed to take it out on me that I was progressive. Just to spite me, he bought a copy of *1984* when it first came out. He said that's what's gonna happen, rotten things like that. Just to spite me, see. One day I was in his room and found the damn thing. I was so angry I threw it down the incinerator. He bought a copy of William Z. Foster's old book for five dollars, *Toward Soviet America*. He showed it to me, and he tore it up page by page right in front of me."

The reporter held her and asked how her son had died.

"They pulled him out of the East River," Sylvia whispered. "Half naked. He used to go to Bellevue Hospital for medication. They treat these things with drugs. One Sunday evening in 1982, he was very disturbed. He understood himself so well. When he felt he shouldn't take something, he didn't. When he felt he needed it, he took it. He was bad that night. At ten he said he was going to go to Bellevue for the medication. As he was walking out the door, I said, 'Michael, don't take too much money with you.' He said, 'Don't tell me what to do,' and he walked out. Monday morning he wasn't home. Tuesday he didn't come home. Friday about four o'clock, two cops came to my house and told me.

"At the morgue, they brought up his body in a glass case all covered with a sheet. And he looked sleepy and he had such a contented look on his face. They brought him up on an elevator. I couldn't even touch him. He was in a case.

"I had his body cremated. The man said to me, 'Do you want the ashes?' What am I going to do with the ashes? I said, 'What do you do with them?' He said, 'They collect them. And then they bury them.' And you know, I get thoughts: How do I know what they did with his ashes? How do I know they cremated him altogether? How do I know?"

The reporter tried to see her again for two months, but she was busy with a Communist Party convention, peace demonstrations, union picket lines. They spoke on the phone. "I hate to say it, but I miss you," she said. "I hate to give you the satisfaction. I know you're not that progressive. But we have respect for each other. Just as long as you don't go any further backward." She laughed.

"I was at a mental illness hearing last week," Sylvia said. "I began by talking about the military budget. I said do you realize what they can do with seven billion dollars that they want to spend on military missiles, that they want to destroy the world? While all these thousands of young people have no place to go? And I told them about Michael. I said I was away one weekend in Cleveland. I said my son was very depressed, and that he tried to hang himself in the bathroom. When I came home, Michael told me. He said he put a rope on the beam in the bathroom and the rope broke, and it cut into his neck. He got very frightened. He put on his coat, he put his collar up, and he ran to Bellevue in the middle of the night. When he got there, the guard asked him what he wanted. Michael told the guard that he'd tried to commit suicide but that the rope broke and he fell on the bathroom floor and the rope hurt his neck. And I said to them, 'Do you know what the guard said to him? The guard wouldn't let him into the hospital. He said, 'Go home and get a stronger rope.' And I said to them, 'That's the kind of society we have.' "

When the reporter saw Sylvia again at Nutburger, her mouth had moved back to the center, and she looked well. "I never did meet the right man," she said. "I was always the one who got the blind date. When I went out with a group of friends, if they had somebody they didn't know who to pair off with, I was it. I didn't like the idea but I accepted it. But inside I resented it. The young men who wrote poetry in those days all had 'dens.' There was a guy named Ezzi, a shriveled-up little thing. I loved that guy. I didn't love him physically, but he was so brilliant. You didn't know how old he was; he was really nothing to look at. My crowd went on hikes to Palisades Park; we'd go hitchhiking and come home at four o'clock in the morning. We'd stop a milk wagon and buy a bottle of milk. We knew what to live for. Whatever we did we did with our whole being.

"This was 1915. I was working at the Arrow shirt factory in Williamsburg. I worked on artificial flowers. They taught me how to work on a button sewing machine. Every time I broke a needle they would mark it down and take two cents out of my pay.

"Oh, I wanted to show you a letter my son sent me once." She handed him a typed page with two quotations on it:

Oh, the comfort, the inexplicable comfort of feeling safe with a person. Having neither to weigh thoughts or measure words, but to pour them all out just as they are, chaff and grain together. Knowing that a faithful hand will take and sift them, keep what is worth keeping, and then with a breath of kindness throw the rest away.

—George Eliot

The second quotation was from an article by Liz Smith in *Reader's Digest*.

The son-to-mother communication transmitted over the longest distance is the birthday greeting sent on November 22, 1968, by astronaut James A. Lovell, Jr. to his mother. At the time of its transmission he was 140,000 miles out in space on his way to the moon.

At the bottom of the page was written, "Love, Michael."

"I wake up and hear him say, 'Ma?' I don't wish it on anyone.

"See, the thing is, I went to work when he was a baby; a year and a half or two years. I had to get out of the house because I was so unhappy with my husband. He was jealous of me—very. I wasn't an attractive-looking woman, and he knew beautiful ones. But he was insecure. And I didn't like humiliation.

"I didn't realize Michael wanted somebody close to him. His father was always running around. He would take Michael to the park, spread a blanket, and fall asleep.

"I got a letter the other day from Reagan. For Michael. They sent a self-addressed envelope with a stamp and they want a reply. I felt like writing, 'You should be where he is.' But I knew Michael voted for Reagan to spite me. He was envious because he knew that I had friends. He didn't have a life. He learned Morse code by himself, and talked a lot to these people, the C.B.'s. The thing is," she said, her voice breaking, "he really loved me very dearly."

"He would have been forty-eight years old now," Sylvia said.

"Then he was—"

"That's right, young man. He was your age."

"Did you ever read Khrushchev's speech in 1956?" he asked her.

"I didn't bother," Sylvia said. "Ben Davis said not to, and his vision was deeper than all mankind. Look, I was in the Soviet Union in 1937 when Stalin was president. The big shots used to walk around with their *canes* and their *ladies*, and the old women used to go about with a stick and clean up the papers and do the sweeping. These bureaucrats had finally reached the day when they had servants and felt like millionaires. I spoke to a lot of people about them. 'Their day will come too,' they said. And it was true. Shortly after I came back here, the Soviet Union had the Moscow trials."

"How did you feel about the trials?" he asked.

"What could you feel?" Sylvia replied. "I felt there had to be a clean sweep, and there was."

"But then what did you think when Khrushchev said all those people were innocent, and the trials were rigged?"

"Listen," Sylvia said, "I don't think about the individual."

F.B.I. Agent Goldberg
and the Car Thief

Solly's best friend.

—G.L.

I arrested Davey Lapidus. We got him on car theft. Caught him in the act. Took me where he stole the cars. A real skunk, low class. A thug. Greasy-looking, tough, surly, cheap crook. Head down, slinking around. He said: "I hate cops. I'll kill any cops in my way." But he really was a profitable car thief. He made a lot of money.

He asked to see me. Says: "I'm in the same place with Rubell. Maybe you'd like me to ask him some questions."

I said goodbye. You don't let a punk like that set you up.

He started telling me about it anyway.

We learned about Rubell through Lapidus.

Solly was weak. Look how he talked to Lapidus, opened his heart to him. Solly opened his heart to a car thief.

Every day I'd write a three-page memo from what Solly told Lapidus.

Solly was that vulnerable. He needed someone to talk to.

The House of Detention was tough in those days. A top Communist, Joe Horton, had his skull bashed in there. Horton had been standing in line for lunch, talking about how he hated the United States. Some little guy called him a son of a bitch, picked up a pipe and hit him. The warden called me up when it happened. There was blood all over the floor. It was a crime on government property.

After the Horton case, the warden and I became friends. He gave me carte blanche.

Ballinzweig was in there too. I asked the warden to bring Ballinzweig up. He was to be brought through the prison door leading to security quarters where prisoners were interviewed.

I was waiting in the interview room. Ballinzweig came through the door. The minute he saw me, he turned and went back to the door, stood there, waiting to be readmitted. Wouldn't speak to me. He was holding all these engineering papers he worked on while in prison.

Ballinzweig was at least on the same level as Solly. But he didn't recruit like the Rubells did.

I had dozens of cases like the Rubells.

Dolly was a vibrant recruiter. She worked at it. She was smart. Always talking with people she might be able to use. The squad room talk was that Dolly was the driving force.

We did chalk talks. On a chalkboard. Points. We'd tear up each point that was proposed; try to develop leads. Dolly was always mentioned. She covered her tracks very well. Solly was a wimp. She led his whole life.

Everyone in the office knew she was the driver.

One reason she wasn't nailed: this was the 1950s—"this is a woman; you're picking on a woman."

Women prisoners who go bad are vicious. Men can still be nice guys. Dolly was vicious.

Squad room agents felt if we had gotten them apart, we could have broken him. Dolly seemed to feel that too. She insisted that Solly be executed first. She raised a hell of a row.

They wouldn't let me talk to Solomon. I think I could have broken him. I'm low key, forthright. I have luck in that regard. Ballinzweig was surly and hostile. With his notebook, his engineering, working on complicated formulas. I didn't like Ballinzweig.

Solly was vulnerable. He knew about Joe Horton. I would have had an edge because he was in jail. I knew that jail. Prisoners had access to each other. Today that jail wouldn't exist.

It was open and dangerous.

Solly, 1953

He didn't flutter with the breeze.

—G.L.

Mornings in deep autumn, with the ebbing of his hopes, he noticed the leaves and maple-tree seeds blown by the wind descending slowly like helicopters over the death-house wall. The icy Hudson River wind. He began another letter to his children—"my precious children"—he talked about playing horsie with them and what it was like gathering them in his arms at bedtime, and again, again about his and Dolly's innocence: "All the government had as evidence, children, were those *Freiheit* thimbles. Thimbles your mommy and I gave to our progressive friends for donating to a peaceful world by reading the *Freiheit*. For this, these cunning madmen plan to kill us." He tore the letter up, and began another, telling them he hoped they were taking their piano lessons seriously. He told them their mother (alone in the women's section of the death house) was a diamond, that no amount of government filth could scratch her honor.

The guards led him out into the yard again in the afternoon. The wind stung his ears. He watched a seagull sail upward in wide circles, lifted by the wind, and fly into the wide-open sky until he could no longer see it. And he saw Delancey Street and Columbia Street, the crowd surging by the pushcarts, the chickens in their wooden boxes cackling, the merchants shouting and fighting, and Solly saw himself hurrying home to Dolly and the kids. Rocking them all in his arms, crying out, "It's over. Everything's hunky-dory." His legs almost buckled. He looked at the white streaks of calcium carbonate running in broken lines from brick to brick along the wall. He thought of coal and iron ore dug from the earth, trucks carrying it to the mills, iron and steel pouring from furnaces, parts sent to the prison. Mechanics molding them into an edifice, a death house. . . . What could he tell his children to make them understand? One parable, one picture. Peekskill, the Scottsboro boys, Gastonia, *Kristallnacht*, Fuchik's letters, Spain, Dmitroff's speech to the Nazi court. . . . And he remembered something that said it all. The American captain who had told Solly of being on the outskirts of Düsseldorf in early 1945. The captain was preparing with his men a siege to liberate the city from the Nazis. A German worker, a printer wearing an apron, approached the captain. The German had asked the American captain for permission to hold a meeting of his Communist club, the first that would be held since Hitler took power. He handed the captain the written announcement of the meeting for his approval. It contained the date, time, and place, and the words, "Those who fluttered with the breeze are not invited."

Only a Communist—no, Solly would have to write "progressive" —could have the perspective to call twelve years of Nazism a "breeze." He sat down to write the letter. My precious children, do you now understand why your parents are dying?

And again Solly could breathe.

The Uncle

Shadow of a moustache.

—G.L.

I met Solly in the fall of 1938 at City College. I knew him for two semesters, in the alcoves mainly. He was there early and late.

He was not too bright.

I could see Solly getting involved with the Russians, trying to help: this aspect of looking for a parent.

A very strange, unhappy young man. Lonely, always there in the alcoves, always away from home.

He didn't have depth.

When the Springers adopted the kids, they looked for people who had knowledge of the Rubells. They wanted to provide continuity, not treat the parents as outcasts.

I saw the kids quite often after the execution. I played chess with Joseph. He used to play chess with his father. So I was Uncle Henry.

The Springers had a family conference every week where anyone could bring up any subject. They operated by majority vote.

The Jewish community was concerned that Communists were raising the kids. The Jewish Child Care Association came with the police and took them away. Joseph and Amy held hands all the way to Pleasantville, New York, where they were put in a shelter.

Acting purer than the goyim, protecting the good name of the Jews: this is what I call a Jewish judge sentencing the Rubells on the eve of Yom Kippur. I think it was part of a primitive purification rite for him that was very vulgar.

*   *   *

In order to wrest control from the Communists, a WASP, Dean Smyth of the New York School of Social Work, was appointed coguardian. The kids' grandmother, Sarah Rubell, was the other co-guardian, but Smyth was main man.

The other grandmother said that if the kids were sent to her, she would throw them out the window.

Sarah Rubell said to the kids: "Look what your mother did to my son."

The Springers would bring food and clothes for the kids. Sarah would hide them. No American culture, no Eastern European culture either. *Prost*, common.

But this doesn't get the mood. She would speak against blacks. She would rail against this woman who took her son away. Doing this in front of five- and eight-year-old kids.

Joseph read the *Daily Worker*. After Amy went to sleep, he wanted to engage in political discussion: never a cultural or recreational matter. He announced his desire to become a lawyer. Vindication was the key word.

The adoption process was still under consideration. Dean Smyth allowed the kids to live with the Springers more and more. To me the amazing thing was their continued sanity. Joseph was a consummate actor. When Dean Smyth visited the Springer house, Joseph wanted to demonstrate what excellent adoptive parents they would be. He would eat an apple and say, "You know, Dean, Mrs. Springer says an apple a day keeps the doctor away." He'd sit down and play the piano and say, "You know, Dean, Mrs. Springer says culture is very important."

Joseph had a bar mitzvah. The dean needed it to satisfy the Jewish community. But he treated it very seriously. Not really a put-on.

Joseph sang and he recited. Dean Smyth cried like a baby. At the end he told Joseph he was magnificent. He said, "I wish I had taped it." Joseph said, "I'll do it all over again."

The dean arranged for the adoption by the Springers. In the wee hours of the morning they all descended from different parts of the city, pretending they didn't know each other as they walked up the steps of the court. The dean had pneumonia and came out of a sickbed to get it done. He died the next day.

The community wanted the kids to be punished for what their parents did.

I didn't have a kid of my own. What do you do with children, you play. I became the uncle. I'd do multiple accents. I'd wear my glasses on my head.

I see Solly's face before me.

A young guy with a moustache, which struck me as strange. My concept of a *yeshiva bocher*, somebody who had not come of a more cultured background. He wore a suit. Most likely he had one suit.

Now Joseph was growing a little stubble of a moustache. He turned his profile and said, "Who do I look like?" I said, "You look like Joseph." He said, "No no no." And I said, "You look like Joseph." And he said, "Come on now." I said, "You want me to say you look like Solly? You look like Solly. Does that make you happy?" He said, "Yeah, it does make me happy."

Surveillance

May I come in?

—G.L.

"For years," the woman said to the reporter, "I kept a nun's costume with a magnetic chessboard in a locker in the old Penn Station. I was sure I was going to get swept up when the arrests began. They had concentration camps ready."

A man watches a cabin in Goldens Bridge, New York, in 1949. He watches the movements of a young couple and their two kids. He watches the father, recognizes the type: a candy-store boy. Both of them, *schleppers*. He observes their comings and goings.

In time, he will knock at their door. He will drop a *Daily Worker* he is holding and, after they react, pick it up sheepishly, as if he is not sure of their response. They will glance at each other, and welcome him instantly. He will drink the couple's coffee and eat their food, and bounce their children on his lap. He will play the harmonica for them.

The kids flap after the ducks on the lake, calling and laughing. The father carries the little one on his back, playing horsie, and tossing her into the air, sings:

> *"Fly higher and higher and higher*
> *Our emblem's the Soviet Star*
> *Let every good comrade shout Red Front!*
> *We're building the USSR."*

The little one cannot get enough of her father. The boy wants to grow up to be like Ben Davis.

233

The mother, away from her therapist, the rasping New York streets, is ready to scream. But how she loves her babies. The cold lake water cleanses the smell of fear that she carries with her. Even in the water, sometimes Solly and Dolly look anxiously to the shore to see who is there. There is their neighbor, the advanced thinker, the man with the harmonica.

> In the jail bullpen the guard averted his eyes and said in an unnaturally soft voice, "Nick, your mother is here to see you. . . ."
> This was hell! This was worse than frying!
>
> —*Knock On Any Door*
> Willard Motely

The boy read the novel after his parents were executed. To learn how it went.

In 1975, in a very small room of the famous Barr Building on Olive Street in St. Louis, a woman was on her lunch break. She was a newcomer to the city. She noticed a man her age who came into the room from time to time: a thin, stern-looking person with white hair.

One day he told the newcomer that he was one of those who spied on the Rubells. He described the cabin on the beach, the children playing.

The woman told the reporter in 1988: "I left home at twenty-one. When the Communists came around, I was ready to join them.

"I married one of the comrades. He was, like most of the others in the Party, a misfit and a loser. My life was even worse than before. I divorced him and dropped all my old friends.

"Three years later rumors reached me that the F.B.I. were looking for me. They visited me. They did not say I was going to jail but let my own fears work on me.

"They suggested I go back into the Party and spy. I would receive twenty-five dollars a month for expenses. I refused. That was the end of it.

"Later, I was on a picket line for Women Strike for Peace. The Red Squad's photographer was there. He called me a *schoene maydel*— that meant 'nice girl.' This was his way of telling me he knew I was Jewish.

"As time went on I was generally burned out as far as any other activity was concerned. When I met this man and he told me about the Rubells, you can see why I reacted the way I did. It was partly what he did and partly what I had lived through. I don't know why he even trusted me enough to tell me what he did. I never found out his name. There was nothing about him that made me think he was not telling the truth or that suggested that he was delusional. I have, in my lifetime, met truly delusional persons and he was nothing like them.

"If someone is suspected of spying, I think the government has a right to keep them under surveillance. But to go out of your way to be friends with people, to eat at their table, to maybe hold their children on your lap—and then coldly turn around and hand them over. . . .

"Well, anyway. Just telling you all this gives me a strange feeling. It makes me tired, if you want to know the truth."

The older child remembers the apple his mother kept on the windowsill of her cell, and many details about both of them. His father's arms around him, and his mother's.

The younger child does not remember them.

Davey "Car Wreck" Lapidus

Don't flush, Solly.

—G.L.

I know my jails. This wasn't so bad. But Solly was a milk shake.

We met; we talked; we walked. I reminded him, he said, of a comrade with a harmonica at Goldens Bridge.

I had credentials. Former member of the Young Communist League. Friend of Harry Brimmer, also known as Jay West, who was in another cell. The Party was ignoring Dolly and Solly completely, so Big Jay never acknowledged Solly in the yard or spoke to him. You should have heard Solly speak Big Jay's name. The earth shook. A top Party leader, Jay had been an organizer in China and Berlin and Harlan, Kentucky. Big build, high forehead with a shock of black hair graying at the temples. Squeaky Donald Duck voice.

Solly desperately wanted the Party to know just how significant his contribution was (as if they didn't). He told me and let me know just how much it would mean to him for Big Jay to know everything. I promised the milk shake.

I told him about my car episodes. He cursed the system.

Not that I didn't like Solly. I liked him. I was still rather progressive, but not the whole hog.

I had been at Peekskill; I knew the score. I had the Little Lenin series in my bunk; I remembered Maury Ballinzweig from Camp Nitgedaiget. I'd known Mendy—Zitzi Mendelbaum—before he'd gone to Spain. Solly and I both knew Mendy's historic words on the rooftop of 617 Livonia Avenue with the other boys before he left for Spain: "I'm just getting into the struggle a little sooner." Brooklyn,

1936. Mendy was killed in his first action in Spain. When I quoted those words to Solly, his eyes filled.

Solly got manic and talked for hours; he was morose and stood by himself in the corner. "When I get out of here, I'm putting you on the right track," he promised me.

He was confused; he'd forget what he'd said. The next week he'd say he would set up drops for me in Cuba, Puerto Rico, and Caracas when I got out. "These are revolutionary strongholds," he said. "I've worked out an escape route to Mexico by a small boat. It's all arranged."

Then, the next time, he said he'd be out soon whatever sentence he got: "In five years, I promise you, sweet guy, we'll have a Soviet America," he said.

One night Solly drew a diagram of the operational setup of the ring. He said there were two units operating in Manhattan. Solly headed one unit; the other was headed by two others, both of whom had fled. Joe Klein was already in Europe at the time of Solly's arrest; the other man had fled to the Soviet Union a week after Solly was jailed.

Solly said that for years he'd been in direct contact with a Soviet he met several times a month. "Oh, I've shared many a whiskey sour with my friends," Solly said, worldly Solly. "They've already given five thousand dollars to Henky for my defense."

When he finished, Solly tore the diagram into little pieces and threw them in the toilet. He didn't flush it. When he left, I took the scraps of paper out of the water and dried them. I put them in an envelope, and gave them to Goldberg.

Solly told me his life story. Someday bridges and boulevards would be named after him and Dolly in a Soviet America; he wanted the facts to be straight. He'd been a hot yeshiva student. Went to a Y.C.L. meeting at fourteen. They told him rabbis were politicians with beards, and gave him William Z. Foster's *Toward Soviet America*. He got a hard-on. The Party, the shock brigade of the proletariat, would overthrow that insatiable bloodsucker, the capitalist class.

Solly would carry a long needle with him to demonstrations, and stick police horses in the flank to make them bolt.

Solly wanted above all to implement his beliefs with action, he said. Something that would tip the balance of forces in favor of the future.

"And it happened, sweet guy," he'd say. "It happened. It wasn't easy going either. Not everyone is capable. It takes training. You don't just get something of value to the Soviet Union and pass it on. No way. There can be many months of waiting. You have to control yourself. Davey, do you realize that when the Canadian ring was destroyed, I lost contact for almost two years?"

He told me of his signals: a circle with a cross in the center of a store window on 14th Street. A hole in the cement floor of a movie theater that was used as a depository for transmitting information. Gum on a subway window—red for danger and white for all clear. "The simplest things are the best," Solly said.

"Solly," I asked, "why didn't you escape when you could have?"

"I had to take care of friends. I knew what was happening for two months, but others had to be warned. One more week and I would have been on my way to the Soviet Union."

"And if it's the death sentence?"

"Look, I played the game and I lost. I'll take the results."

Solly wept at night about his kids. A letter came from his sister that the kids wanted him to come home, that they did not understand what was happening, or that they understood too well. I put my arms around the milk shake.

"What is Dolly like?" I asked him one night.

"Dolly . . . is the most beautiful person I have ever met. She is truly beautiful in her soul. A keen analytical mind. She does not give an inch, never compromises her principles. She is in pain so much of the time from her back, her headaches, and the suffering of the workers. She has such revolutionary anger; she never deviates from it. She referred to Eisenhower the other day as a 'guttersnipe in striped pants.' And 'a privileged fascist dog.' And 'a homophobic faggot who will fuck anything in skirts.' I mean, she talks that way to me. I have learned so much from her integrity."

He told me Dolly was furious when the newspapers criticized returning prisoners of war from Korea for praising Communism. " 'They've seen a real system that works for the people for the first time,' she said, 'and their hearts rise up within.' "

Solly got sentimental, and began humming concentration camp songs and Red Army troop marches. He said that when he met Dolly, life began. She helped him with his studies and typed his homework; although, he said with a twinkle, they did their share of smooching.

Trolleys were still running then. There was a ferry at the end of Christopher Street, and they rode down to it. They read the *Daily Worker* and lists of lynchings from the Civil Rights Congress as the sweet salt spray kissed their faces. They learned about Sartre's cockroach philosophy and other Freudian worms of reaction, the dangers of sectarianism and opportunist tendencies, and how to talk to the workers.

When Stalin signed the pact with Hitler, they shouted Starve the War and Feed America! Food for the Unemployed—Not Fodder for Cannon! Keep America out of the Imperialist War! Not One Cent, Not One Man, Not One Plane for the Imperialist War! The Yanks Are Not Coming! Solly told me of the merry days Dolly painted his hair gray, put him in a wheelchair all bundled up in blankets and wheeled him down Bleecker Street. She carried a placard: "My husband is legless because of fighting in the imperialist war! He can't even get it up! Remember 1917! Don't let Wall Street trick us again!—Sex-starved housewife."

Dolly handed out *A Letter to Mother*. Solly gave me a copy of it. The cover of the pamphlet had a drawing of a bent-over little old lady, a picture of her boy on her table, letting a piece of paper fall to the floor: "Telegram: Killed in Action."

Dear Mother,

Happy Mother's Day.

I wish I could send you something that you need like a new chair or a nice dress, but every penny I get goes for room rent and eats. It sure makes me sore that my dear mother can't have some nice things when the swells spend whole fortunes on a single swanky party or a country home, enough to keep a couple of dozen families like ours going for a whole year.

Did you have Tommy's tonsils out yet? Better take care of it before all this economy stuff goes through and they begin to shut down all the free clinics and hospitals. Things are getting plenty tough but Roosevelt ain't talking no more about the unemployed. Looks like he has gone over to the fat boys on Wall Street bag and baggage. No difference now between him and the Republicans.

You've guessed it, Mother. I'm sore. And I'm worried too. I'm worried about a lot of things that are happening but most about this country getting into the war. All the fellows I know feel the same way. None of us want to be smashed up in a Wall Street war.

I heard a fellow talking just the other day: he said we have a big fight on our hands right here—for jobs and security and a federal health-and-housing program. Said he was a Communist. Said that we got into the last war for the benefit of big business and the munitions makers and we don't want any more of it. Mother, he said, Give peace a chance. Sounds good to me.

Now I see why the newspapers and the millionaires don't like the Communists. But the Communists are for people like us. I'm going to read some of their stuff to find out what it's all about.

I am going to send you a little booklet that my friend Jim gave me. It's called *I Didn't Raise My Boy to Be a Soldier for Wall Street*. It only cost a cent but it's sure got a lot of common sense in it. Mrs. O'Connor, Mrs. Goldstein, and Mrs. Fabrizio ought to read it too. Jim's mother is getting the neighbors together for a Mother's Committee to Keep America out of War. You ought to do that, Mother. Get off your fanny. All the neighbors would go along with you.

Tell Tommy and Mary that if I get a job I am going to send you all something nice for Christmas. But there are no jobs. I am pressing my suit the way you told me to so it still looks pretty good. I want it to last till I get work. I wish I had a shirt to go along with it.

Well, this is a long letter but I just had to tell you all this. Remember me to all the neighbors and any of the old gang on the corner. Love to you, Dad, Tommy, and Mary.

Your son,
Bill

Then Hitler attacked Russia. Stalin was heartbroken. Browder made his famous statement: "What nerve! That's really brazen, don't you think?" The character of the war changed. Fascism lost its progressive character. Solly and Dolly carried the new placards: Starve the Shiftless and Feed the War! Not One Cent, Not One Man, Not One Plane for Peace! Down with the Appeasers of Hitlerism! Defend America by Giving Full Aid to the Soviet Union! The Yanks Are Coming! Defeat Anti-Semitism! Forward to a Worldwide People's Front Against Hitler Fascism for the Defense of the Soviet Union!

Solly and Dolly threw out their books and pamphlets with titles like *New Germany—Where the Trains Run on Time*, and *America for Americans First: Refugees Crimp Our Style.*

Solly stopped reminiscing. "The thing is, Dolly is a tank."

I thought of the reason I could never testify against Solly at his trial. I'd never want Mother to know. She's not only my mother; she is the famous Mother Lapidus.

Mother came to this country from czarist Russia.

She lived in a town that was friendly to the Jewish enclave within it. Things had not been bad.

In this town, church bells rang for the call to prayer, and on Sundays and holidays. On this particular day—not Sunday or a holiday—the church bells rang. The peasants, the town doctor, the school principal, the intelligentsia, and the priest gathered.

The Jews went into a panic. Yet it was a friendly town. They waited.

The group came out of church. They knew all the Jews and where they lived. They knocked on doors and asked the men to come to a meeting. They called them by their first names and smiled. My grandfather had evaded Petlura's soldiers. But these men called him by his name and he went. Five hundred Jewish men gathered. They were taken out of town to a building in a forest clearing.

The town could not decide how to kill them. In the meantime, they had to feed them. They let the women in the town know they could bring food. For a week the women, including my grandmother, came with food for the men and saw them and talked to them.

At the end of the week, on Friday, they didn't permit the women to bring food. There was no contact during the next week. The women wrung their hands and tore their hair.

A young peasant boy from the nearby French sugar refinery wandered into town. The women controlled themselves and said to him: "We're not going to hurt you. We just want you to tell us: what happened to the men?" He took them to the mass grave. It was a block long.

They had thrown a bomb into the building. A young Jew within the building picked it up and threw it back. It didn't detonate. The rabbi and the older Jews were critical. They said you must not fight back.

When the bomb failed, the town tried shooting the Jews in groups. But they ran out of ammunition, or didn't want to waste it.

So they cut their throats.

They piled the Jews into wagons. They drove them around the town and to the grave. The town doctor advised them to put lime on the grave so that a mass epidemic would not result.

One man survived. He had been at the bottom of the pile. When they emptied the wagon, he surfaced. They left him for dead. He was only slightly wounded in the leg. He crawled over the bodies and out of the grave. He ran into the woods and hid.

My grandmother went out of her head. She spent the days reading doom poetry to my mother and the other children. Poetry by the Zionist Bialik. The poem began: "God sent me to you to warn you." It ended: "Go down to the potter's house, buy a pot, throw it on the ground. That's how the Jewish people will be broken. And bow your head and say no more." She read these poems. That's what she did. She said that animals in the woods were calling: "Don't call me man."

One day my mother went by a synagogue. The children within were saying the kaddish for their dead parents. She listened to the weeping.

Soon after, my mother left for America.

Mother was a charter member of the Party. She was at the rally in Madison Square Garden when Mother Bloor spoke. The Communists were forbidden to display the red flag. And so Mother Bloor wore this beautiful red blouse with big butterfly sleeves. She started to talk and spread out her arms, and the red flag blazoned freely. The crowd roared.

My mother. Her leather jacket, beret, blue work shirt and red tie, heavy work shoes. Her borscht with cream, her black bread. That was in my youth. Then came the Popular Front. Browder called Communism "twentieth century Americanism." Mother now had ribbons in her hair, spoke with a reborn Yiddish accent, wore skirts and lipstick.

Mother studied at the Yiddishe Arbeiten Universitett—the Jewish Workers University, run by the International Workers Order on 14th Street. She worked in the factory by day and after work studied Marx in Yiddish until midnight. Some of the other students couldn't even read the clock. The legendary Pop Dinwich singled Mother out one night. He took her aside and said: "My child, you want the right things for the people. You must go out and be with the workers." Mother went, and never came back. I was seven years old. But I always saw her on May Day when she spoke at Union Square.

Mother believed in the Soviet Union one hundred percent. When her brother wrote her from Russia in 1923 that he was not surviving, Mother felt sorry for him. But upon reflection, she decided that if he had believed deeply enough in the Socialist transformation, he would have established deeper roots and found his way. She never heard from him again, and never mentioned him.

My mother stands five feet tall in her heavy orthopedic shoes. She has a jutting jaw and a lined face. She speaks with a Yiddish accent in a fractured English that is careful, reflective, and charming. Like her friends Manya Poffnick and Sylvia Pollack, Mother has a wonderful way of communicating with the workers. And unlike Manya and Sylvia, there is an air of serenity to Mother, a calm, that is comforting to be around. She really is becoming a very nice little old lady. She has little busts of Stalin and Robeson on her bookshelf. "Remember," she says to me, "there is only one Soviet Union in the entire world." Who can deny it?

When I told her I was going into the car profession, she told me a story her mother had told her. There were a bunch of businessmen on a ship. They had superb merchandise with them, and they were the center of attention. Suddenly a storm erupted, and the ship went down. The businessmen drowned. The survivors went to a nearby town. During the sabbath service, one of them spoke to the congregation. He was inspiring and wise, a student of philosophy and a poet. The other survivors said: "How come we didn't notice you when we were on the ship?" He replied, "The merchandise I bring with me doesn't sink."

Mother always told me that the Party released untold creative sides to her nature, making her venture into realms that would ordinarily have been denied to her in a male chauvinist oligarchy like the United States. For two years Mother became Patrick O'Shaugnessy, head of the American Legion post in Doberman's Creek, New York, patriot, boozer, and cocksman. Patrick spearheaded the war drive in Doberman's Creek after Hitler invaded the Soviet Union, headed the war bond drive, sang in the barbershop quartet at Clancy's Pub, and shot at least eighteen shirkers during the legion's weekly "faggot hunt" of men spending the war crocheting or writing poetry in the eaves of their grandmother's houses.

At the height of the campaign against Orientals in California, a comrade named Molly Figman, donning pigtails and eye makeup to make herself look Chinese, pitter-pattered down the street in white socks and sandals. Mother would whip out her pistol and scream, "Send the Chinks back to China!" and chase Molly down the street. Soon a crowd joined in the fun. Molly and Mother led the witless crowd to Union Square, where a Negro on a soapbox was waiting to deliver a lecture to them on the Chinese Soviets. The comrade began his address on the anti-imperialist struggle of the Fukien Soviets. The crowd misunderstood him and somebody yelled, "Hey, Nigger. Don't you know there are white women here? You let a nigger talk and right away they use dirty language." Mother had to plead with the crowd to keep their minds on the Chink menace, but the progressive nature of the meeting was seriously undermined.

Now that Mother was getting older, she was beginning to take a genuine interest in me, and even visited me here, since she had to see Jay West anyway. (No one was allowed to see Solly or Maury.) She was very impressed that I was in such important company. She had known Solly (and Maury Ballinzweig too) since they were young men. And when I hinted to her that I was involved with Solly in a progressive way, she responded to me with incredible warmth and electricity. Her eyes filled, she touched my arm, and said, "Davey, if you can be of any help to our Solly, you will fulfill all my hopes and dreams for you as my son. Never did I imagine you could play such a crucial role in the people's struggle. If Solly trusts you, my son, so do I." Mother had never called me son or, in fact, Davey before. She had always addressed me as "fellow worker." I trembled when she touched my arm.

And even when Mother heard the ridiculous charge that I had also been a "pimp" for a number of years, she did not bat an eyelid. I was tremendously relieved. The charge was ridiculous on the face of it. The women in question were just a couple of young sluts of limited education. If other men had been as understanding and giving of their time as I had been, perhaps their fates would have been different and less of a blot on the educational and economic systems that just used them and threw them away.

Mother said that she knew positively that Solly and Dolly were innocent—because they were pure of heart, because they knew the score, because they aided the forces of peace, and above all because they helped the people. "Whatever they did," she said, smiling, "they didn't do it."

It would have killed Mother if I testified openly against Solly—and just at the moment when we were getting along so well.

Solly had wanted more time to prepare for cross-examination, but the trial started. He had two years without salary to explain. Henky Rubin told him to say he was selling scrap iron. He had three trips to Pennsylvania, two to Syracuse. Henky said they were hot scrap-iron towns.

Solly told me that Bobby Metzger, Joe Klein, Sophie Rich, the whole gang, were "all my boys."

Fingering his cigar, the light flickering in the dark cell, he repeated proudly, "All my boys."

"Aren't you worried about them, Solly?" I said.

"They won't talk. None of them will talk. They'd cut their own throats," he said.

At night, he said, Dolly was writing a history of the world from a progressive perspective. She was up to 1939 and the Hitler-Stalin pact. When he visited her, she had all the pamphlets from before and after the pact. She was seated on the floor reading two at a time. One pile was labeled Peace. The other was labeled War. Solly tried to talk about the Case, but Dolly interrupted him: "The Party was correct! Always correct!"

Solly told me that he was worried that the F.B.I. would find the passport photographer. What passport photographer? I said, genuinely interested. Solly and Dolly had a hundred pictures taken with the kids just a few weeks before their arrest. It would show intent to flee.

When I told Goldberg, he assured me I should no longer worry about getting my parole.

Then he knew he was going to die. And Dolly.

Solly couldn't hold anything back. He looked like his legs were falling off. He lost his watch. He couldn't eat. His voice went up a decibel. He smoked the burning end of his cigar. Dolly was terrific, he whispered. Dolly wanted him to die first.

"That's wonderful, Solly," I said.

The Trial

Hershie, Solly, Dolly, and Manya.

—G.L.

Mr. and Mrs. North America and all the ships at sea—dots and dashes with lots of flashes from border to border and coast to coast: for the red white and blue . . . the great white way . . . and the stars and stripes forever . . . this is your favorite newsboy . . . your whale of a guy . . . your Broadway gigolo on a furlough . . . your Hiawatha gewgew man . . . Mrs. Mayfield's little boy Howard, taught at her knee to Love It Or Leave It . . . Howard May They Wave Forever . . . Howard Traitors Are Treife . . . Howard Toss Me Another Red Herring, Harry—Howard Mayfield . . . far from the guys and dolls at Lindy's . . . Love to Leo and Sugar to Sherman at the Stork . . . Howard Mayfield . . . live from left field . . . the trial of the century, for you, Mr. and Mrs. America, the trial of the scummies and peculiars, the Rubells, Solomon and Dolores, and Maury Ballinzweig . . . keep the nova fresh, Leo, this won't take long.

Maury Ballinzweig never took the stand at all. He read the *Gourmet Diner* much of the time.

Sid Smorg was not cross-examined by the defense. A wise decision.

The jurors took their seats: a guard in the Brooklyn Navy Yard, a rayon converter, a caterer, a pulp producer, a heating consultant, a brakeman on the Erie railroad, a furrier, a broker in a securities cage on Wall Street, a tractor operator at the Brooklyn Army Base, an official of Morton Salt Company, a milliner, a cat trainer.

Juror Y: "I don't believe in capital punishment."

Judge Milton Goldman: "You may be excused."

*　　　　*　　　　*

Judge Goldman to the jury: "If you can't keep your mind open, if you are prejudiced before you even begin to hear the evidence, I want to know about it right away."

Hy Briské was the youngest member of the prosecution team. He looked like a handsome ferret. His T-shirt said SUPERJEW on it. He skipped up and down the aisle. Solly's lawyer, Henky Rubin, began: "What does Communism have to do with this case?"

Hy flung his wrists out: "Oh . . . noth-ing! . . . Noth-ing!"

Hershie Stern, Dolly's brother, burped and belched his way to the stand. He had a cross-eyed, fat look to him and a smiling joviality. The buttons popped off him.

"Solly said the Russians were bearing the brunt of the war and we had to help them. Dolly backed him up. So I went with it. It was okay. I mean, it was shit, but I was twenty-three, right?

"Then," Hershie said, "Solly gave me five thousand dollars to get out of the country. He said Rolle was arrested. Smorg had been his courier, and he would be apprehended next. Then it would be my turn. I took the five thousand dollars but I ain't going nowhere. When Solly left, I turned to my wife Jelly and I guffawed. She wanted to flush it down the toilet."

"Didn't you have qualms?" Hy asked him.

"Didn't I have what?"

"Qualms. About keeping the money."

"Why, Hy?"

"It was Solly's money."

"No, Hy. I had no . . . *qualms.*"

"Why not?"

"It wasn't Solly's money. It was the Russians' money."

Hershie paused and rubbed his hand against his mouth. "You see, Solly had said at first it was all for the sake of science. But it turned out to be C.O.D. Just C.O.D."

"So why did you take the five thousand dollars if you didn't intend to use it?"

"We didn't want Solly to know we were gonna stay put. We were dangerous to him that way. We were in his way."

*   *   *

On the following day, Hy said, "Did you draw up a sketch of the bomb that Solly Rubell wanted?"

"Yes I did," Hershie replied. "I wrote out all the information for Solly."

"Did you prepare descriptive material to explain your drawings?"

"I did."

"And you gave Solomon Rubell all of this information?"

"Yes."

"Have you prepared for us a replica of your sketch, the one you gave to Rubell that day?"

"Yes I have."

"And it is very much like the sketch you gave him in 1944?"

"Very much like it, yes."

"Who was in the room when you handed the material and the sketch to Rubell?"

"My wife Jelly, my sister Dolly, and myself."

"We offer this in evidence, My Honor," said Hy.

"This is diabolical!" shouted Henky Rubin, running down the aisle. "What will happen to our vital juices? I insist that the court impound this exhibit so that it remains a national secret."

Judge Goldman looked at Hy Briské. Hy looked at Judge Goldman. Duboff, the senior prosecutor, stared. They all looked at Henky Rubin.

"In the name of all that's good, please, Your Honor, don't let the enemy be apprised of this material." Henky was trembling.

"Henky, I know how you feel, and I love you for it," said Hy.

"I do too," said Duboff. "I love you more than Hy does."

"No you don't, ficklepuss," said Hy. He turned to Henky. "Look, this is incredibly generous, coming from the defense. Albeit a little weird."

"Nothing weird about it," said Henky. "I love my country, and I want to keep it that way. I'm not going to allow a foreign power to use this stuff to undermine our national security."

"If I had made this suggestion," Hy said, "there might have been criticism of my trying to ramrod something through. But you, you heavenly creature, you did it yourself. I thought you said Hershie was a moron, that he couldn't find his own mother's pussy."

"He spotted the pussy," Henky said.

Judge Goldman said, "There might have been some question on appeal. But since the defense is making the request, the question is removed entirely."

"We are all Americans," said Henky Rubin. He joined hands with Hy and Duboff. "We may have our little disputes, but we don't want to see our country double-crossed."

"Your hand is warm, Henky," said Hy.

"The sketch and material shall be impounded," said Judge Goldman.

"May I have a glass of water?" Solly whispered to Henky, his face chalk white.

"Sure thing, Solly," Henky said.

In his excitement, Henky handed Solly an empty glass.

On Friday afternoon, Hy said, "Your Honor, I have a busy weekend ahead. I'll be at the Athletic Club with Commissioner La Farge, Judge Delaney, and Father Balaban tonight; then we'll shoot over to Jack Dempsey's for bourbon and poker with the boys. Tomorrow I'm hosting a communion breakfast for His Holy Eminence Spellman."

Judge Goldman said, "My boy, I wash my hands. What you do on your own time is none of my business. Far be it from me to dampen your boyish enthusiasms and noble endeavors. Plug on."

Solly's turn would come soon. Solly in his shiny suit. Negro-lover Solly, the lamb Solly, nebbish softness, yeshiva madness, schmuck face.

He'd read *Jews Without Money*. He *was* Jews without Money. He'd been a Jimmy Higgins, a nobody in the Party; he'd struck out on his own and reached the stars. Now he was on the cutting edge; he was on history's express train.

Never taken a penny. Oh a penny sure. To get a maid for Dolly. Dolly, Solly said, was a diamond—no filth could scratch her honor.

This couple was principle plus. They wanted vitamins for the entire human race. Hy Briské was the brilliant, vulgar Jewboy, the Irgun type, the patriotic bullshit artist. Jews, he said, should get down on their knees and kiss the earth for what America had given them. He sincerely hated faggot Jew Commie bastards. Their ingratitude, their betrayal, their worship of Stalin.

If Solly had his way, he might have exterminated this scumbag, but only if he was told to do so. His first approach would have been to attempt to correct Hy's thinking.

Hershie concluded his testimony on Monday afternoon.

"Your Honor, Hy speaking, shall we break for your synagogue attendance?"

Hy turned to the jury. "His Honor is going to pray now in the ancient way of his people for generations," Hy announced.

"Beautifully put," said Henky Rubin. "I couldn't have said it better myself, Hy. This is what America is all about."

The sweat poured down Solly. Pools of it flooded his eyes and mouth.

Marv Duboff asked Solly if he had told Hershie the Soviet Union had a better form of government. Solly held up a finger as he talked about the first land of socialism, just as he had done when lecturing many other politically backward elements. "You see," said Solly, "I believed the Soviet Union was bearing the brunt of the war against Nazism. As every intelligent person of a progressive nature was prone to incline, I discussed the war with Hershie. And our discussion deepened. I explained how the Soviet Union had improved the lot of the underdog, ended illiteracy and most death as we know it. It had brought about reconstruction and given the workers free medical care, health care, and education."

Solly beamed, his finger up, bringing true understanding to Marv Duboff, Hy Briské, Judge Goldman, and the jury. "I felt that it was interesting that the Soviet Union was carrying the heaviest load, I felt it was a little unfair. My people were being gassed in ovens, and here was this one country taking action against Hitler with insufficient help from the richest country in the world."

"Would you like to overthrow the American capitalist system?" said Duboff.

"I heartily approve of our system of government, its Constitution and Bill of Rights. Oh no, Mr. Duboff, I just believe in live and let live and allowing The People to think for themselves and make up their own mind. I believe in The People. I know they will reach the correct conclusion if their minds are not clouded with irrelevant information."

"Mr. Rubell, were you a member of the Young Communist League?"

"Well, gee, I guess I refuse to answer that question on the grounds it might tend to incriminate me."

"How about the Steinmetz Club at City College?"

"I'd like to assert my constitutional privilege against self-incrimination," Solly said.

Judge Goldman addressed the jury: "You are to draw no inference whatsoever from the witness's refusal to answer on his assertion of privilege."

"*Huh*! Course not!" Hy shouted.

"Now, Mr. Rubell, let's get back to your discussing with Hershie the Russian advances," said Duboff.

"Well, I meant their advances in the winter campaign against the Nazis."

"Didn't you also talk about their economic and social advances, all the wonderful things they were doing for their people?"

"Certainly. But I would also want to stress here that I felt deeply that the Russians contributed the heaviest share to eliminating Hitler."

"And you felt that the Russians should be getting more help than the Allies were giving to them?"

"I felt it was vital that Russia get everything it needed to enable it to defeat the Nazi butchers."

"What was your opinion of Great Britain sharing in our secrets in 1944 and 1945? Didn't you feel that Russia should share as well?"

"I felt, Mr. Duboff, that we had an enemy we were all facing, and that we should help each other as much as possible to defeat that enemy."

"You wanted us all to fight just a little bit harder?"

"It occurred to me that if we had a common foe we should get together commonly."

On the lunch break, Judge Goldman sat at his table at Lindy's reading Howard Mayfield's column on page 5 of the *Echo*.

Did ju know Edna St. Vincent Millay, the love-poem writer, bought new sets of store teeth along Broadway every year? . . . America's Swedeheart, Greta Garbo, is pouting . . . Whittaker Chambers, the Marx of Time, is back on the

*payroll . . . Sudden thawts: Joan of Arc was too sexy to wear dresses . . . A
liberal is a fellow who has both feet firmly planted in the air. . . .*

Howard's column mentioned the Rubells: "Out of the Frying Pan
into the Fire." There were orchids for the judge for keeping an open
mind and for keeping the trial sailing along at a Hy Briské pace.
Kudos to Hy and Duboff for dancing to a different drummer. And a
kick in the pants to Commie-lovers, pinko pimps, and pansies.

The judge did not like his picture in the column. He picked up the
phone on the table and called his secretary. "Tell Howard if he
wants a fresh photo of me, he may have one." He hung up and
called Hy. "I'm in a tough spot," the judge said. "All this publicity,
this spotlight. It should be just me, my God, and I. You know?
Instead I'm the center of the universe. The picture of me in
Howard's column is a poor reflection. I need time to ponder away
from the glare of publicity. I want peace, calm, breezes, water,
goyish refinement, and good food. I'm thinking of the Concord
for the weekend. Hy, I'm thinking sentences. What do you think?"

Solly tried to eat his egg sandwich on white bread. The same tune
always came back to him:

> *Fly higher and higher*
> *Our emblem's the Soviet Star*
> *And every propeller is roaring*
> *Red Front!*
> *Defending the USSR!*

It was "The Song of the Red Air Fleet." For a moment he relaxed,
waving his sandwich in the air. There was a smile on his face; his
eyes were closed. It was the same daydream: Solly at the window,
suddenly barless, sighting the star, and then the roar of the propel-
ler, hovering overhead, Solly stepping through the window helped
aloft by outstretched Soviet arms, and away he went.

Solly opened his eyes.

Duboff was refreshed for the afternoon session after a hot pastrami
at Toots Shor's.

"Did you ever make any contributions to the Civil Rights Congress?"

"Yes, I believe I did," Solly answered.

"That is known to be an organization deemed subversive by the attorney general." Duboff paused significantly.

Solly said, "I don't know."

"Was that all you did?" Duboff asked, bowing deeply.

"I don't think I know what you mean, Mr. Duboff," said Solly.

"Don't be coy with us, Mr. Rubell. Did you ever give money to the Communist newspaper, the *Freiheit*?"

"I might have."

"Did you express yourself in other ways, soliciting, speaking?"

"What do you mean?"

"Did you ever collect money in your neighborhood for the Civil Rights Congress or the *Freiheit*?"

"I did give money; I didn't collect it."

"No? Let the thimble be brought forth."

Hy Briské rushed down the aisle with quick little steps, holding a tray, his hand under it, gurgling. He extended the tray toward Solly. A tiny object perched on it. Holding his nose away from it and sniffing, Hy held up a thimble between his thumb and index finger.

"*What is this?*" Duboff shouted at Solly.

"Can you see it, My Honor?" Hy said to the judge. "It's really awful. Show it to His Honor, Mr. Duboff."

"Wait a minute," said Duboff. "What is this thing, Mr. Rubell?"

Solly's voice trembled. "A thimble. Just a thimble."

"It was in your home when the agents arrested you. What does it say on it?"

"*Morgen Freiheit*," said Solly.

"Mr. Rubell, there were hundreds in your home."

"They were given to new subscribers to the progressive newspaper, the *Freiheit*," Solly said. "It was all legal."

"The *Freiheit* is known to be a newspaper deemed subversive by the attorney general," Duboff said. "Let the thimble be shown to the jury." Duboff handed the tray to the jury foreman.

"Now bring us the picture of the angry-looking Negro," said Duboff. Hy handed it to Duboff.

"This picture has the following words on the back: 'Paul Robeson as Othello. Thank you for your contribution to the Civil Rights Congress. Stop All Lynchings.'

"Now, Mr. Rubell, you did a little bit more than just contribute."

Solly said, "I just helped."

"Is it not a fact that the Civil Rights Congress is a Communist organization exclusively?" asked Duboff.

"I object to the form of the question," said Henky Rubin.

"The form is all right," said Judge Goldman.

"I don't believe it is a Communist group," said Solly.

"When did you join it?"

"I don't remember."

"Who invited you to join it?"

"I don't remember."

"How did you first learn of it?"

"Somebody asked me to join."

"Which somebody?"

"I don't remember."

"Perhaps that someone was a member of the Communist Party?"

"I don't know, no."

"Where were you solicited?"

"I don't remember."

"Mr. Rubell, were you a member of the Communist Party?"

"I refuse to answer on the grounds that it might incriminate me."

"Were you also a member of the International Workers Order?"

"I just have an insurance policy with it," said Solly.

"Is it a public insurance company?"

"Yes, Mr. Duboff."

"Is it not a Communist organization?"

"I don't believe so."

"Is it not a fact that its members are exclusively members of the Communist Party?"

"I don't know whether that is a fact."

"How did you come to join it?"

"I don't recall."

"When did you become a member?"

"I don't remember."

"Who invited you to join it?"

"I don't remember."

"Mr. Rubell, do you remember that we are in the midst of a war in Korea against the Communists?"

"Yes, sir."

"How many years have you been a member of the International Workers Order?"

"I can't remember."

"What kind of insurance do you have?"

"A two-thousand-dollar policy for life insurance."

"Where is the policy?"

"My policy?"

"Yes, your policy."

"Well, it was in my home."

"Where do you send premiums?"

"To the secretary."

"Where was he?"

"I sent it to his house."

"Where?"

"Somewhere in New York City. I can't recall."

"You're telling us you send the money to the secretary at his house? Doesn't the International Workers Order have an office, a room, a cell, something?"

"Yes. I'm sure it does."

"But where?"

"I don't know, Mr. Duboff."

"Your policy is at your house?"

"Yes, Mr. Duboff."

"Would you bring it with you when you come here tomorrow?"

"But—"

"Get the policy! Bring it here!"

"But I have no home," said Solly. "My home is gone. My things are somewhere else."

"No speech," said Duboff. "Just the policy."

"I don't have it," said Solly.

"He doesn't have it," said Henky. "I will try to get it. The Rubells no longer have an apartment. The lease was canceled. Their furniture was disposed of."

"We don't want the furniture," said Duboff. "The policy will be fine."

*   *   *

The trial was adjourned for the day. Solly collapsed on his bed.

In his cell, he read the *National Guardian*. There was a Soviet cartoon illustrating the Soviet Union's relationship to the People's Democracies. Two sparrows wanted to live by themselves. But they ran into a lot of trouble with cats, dogs, and children. Finally, they realized they had to live with the other birds for their own protection. So it was that smaller nations needed to join the Soviet Union so that they could be protected.

Solly clipped the cartoon for Dolly. He captioned it "Educational Reading."

Duboff resumed his cross-examination of Solly the next afternoon.

"How long have you known Sophie Rich?"

"I'm not sure exactly."

"How often have you seen her since you first met her?"

"I don't remember. She had been Joe Klein's sweetheart, and he would come to the house with her. I think I also saw her at musicales."

"When did Joe Klein leave the country?"

"I'm not sure, sir, but around 1948."

"When was the last time you saw Sophie?"

"It's hard to say."

"A couple of weeks before you were arrested?"

"I'm not sure."

"A week before your arrest?"

"I don't remember."

"What did you chat with Sophie Rich about the last time you saw her?"

"The price of eggs, that sort of thing. I says, How are you, Soph?"

"Did you talk with her about anything else?"

"Nothing else in particular."

"Did you give her some money?"

"Can't say that I did, no sir."

"Did you send her on a trip to Pittsburgh?"

"No, not at all, sir."

"Are you sure?"

"Absolutely."

"Didn't you give her three thousand dollars to bring to someone in Pittsburgh?"

"Totally untrue."

"You're certain?"

"I am certain."

"Where did you see Joe Klein?"

"At his apartment in Greenwich Village."

"What was the address?"

"I can't remember the exact street. It began with a p. Either—"

"Wasn't it 29 Perry Street?"

"Right, that's it, Perry Street."

"Was that very hard to remember?"

"I just told you it was."

"How often did you go to that apartment?"

"A number of times."

"How frequently?"

"Not very frequently."

"Were you there with Maury Ballinzweig?"

"No, Mr. Duboff."

"Were you there with Jed Levine?"

"No, not at all."

"When did you last see Klein?"

"In 1948."

"Where is he now?"

"In Brooklyn, I believe."

"You don't know exactly where he is?"

"No, I wouldn't know for sure."

"Don't you know that he is in Russia?"

Henky jumped up. "I object to that upon the ground that it is incompetent, irrelevant, immaterial, and highly inflammatory—"

"Oh, *sure* it is!" said Hy.

"I move for a mistrial," Henky said.

"Denied," Judge Goldman said.

"Mr. Rubell, you were interviewed in this building the day after Hershie was arrested, weren't you?"

"Correct."

"You were interviewed by Mr. Steve Tabackin of the F.B.I."

"Yes I was, sir."

"And you were arrested a month later?"

"That is right."

"Did you see Mr. Tabackin in the following weeks near your shop or home?"

"I noticed Mr. Tabackin hanging around my shop. One day I saw him peering through the open window. His nose was in my shop. He winked at me."

"Did you think you were under surveillance?"

"I don't have a thought on that."

"Didn't you find it unusual that an F.B.I. agent was peering through the window of your shop?"

"I thought that was his business, Mr. Duboff."

"And what were your thoughts?"

"That he might be looking through the window in order to find something."

"What might he be hoping to find?"

"I really don't know."

"Weren't you upset by his looking through your window or standing outside your shop?"

"No, that was his business, Mr. Duboff. I didn't manifest anxiety because I had no guilt."

"Why did you think he was standing there?"

"It didn't occur to me to think about it. That was his concern."

"It made absolutely no impression on you?"

"It didn't concern me."

"But it made no impression?"

"I thought he was seeking something."

"But it had nothing to do with you?"

"Perhaps yes, perhaps no, but I was not concerned."

"But did you think Mr. Tabackin's nose, perched as it was in your window, or his standing outside your shop, had any connection to you?"

"Perhaps yes, perhaps no. It didn't occur to me to think about why he was doing it."

"You didn't ask Mr. Tabackin why he was sticking his nose through your window?"

"I wasn't going to order the F.B.I. around, Mr. Duboff."

"You knew that your brother-in-law had just been arrested?"

"Yes, I did."

"Did you discuss with your wife the fact that an F.B.I. agent was hanging around your shop?"

"Nope, never did."

"You didn't mention it to her at all?"

"Can't say that I did."

"Even if you were innocent, Mr. Rubell, wouldn't you have guilt-free anxiety about an F.B.I. agent watching you at a time when your brother-in-law had already been arrested?"

"It couldn't have anything to do with me, so I wasn't concerned."

"But what if he was mistaken and *thought* it had something to do with you?"

"I didn't relate to it on a personal level."

Dolly followed Solly on the stand. She was no more a social bug there than anywhere else.

She cocked her head and held it high because of the pain in her back and her migraine headache. But it made her look prissy—stiff and haughty. And she was very pale.

Duboff quoted Dolly's testimony before the grand jury two weeks after Solly had been arrested. She had been asked, "Did you ever talk with your brother about his espionage activities?" Dolly had replied then: "I decline to answer on the grounds that this might tend to incriminate me."

Duboff said now, "Did you give that testimony at that time?"

"Yes."

"Was that the truth?"

"Was what the truth? That I answered the question that way?" Dolly said.

"That you answered that to disclose whether you had talked with your brother about espionage would tend to incriminate you?"

"I don't remember what reason I may or may not have had at that time to give that reply."

"Was it an untruthful reason?"

"No."

"And today you feel you can answer that question and that there is nothing incriminating about it?"

"Correct."

"But at the time, when testifying before the grand jury, you felt it might tend to be incriminating?"

"I suppose I had some reason for feeling that way."

"What might that reason be?"

"I really couldn't surmise at this time."

Dolly was asked by Duboff about another grand jury question: "Did you discuss this case with your brother Hershie?" She had refused to answer on the same grounds.

"Was that question asked and did you give that answer?"

"I did."

"Was it true?"

"Yes, because my brother was under arrest."

"But how would that tend to incriminate you, if you're innocent?"

"It wouldn't necessarily. But it might have, and as long as I felt there might be some possibility of my being incriminated, I had the right to use the privilege."

Dolly had invoked the same privilege before the grand jury when asked these questions:

"What is your middle name?"

"When did you consult with an attorney for the first time?"

"Did you invite your brother and his wife to your home for dinner?"

"Have you ever met Sid Smorg?"

"Do you know if your husband is working for the Soviet Union?"

When Dolly was asked if she had loved her brother, she said yes, she had loved Hershie deeply.

The jury believed that this was true.

Hy Briské circled around the one witness the Rubells could muster, the little lady wearing sneakers, brown ankle socks, a red cap, and a button on her jacket that said Shoot First!—Manya Poffnick.

"What is your profession, Mrs. Poffnick?" Briské asked her.

"I am an activist all over," she replied. "I am also a cafeteria worker."

"And what, Mrs. Poffnick, can you tell us of the Rubells?"

"I know the Rubells as good progressive people; they would never hurt a soul. I can tell you Sol Rubell fulfilled his thimble quota many times over. I saw them selling subscriptions for the *Morgen Freiheit* hours before they were arrested."

"And do you know Maury Ballinzweig?"

"I know him too well," Manya said.

"Could you explain your meaning?"

"Forget him. To me he's not a human being. But he's innocent. He thinks he's got four balls."

"Could you tell us about the espionage activities of Solomon and Dolores Rubell?"

"Dolly Rubell would give her last dime to a person in need. Solly too. They were ordinary working people who wanted to help the workers. That's the only crime they were guilty of."

"Mrs. Poffnick," Briské said, "according to the *Daily Worker* you are a widow."

"I was married in 1929 and he died in 1932. Peculiarly enough, his name was also Poffnick. He was a dressmaker. A very nice human being."

"And you have one living son?" Briské asked.

"I have no children," Manya said.

"You have no children? But Mrs. Poffnick, according to the *Daily Worker* of June 5, 1951, you spoke at an antiwar rally at Randalls Stadium and you said, quote, I had two sons. One was in the Second World War, and was killed. And you want me to lose the second one in Korea? *Like hell!* I don't want my son or anyone else's to be lost in Korea. For whom? For what? We have no business there. Before this war, I never even heard of Korea, for Christ's sake, unquote. Did you make that statement?"

"Sure," Manya said. "It's the truth. We have no business in Korea."

"But you have no sons."

"What the hell's wrong with that? I told a little lie."

Manya Poffnick was excused.

Hy Briské was chatting with Judge Goldman on the phone from Goldman's table at Lindy's.

"I've been praying, Hy," Judge Goldman said. "I have to give them the chair, don't you think?"

"*What is this shit on my plate?*" Hy screamed, tossing a plate backward over his head. "Excuse me, My Honor, I certainly wasn't talking to you."

Someone had placed a leaflet on Hy's plate claiming that Dolly and Solly were innocent.

"In answer to your question, My Honor: sure."

The Rubells were sentenced to death. The judge said their crime would "live in infamy." Maury Ballinzweig received twenty years.

The *Daily Worker* wrote about the Rubells for the first time. "Fascists are overjoyed," it wrote, "that a simple little Jewish-American mom and dad may be murdered in the interests of the war-makers and Jew-haters." The Committee to Resurrect the Rubells went into action. They collected on every street corner.

At Sing Sing, Solly had a tooth extracted. Then he had the flu. His mother visited him. Solly was held up by two guards.

"What kind of animals am I dealing with here?" Henky Rubin screamed at the sentencing.

"What kind do you want?" Hy asked.

What Can We Do to Help?

Would a noose do?

—G.L.

The Party's Committee to Resurrect the Rubells met that morning. Their guest, Ziggy Weissberger, bore instructions from closest friends. His words would be correct.

Trusted, solid, Ziggy sat in a swirl of smoke and dust on the ninth floor of 35 East 12th Street.

"Comrades, I come before you from the first land of socialism; from Paris, where peace is on the front burner; from the docks of London and Algiers. Everywhere I was asked, What is wrong with you Americans? Why do you want war? And I promised them that there was a vanguard party here that would soon make America a word of sweetness again on humanity's lips. America, I said, despite all the evidence to the contrary, is still in the ranks of humanity.

"And everywhere the working class is sizzling. At a peace conference in Paris I saw a springtide of peace burst out like flame. It had taken hold of the cities, the villages, the farthermost mountaintops; it hissed through the factories and mines. A handsome Parisian, his face gleaming, told me: 'It's beyond anything we ever dreamed. The people have taken it out of our hands.'

"Thus we see capitalism's deep crisis. All the king's horses and all the king's men cannot save it. Even as the Socialists stab the working class in the back, there is one party that fights unyieldingly for it. Our Party.

"We do not sit in our ivory towers and ponder; we don't write poetry in chapels, kiss our *tzitzith*, weep like the rabbis. No, comrades, our voices are deep, not high; our ideology is thick, not thin; we see the shore, not the waves; the brick, not the mortar; the heat, not the oven; the tit, not the bra; the ocean, not the pond; the rope, not the thread; the forest, not the trees; the cunt, not the panty; the gorgeous tree of Communism, not the fig leaf of socialism; the sky, not the ceiling; the stars—yes the stars, comrades—not the bars. There will be no bars on our vision, comrades, and if necessary, there will be no vision on our bars. We'll hurl the dirt over our graves and roll over with joyous laughter if we must!

"And so I come to the Rubells. Everywhere I was asked about them, that plucky couple whose courage has amazed and delighted peace-loving people everywhere. This couple will never die, comrades, as surely as they will soon not be amongst us anymore. Why are the Rubells being singled out by the mad war-dogs of fascism? Because they became the focus of the entire world's hatred of Washington's war policies and its attempts to McCarthyize America in the image of the swastika. Because they were for peace and would not give the Jew haters and the war plotters what they wanted, they are in the death house today.

"For fighting to defeat America's war drive, Eisenhower's power-hungry lust, they have been targeted to die. The Rubells reached the masses and struck deep chords of understanding within them.

"For this they will die, and soon.

"What can we do to help?

"By dying, the Rubells will live forever. People are tired of Sacco and Vanzetti. The Committee is flourishing. It informs the world of America's fascist drive to dominate the world. Dolly and Solly Rubell, of revered memory, will be powerful symbols for us. Antifascist heroes. Victims of anti-Semitism. Dutiful and loyal, they sacrificed themselves for our cause. It brings tears to my eyes to remember them.

"Even though we are eager to save their lives, let us examine the dialectical realities. Dolly and Solly worked very hard. They have many friends in many places. Once their lips are sealed, there are unlikely to be any more indictments.

"The vilest suspicions about the Party are fed by this case: that we receive Moscow gold, that the Party is under the thumb of the Soviet Union, that in effect we are its American branch.

But the way things look now, Dolly and Solly will not say the wrong thing.

"Solly Rubell has always looked better with his eyes closed; this is a fact.

"And so, comrades, let us light candles of remembrance, let's do what we can. But if perchance we lose Dolly and Solly, they will be vindicated by history and live forever anyway. Any questions?"

Johnny "Apple Seed" Beaver, the People's folk singer, sat in the front row in his lumberjack shirt, overalls, holding his corncob pipe and guitar. His freckled face was grinning as always. "Hey there Comrade Ziggy, I reckon we got our work cut out for us. I'm just a poor guitar picker. Let me see if I understand the Party position correctly. Lots of love. . . ."

"Love is the key motif," Ziggy said. "Praying, stroking, hugging, marching, meowing, pleading, sobbing—that should do it."

"What about the children?"

"The children are terrific photo opportunities. Keep them in short pants forever. Public trust fund, that sort of thing. We will raise millions."

Molly Leash, people's poet, moved to tears, stood up and recited:

> *"Passing Lord and Taylor today*
> *Sumptuous window display*
> *Dolly, Dolly, Dolly Rubell*
> *What's that lousy* shmatte *you're wearing*
> *In your lonely prison cell?"*

V.H. Spellman inquired about party slogans and chants. Suggestions included, "Vindicate the Rubells," "The Rubells—Antifascist Heroes," and "Don't get Bluebells—Release the Rubells." Spellman suddenly said, "Aren't we going to do anything to really save them?"

A stream of tears poured down Weissberger's cheeks. "Comrades, I speak to you filled with disgust, self-loathing, and a bubbling joyfulness. I am a Communist. I eat shit. I am proud to eat shit. 'It takes a tough man to make a tender chicken'—Stalin, 1939.

"This is an objective situation. Personally I loved Dolly and Solly. I would sit and eat kasha with them forever. I am doing exactly what they would do in my place. They are with us, and would approve of what we are planning. (It might make them a little uncomfortable, in this particular case.) Objectively, their usefulness and vitality are directly proportionate to their state of breathing or not breathing. They would be in favor of doing whatever would strengthen the international vanguard, the relationship of forces. Can we do any less?"

The meeting was adjourned.

The Autobiography of Hy Briské

Freedom's frisky advocate.

—G.L.

My anus may rhyme with heinous, but I'm still the sharp lad I was at three in my father's Tammany chambers.

I will take to my grave the things I was right about: world Communism and the Rubell case. The memory of proudly sitting beside Joe McCarthy as he ripped into a silent witness: "Got some pussy stuck in your throat? Would you share it with us?"

And the first glimpse of the boy across the room at a Chinese restaurant in Washington. I told the waiter to bring him an egg roll on me. Only later did I learn that the dark brooding stranger was a Manila houseboy working in the White House.

When I discovered that Fifi Dorsay knew more about the Communist menace than anyone I ever met, and that he *cared* about it, I knew I had to have him by my side. You should have heard him talk about the Communists: "They're horrible! Their food is unclean! They smell!" I knew in my guts this man was the expert the committee needed to ferret out subversives.

When Eisenhower refused to discuss it, I confess I went bananas. "I'm really getting sore, Dwight David," I said. "He's cleaning your bathtubs, for God's sake, when he should be beautifully decked out, in shades, in the sun, oiled and perfumed, reading and writing and giving dictation!" I screamed, but to no avail.

I got stares and blank looks. It was then I realized there was creeping subversion within the White House gates, probably aided and abetted by pinkos and lulubelles. I couldn't sleep nights. I was hot and flushed. There was no relief.

Thus the genesis of the altercation that broke Joe McCarthy's spirit.

"Give me Fifi," I told Eisenhower over a dish or two of ice cream one afternoon, "and you can do whatever the fuck you want."

"The man can hardly read or write," he said.

"Let me worry about that, bub," I replied. "I'll dot his i's and cross his t's for him. What about Fifi's book, *Reflections on Comunism*?" (Fifi deliberately misspelled it to tease me.)

"What book? It's three pages."

I read aloud from it:

Comunism is shit. It bothers me, it's so bad.
They don't take baths, they don't believe in God.
Most of them are liars and Democrats.

I ventured to point out that simplicity could be bliss.

"Anyway, the army's going to draft him," he said.

This was too much. "I've really had it up to here with you," I shouted. My ice cream dish overturned as I stood up. "When I get headaches like this, it's ridiculous. You've ruined my day."

"Look, Hy, you're taking this too hard. Why don't you take a vacation?"

"I would have loved to. How can I now? You've spoiled everything, you nitwit," I shouted.

"I'm the president—"

"Just cut the shit, Dwight. Frankly, I think the whole operation stinks."

"What? What operation? What are you—"

"The so-called White House. Your administration. I want to find out what's going on."

"Are you calling me a Communist?"

"This is making me nauseous. I'm not gratified. Who else can I speak to about this?"

"No one. I'm the president!"

"I'm gonna tap the pope on this one."

"Hy—Hy."

"This just isn't good enough. I want a real man."

"For a guy who's done responsible work on the Rubell case and seems to understand the Commies, your behavior about this houseboy is simply incomprehensible," the president said.

"Cut this vague shit," I demanded. "Give me Fifi and all is forgiven. Otherwise I'm going to make your days miserable. I'll make you crawl through mud. I'll make you sorry you were born."

Perhaps in retrospect I should have softened my language. But I knew what Fifi could contribute to the fight against subversion.

The rest of those events are history: the investigations and hearings I conducted with Joe. Some say I took Joe down with me. But that's obviously ridiculous. Joe went down. I am here.

Joe wanted to be loved. I regarded the hatred of me as a cool ocean spray.

One of Joe's fans, Gus Avery, would greet me by asking: "How are all the dirty Jews?" Ordinarily a remark like that would raise my hackles. But this was a dedicated anti-Communist whose concern was the disturbing number of Jews in the Communist Party. "Dirty as ever," I would reply. He loved that. He was a heavy hitter from Detroit, chairman of the "Hail America Committee." Gus always wore a yarmulke when he sat on the dais at my "Patriotic Jews Against Subversion" dinners. In fact, many of Joe's followers were very intense in their love of country and their hatred of Communism. Like Joe, they were often earthy types who liked to take their shoes and socks off at my "Patriotic Jews" events, occasionally even their pants. Once, at the end of an America Lovefest evening, Joe, Gus, and a bunch of other shakers and movers on the dais—Cardinal Lefebre of Detroit and Art O'Malley of Chicago and Danny Toto of Toronto and Mario Calabrese of the Bronx—gaily tossed used American-flag condoms (dripping ones—can you believe it?) over my head across the stage at each other. But Art's toast—"Hy is one Jew we can trust"—was right as rain, and things were copacetic.

Joe is long gone. Howard Mayfield is gone. It was Howard who wished Dolly and Solly a happy electrocution in his column. In the mid-seventies Howard awoke one morning to find that all his engraved gold cuff links ("Mr. Broadway") were gone. He wandered down Broadway, where the curlicue neon lights had danced in celebration when the Rubells were cooled. Hubert's Flea Circus had turned into a fellatio shop whose prize attraction were wolfhounds.

Lindy's was now Extasy Fantasy. Howard wandered in that morning, and there was a row of girls in booths with windows. Windows were raised and customers got quick feels for a dollar; two dollars for tit sucking and cunt lapping. Then they ran into bathrooms and gargled. Near the site of the Paramount where Sinatra had sung, a video theater the size of a dime played "I Spit on Your Grave."

Thus the decline of morality and decency in the heart of America's greatest city, the center of the free world.

I came upon Howard in 1980 in a hotel lobby in Yonkers, alone and dozing, a newspaper on his lap. He was finished. When he saw me, he struggled to get up. Yes, Howard too wanted to be loved.

Jack Lait, Lee Mortimer, Pegler, Leonard Lyons—gone.

Others are irrelevant, forgotten, ill.

I am in perfect health, wealthy, and famous.

The Rubell case was a lead-pipe cinch.

The F.B.I. broke the Soviet code of American agents. That was for starters. Then we had the hermit and we had Hershie. So what's the wailing about?

Sometimes somebody being cute asks if I feel sympathy for the Rubells. I don't understand the question.

But of course I'm the lowest turd in the world, and their shit doesn't smell. At least anymore.

I'll say this. I had a chance in life. My family's name got me through doors. Of course then I had to prove myself—and I did so splendidly.

They were *pishers*. They had nothing. Dolly wanted to be a ballet dancer but she had two left feet. She was probably tone deaf too. Solly grew up not getting laid, not having understanding parents, not tasting the world or being as smart as some of the others. I figure Solly and Dolly were the kind who didn't fuck for three years after they met because they didn't know where to put what.

They needed a push in life, somebody behind them. So they went to the Soviets. And they got a quality friendship. And for a while they were somebodies.

Maybe it was that simple.

The Rev. Very Big Bob

Fish fries.
—G.L.

I

The Rev. Very Big Bob was about to begin his Thursday radio show when he heard shouts: "Massa Big Bob! Massa Big Bob! Good news! We have proof!" It was Bradley, the midget Negro who slept at the foot of Big Bob's bed and was his faithful servant—the epitome of the "real Negro" as Bob called him, not the uppity Communistic nigger types.

It *was* extraordinarily good news, and the Rev. began his program with it: "Flash! Evidentiary proof has just reached your reporter that Eisenhower is the Jew we thought he was all along. Here verily is the West Point Military Academy yearbook of the year 1915. We quote: 'Dwight David Eisenhower. Abilene, Kansas. "Ike." This is Señor Dwight David Eisenhower, gentlemen, the terrible *Swedish Jew'*— emphasis mine—'as big as life and twice as natural.' " Bob slammed the yearbook on the table. "Now tell me that I'm crazy, motherfuckers."

There was silence, interrupted only by the troubled breathing of Rev. Very Big Bob.

"Yes, this is your Rev. Bob. Tonight I'm seated before a roaring fire in my study in brown tweeds, pipe in hand, the sweet aroma of tobacco recalling the winding green and brown roads of my boyhood. The luscious strains of the organ you are hearing: the beautiful Celeste at the reins. Bless you, Sister. I love your hair. We'll take your calls. Here's one now."

"Something is going on, Rev. Bob," a thin, reedy voice whispered. "There is some hidden force, or some hidden power, or something that is influencing our people. They don't act like Americans."

"So true, Christian caller. There is too much treason in the land. The Rubells are not alone. The same force that has agreed on the elimination of Senator McCarthy, the one man who, alone, has aroused the American people to the menace of the hidden force in the government—"

"Yes, yes," the voice said excitedly. "Hidden, hidden. But what is it? Who is it?"

"Oh, we know *who* it is, don't we, Christian caller?"

"Who is this?" the voice was gasping now.

"Who is what? This is still Rev. Bob."

"Is it really? How do I know? Everything is so hidden. How can I be sure? You could be one of them." He hung up.

Another caller, a lady, said "Eisenhower says he understands the Russians. If he understands them he must have a lot in common with them. Huh!"

The organ caroused softly behind Rev. Very Big Bob. "The thing you've got to remember about *them*, brethren, is that they look different from anyone else. Big noses, dark looks. But then on the other hand, they don't look very different at all. That's their cleverness. You wouldn't always spot them in a crowd; they mesh. It's devilishly complex. Or, for example, they'll poison the water with fluoride and x-rays and they'll drink it themselves as well—see what I mean?"

Sister Celeste let out a giggle: "I'll stick to martinis, Big Bob."

"And they'll take their own electric shock treatments to prove the treatments are innocent. Boy, are they smart. I wish I was that smart. You can't think about this stuff all the time, it would drive you loony."

Rev. Very Big Bob read for the rest of the program from the seventeenth chapter of Revelations, which depicted serpents covering the world. He said, "Internationalism is the serpent, my friends, engulfing Christian virtues."

The tapping of shoes was heard. "It's time to go, dear friends, but we'll end this Thursday with a rousing tap dance from our beloved little Negro Bradley. Take it away, Bradley." The sounds of tapping, the organ strains of "Oh! Susanna" filled the airwaves, and the delighted laughter and shouts of Rev. Very Big Bob: "Do it, Bradley. You kill me, ya brave little pickaninny. Brethren, say a prayer for America and put it in an envelope. No coins please. Nice bills. Mail to Rev. Very Big Bob, Stearwater, Arkansas. Godspeed."

The following Thursday, Rev. Very Big Bob said, "I just came back from New York City, that sewer reeking with big-breasted women, subversion and anti-Christian influences. The world's center of intrigue. The House of Rothschild, all them superpowerful money changers operating between New York, Switzerland, London, and lovely Paree. The twins of the antichrist, Communism and Zionism, have their headquarters there.

"I had the honor of meeting with a little handful of fearless patriots not afraid to say the word 'Jew.' Not afraid to expose the octopus of political Zionism or to contribute manfully to the struggle.

"My person was not safe. It was necessary for me to remain strictly incognito as far as my place of abode was concerned. There are thousands of people who would be only too happy to murder me on sight if they could do it without being caught. And if they were caught I doubt seriously if they could be convicted. They might even be honored by the Jew-controlled courts.

"Brethren, do not get caught up in minor, routine issues. Stick to the super-issue, the terrific issue, the awful issue, the bloody issue.

"Last week this reporter presented proof about the Abie in the White House. Yes, Baruch and his gang have captured the capital once again. And the process of mongrelization goes on. Yet tonight I have even more fantastic evidence. I could hardly believe my eyes. I chanced upon a 1912 novel about a Communistic social utopia—*Philip Dru, Administrator* by Colonel E. M. House—in an obscene little bookshop in Manhattan. God sent me into that store, and then he made me want to throw up."

Organ music surged. "I have irrefutable proof that the Swedish Jew was the candidate of Jewish plotters to dominate the world—"

"Oh my goodness, what is it, Rev. Big Bob?" the beautiful Celeste asked.

"It is precisely this, Sister Celeste. I discovered the truth by reading between the lines as I always do. This strange book appeared in 1912. Only a few copies were printed—for obvious reasons. Franklin Delano Rosenfeld was chosen, groomed, and installed in the White House to consummate the conspiracy. This explains why, *the day after F.D.R. was nominated in 1932*, he flew by plane to be the houseguest of Colonel House in Massachusetts! So you see, it's clear as a bell. Rosenfeld served them to the end of his days. Truman was their pawn. And the Swedish Jew—of course, what am I, an idiot?—was their choice in 1952."

"Oh, wow," said Sister Celeste.

"During the war, I have learned that, under the Swedish Jew's military command, white girls were used exclusively in Europe in all the U.S.O.s and cafés to dance with, entertain, and date Negroes. That's his version of Romeo and Juliet."

Rev. Very Big Bob sighed. "Enough insanity. Let's hear from our callers."

A piercing female voice said, "It looks to me, Rev. Bob, like Washington is just a snake pit of thieves, perverts, hookers, and traitors."

"I'm afraid you're right, listener."

"Did you know, Big Bob, that the real America can be found in the archives of the thirteen colonies? Ninety-eight percent of the founding fathers were Christians."

"You can bet your sweet buns on that one," Rev. Bob said.

"And did you also know that the United Nations was conceived in sin?"

"Sure did."

"It's the devil loose in the world, the most diabolical scheme ever hatched—"

"Absolutely." The caller said goodbye and hung up.

Rev. Big Bob said, "Brethren, it's time to go. While I was in that city of sin, I wrote my mother every day. If you would like to read my letters with my dear mother, if you want to walk by my side as I encountered the red-lipped harlots, the temptresses, the hot teasers, mail your request and offering to me. You will hear from me in a plain brown envelope by return mail. Jesus loves you and so do I. For now—I remain Very Big Bob."

II

He began his radio ministry at the peak of the Depression. From the time of his earliest broadcasts from his home in Arkansas, Rev. Bob believed that capitalism would not work. He saw the breadlines, the bank closings, people deprived of their lifetime's savings, dispossessed from farms they'd worked their entire lives. Everywhere, people looked for work and didn't find it. He said, "It is time for the world to look aloft, above the stars, and see there the eternal Son of Justice, who says to all of us: 'Come to Me all ye who feel heavily burdened, and I will refresh you. He who is not with Me is against Me, and seek ye first the kingdom of God and His justice and all things shall be added unto you.' "

His strong, syrupy voice kept millions glued to their radios. They waited for the weekly rituals Rev. Bob indulged in—stoking the fire (they would listen to him puttering with it, exclaiming "Golly ding it"), feeding his puppy Billy (Billy's barks were a treat), tapping his pipe and filling it with tobacco, lighting up with a sigh of contentment ("Gosh a mighty"). He'd mislay his suspenders and talk to himself while hunting for them. They listened to him count the stars in his backyard and answer the doorbell right on the air and chat briefly with neighbors who stopped by to borrow sugar or discuss seed supplies. And they enjoyed Bob's unpredictability: one week he was joyous and full of pep, another he was sad, another angry or pessimistic about the state of the world. You never knew what was coming with Rev. Bob. "Boffo radio," said *Variety*.

But it was what he said about their lives that counted most. "Something is very wrong, and we gotta fix it," he said. Every weekend Rev. Bob and a group of volunteers distributed food and clothing to thousands of the unemployed and their families. Communism, he said, was the enemy. But what was creating Communism? Selfish capitalism. The capitalists had to raise wages, create better working conditions, provide the workers with old-age insurance. They had all the wealth, and assumed none of the responsibility. And why the hell should so few have so much anyway?

Congressmen, senators, and newsmen flocked to his door. "Get the plutocrats," he told them, "retire the international bankers, the money changers, the Wall Street finaglers." He had a new prescription every few months. It was difficult to keep up with Rev. Bob.

Within a year, the money came pouring in from sympathizers. Rev. Bob was forced to construct a twelve-story edifice, the Wee Kirk of the Heavenly Biscuit, and hire a corps of a hundred workers to handle all the money that was coming in. They worked ten-hour shifts. The Wee Kirk of the Heavenly Biscuit was illuminated with floodlights night and day. The lights were staggering; those within two or three blocks of the shrine would sometimes faint from the impact of the glare and crumple up on the sidewalks. Those who got closer shielded their eyes with steel buckets over their heads, making their way by holding on to the sides of buildings. Rev. Very Big Bob used a seeing-eye dog himself to reach his office.

Three years passed. The country had slowly picked up, but Rev. Bob was sorely pressed. So many admirers, so many flowers, but he was still broadcasting from Arkansas. Roosevelt had reformed the system and allowed it to survive. At first Rev. Bob showered the president with bouquets. When he was invited to the White House, he tingled. He arrived with notebooks of proposals. Roosevelt handed them to a secretary. Did the president giggle? No, that was impossible. "Let's do this more often," he told the president. "I'll make myself available." He suggested a private phone line between them as well.

The President sent Bob little thank-you notes, but rarely saw him after the first meeting.

In 1936 Rev. Bob formed the Christian Bob League, so that "the will of the people will be realized." His enthusiastic followers sent in more money and membership cards. Rev. Bob said that Roosevelt had deeply disappointed him by his partial reformist methods that ignored the central problem of injustice that was gnawing at the country. Plutocratic capitalism and the international bankers led by the House of Rothschild were depriving the workers of their fair share of the national wealth.

He addressed a packed house at Madison Square Garden. Confetti rained down on him, men and women fainted in the aisle. A woman who had not been pregnant gave birth in the twelfth row. As word spread of this miracle, the crowd went berserk. Mother and child were carried down the aisle and up to the stage to the outstretched hands of Rev. Bob, while the mob shrieked with joy. "This is God's handiwork," someone called; the crowd shouted thousands of hallelujahs.

An unfortunate incident occurred later the same evening outside the Garden. When a portion of the crowd learned that the mother—not having even dreamed of bearing a child—was not married, they stomped both her and the little bastard to death on the street and walked away furiously. It was a sad footnote to a beautiful and miraculous evening.

As the months passed, and F.D.R. continued to implement social programs that improved the national economy, Rev. Bob became more and more depressed. He did not feel the energy to organize the League or to do much of anything. His radio audience was slipping. He wondered what was the cause of it all.

One balmy day in June, Rev. Bob received a bulky package in the mail. "That Jew in the White House don't want you to know this, but you will be interested in the enclosed.—A loyal follower."

Rev. Bob went into seclusion for seven days. It was such rich reading. So there it was, explaining what he'd suspected all along but couldn't put into words. No wonder Roosevelt had been so unfriendly—that cat's paw for the international Jewish conspiracy. It was so simple. Bob shivered. So unbelievable, so strange, but there it was in learned print. The Illuminati. Sounded Italian and sexy to him.

A secret order. Blowing up ships. Taking over the world with the Jews and the Masons. It went back to 1776. A group of secret societies headed by the Illuminati—led by Adam Weishaupt of Bavaria—conspired to overthrow every institution, dethrone God and become the new rulers of civilization. Responsible for the French Revolution! Sponsored Karl Marx!

Communist traitors now ran the government. How did they do it? With gentile fronts. With ridicule. With scantily clad women, of course, with jazz, movies, with sharp tongues of revolutionary heat licking at church altars, playing in school belfries, crawling into every sacred corner of the home. Every delicious perversion known to man.

Rev. Bob ran from room to room in his excitement, trying to absorb it all, to understand, to grow. And he'd practically groveled at Roosevelt's feet! He read on and on; this stuff was catnip to him.

Tucked in with the other material was *Protocols of the Learned Elders of Zion*. Now he understood it all. This Jewish hidden hand controlled both capitalism and the revolutionary movement. Of course, of course—the Jews had it both ways, they always did, you couldn't keep up with them, they were so damned smart, a diabolic force.

The Yiddish control of Bolshevism was explained so simply—and from the horse's mouth. A leader of the secret Jewish world government wrote the document. It was all a plot to destroy Christian civilization, a plot two thousand years old. They pushed alcoholism, invented pornography, mocked the clergy, popularized Darwinism, Nietzscheism, Marxism. Arranged wars to kill gentiles and profit Jews. They just had it made, any way you turned.

In his next broadcasts, Rev. Bob explained how the Zionists had formed the Invisible Government, led by King Barney Baruch and his satellites. They were preparing the way for the triumph of world Communism. "Behind Communism stands . . . the Jew," Bob said.

Bob plugged the Christian Bob League. "A person who hears the warning of a diamondback rattler and still stands around is a fool," he said. "There are only two things to do: run or exterminate the snake. You can't run from Communism, brethren, for it has insinuated itself into all phases of life everywhere. You can help to stamp it out by becoming active in the Christian Bob League to preserve the liberty Communism would destroy. You can hear the rattle of the serpent. You can *see* it coiled before you. Remember—you can't run. You *must* stay . . . and fight."

In the weeks following Bob's angry broadcasts, the League formed sports clubs around New York City that would teach men "how to take orders and accept discipline." The clubs would train the men in the use of "walking sticks" called kike killers to protect themselves against Jewish rowdies.

In September 1939, a meeting was held at Lucifer's Hall on Columbus Circle. Rick Lloyd, head of the local branch of the League, said, "The government is on the brink of revolution. Communism is spreading and arming. War is declared in New York on Christianity. The Reds are training their men in the use of arms.

"I am not content to walk in the footsteps of Christ," Rick said. "I want to walk ahead of him with a club. Grab your opportunity, men. Some of you will die, but what of it?"

A woman in a blood-spattered dress and a hat with a bird falling over her head came screaming down the aisle. She shrieked that Jewish Communists had broken into a Catholic Church, beaten the priest, and spat on the nuns. The meeting broke up. The crowd headed for the downtown area of Jewish-owned shops. They stopped before each shop and scrawled graffiti and stuck "Buy Christian" stickers on the plate-glass fronts. They shouted, "You'd better get out of here quick, you Jew bastards. If you don't get out, we'll take your store and you with it. You've got two weeks to vacate."

Two policemen stood on the sidewalk watching the scene with an air of calm detachment.

A year later, the Christian Bob League suffered a major setback. A group of its young followers stole ammunition and arms from the National Guard and were arrested and accused of plotting against the government.

Rev. Bob was not surprised at the arrests. He commented on the radio that no one should be surprised at the power of the enemy.

That same week, the representative from Mississippi, John Rankin, had described to Americans the typical "little Communist kike" on the floor of the House of Representatives: "A scavenger who stoops to as base a level as that of the loathsome ghoul at night, who invades the sacred precinct of the tomb, goes down in the grave of a buried child and with his reeking fingers strips from its lifeless form the jewels and mementos placed there by the trembling hands of a weeping mother." Having concluded his remarks, the representative went back to his seat and sat down, glaring ferociously in all directions. Within minutes a telegram was placed in his hand. It bore congratulations and blessings. It was sent by Rev. Bob.

III

The Rev. Very Big Bob went on the air three days before the Rubells were executed. He seemed serene.

"Good evening, radio friends. I love you. I am physically naked tonight in the elegant Wee Kirk of the Heavenly Biscuit, brethren. My body glistens. The beautiful Celeste is at the reins. She plays like an angel, doesn't she? Bradley is home, polishing my sword.

"Outside, the whoremongers, the bulldykes cavort. Flying saucers: a clear sign the final days are near. We count the days till the Rubells are no more. The worldwide revolt against Jewish tyranny is on. The boiling lava of inarticulate resentment is about to gush out.

"The hour is late. They have swallowed up Korea. They have taken the White House. They have stolen the bomb. They have poisoned the waters. They are into our little girls' breeches. Haven't they had enough? It sounds pretty good to me.

"I want to quote you two things the Bible says about the Rubells. Open your Bible, please, to the last book in the Old Testament, the Second Book of Maccabeus 14:6-7. Let us read together: " 'It is the Jews who are called Hasidaeans under the leadership of Judas Maccabeus that keep the war alive and stir up sedition, and will not let the Kingdom enjoy tranquility.' " Then in the tenth verse it says: 'For as long as Judas lives, it is impossible for the government to find peace.'

"Perhaps now we shall find peace.

"I am reminded, as well, of a comment made on the floor of the House of Representatives by that courageous prophet, John Rankin: 'Communism is older than Christianity. It hounded and persecuted the Savior during His earthly ministry, inspired His crucifixion, derided Him in His dying agony, and then gambled for His garments at the foot of the Cross.' Well said, Big John.

"But my friends, even with the burning of the Rubells, we will hardly be out of the woods. We have black men crowding white ladies on buses. We have drunken debauchery and fluoridation. Our precious bodily fluids are being drained from us.

"We have the mental-health scam at work this very moment. Patriots and Bible-believing Christians are declared 'insane.' If you are moral and oppose Communism, you can be certified mentally ill. It is happening as I speak. Psychological methods are being used to create a new breed of amoral men and women who will accept a one-world socialistic government. If you are a God-fearing Christian, you are in danger of being kidnapped, placed in a mental-health prison, and mentally murdered by electric shock treatments, chemotherapy, hypnosis, and lobotomy.

"Part and parcel of this whole shitload of subversion is the Council on Foreign Relations. Its fourteen hundred members control the U.S. State Department, cabinet posts, the press, and A.T. & T. This is an invisible government, my friends, that sets the major policies of the federal government. The goal? To convert America into a Socialist state. *This is the plan*: the same old internationalists' no-win policy against the Russians. Containment, not victory.

"I'm disturbed. I'm troubled. Even if they do kill the Rubells—and who can be sure? I mean, why should they?

"Please stand with me. If we lose our battle, nothing you have will be worth anything. Senator McCarthy is marked for death by these Christ-haters and so am I. It is up to you to see to it that the maximum good is accomplished before my time comes to go, whether I am taken by the hand of nature or by the manipulations of the enemy.

"Naked and alone, in the cool night air, I await your generous calls. Here come my fourteen little helpers. Move your butts, boys.

"As a special offer, for a ten-dollar contribution—for those who call within the next half hour—I will mail you in a plain brown wrapper . . . a picture of the Council on Foreign Relations, the scene of the worst debaucheries of the twentieth century! It will send needles up your spine. It will send you spinning. This is a high you can't miss. Share it with the boys at the clubhouse after you pull down the blinds. Some of you have etched for me your warm memories, your first recollections of the 'it' girl, Clara Bow, of summer nights in jalopies with your first dates, the girls' mouths tasting of candy and licorice. You didn't think you could recapture those feelings, but now you can. Just write 'Hot Picture' on an envelope, add a ten-dollar bill, and mail it to me, Father Very Big Bob, at the same old address."

Rev. Very Big Bob was silent for a full five minutes. Listeners wondered if he had fainted or was jerking off. But occasionally they heard his rasping breathing, the start of a word, the pulling in of breath. Rev. Bob was struggling with something he wanted to say.

"It is my sad duty to relate news that sickens me to death. I have discovered beyond a doubt that J. Edgar Hoover, director of the F.B.I., is a tool of the Communists. One has only to study his new book about Communism to see this. It is veritably a manual for revolution, with tips and rules and guidelines to follow to overthrow the U.S. government.

"In fact, Hoover is the surviving constituent of the 'big four' fanatic Bolshevik conspirators of the master plan for world conquest. He is the Communists' trojan horse of the century!

"Look, it is not easy for me to say this. I can hardly breathe. The big four Bolshevik madmen assembled in Petrograd in March 1917 to direct the revolution. Just listen to me. Lenin arrived from Switzerland, Trotsky and Hoover came from the U.S. (Trotsky was living on St.

Marks Place in Greenwich Village where they fuck night and day), and Joseph Stalin from Siberian exile. The Communists' tool, Hoover, ordered the liquidation of the following non-Communists first in the U.S.: the police, stockbrokers, especially lawyers and clergymen. I quote the book, his book; it's all there: 'Don't hesitate to use illegal methods . . . use any weapon: knives, hatchets, or guns to achieve your aim . . . tear capitalism down completely . . . inspire civil rights demonstrations, integration, strikes. . . .' Hoover's atrocities against non-Communists surpass those of Genghis Khan or Attila."

Rev. Bob paused. "So you ask, am I happy about the Rubells? Who could be happy under these circumstances? We have much bigger fish to fry, dear Christian friends."

Shoot First

Choke on it.

—G.L.

Manya Poffnick had had a few beers on an empty stomach before she testified that day. On the way out of the courtroom, Hy Briské blew her a kiss. She felt heartbroken about it, and was terrified that the Party would expel her.

But the Party leaders were friendly. Not an angry word, even from Henky Rubin. Manya pondered this for a long time. Now why was that creep, the head of the National Review Commission, V.H. Spellman, who loved to make comrades crawl, patting her on the behind? V.H. knew which side his bread was buttered on.

The F.B.I. watched her from windows. The Party was shot through with informers and opportunists. It was no good. If Stalin only knew what went on. "Stalin," she said, "is as right as steam heat."

"I fucked up. What are they sending me flowers for?" She was musing aloud in the bathroom of the automat on Union Square where she washed every morning. "How did I wind up in bed with scumbags? Their pipes, their tweeds, their corduroys! Spellman, I think, is a prostitute. But he's not F.B.I. Still, he is not sincere. He thinks one thing and tells you another. Eugene Dennis wants to be by himself. He can't be with people. How in the world does one of that join the Communist Party? Dennis is a question. Gus Hall— him! That momzer! Him I knew before he went to the Lenin School. He's never suggested a logical thing. When he speaks, I have to hold on to my chair with both hands to stay awake."

She opened the door, and headed for the front where she worked as a countergirl. She wore her usual button: Shoot First.

Manya didn't have her own apartment. She slept four hours a night in comrades' living rooms, rising at dawn to join picket lines before going to her job at the automat. She had one dress, three pairs of sneakers, two blouses, and two sweaters. In 1932, when tuberculosis was widespread, she was ill with a bronchial condition. She bought a bottle of Lysol. If it turned out to be TB, and she was confined to a bed in a place where she might infect others, she would take the Lysol and get it over with. The diagnosis was not TB. She called friends: "Good news! It's not the lungs, it's the heart!"

(Later, in the seventies, she had a studio apartment in Morningside Heights, and it was like a monk's quarters, like Maury Ballinzweig's. She had joined the Black Panthers. The reporter visited her there. She sat on her bed with a bottle of beer in her hand, an old woman overtaken by leukemia and diabetes, phobias and allergies. There were two cups, two plates, two forks. She had one tiny table on which she had placed, for her visitor, coffee, cookies, candies, gefilte fish. Everything kept plopping off the table, and the reporter kept picking things up off the floor. "Your table is too small," he said.

"That's right," Manya said. "I had a bigger one. I gave it away. Somebody needed it.")

After the revolution, a young man came from a big city to Schedrin and said to Manya, who was twelve years old, "Why don't you get in touch with the Bolsheviks and see what's doing?" She had already tried the Bund—boys with suits and ties, neat, clean future lawyers and drones. Forget it.

Manya had taken off, walking fifty miles barefoot. As she walked, she thought: how do I find a Bolshevik in the big city? Suddenly she thought she spotted one, and ran after him: "Young man, you I was looking for." He said, "For me, you were looking?"

"Personally, no, believe me," Manya said. "I'm looking for a Bolshevik."

Her intuition was right. Later, he visited her in Schedrin. She became an organizer for the Bolsheviks, distributing leaflets from village to village.

*　　　*　　　*

She hounded the Party leaders and Henky Rubin. "Why are you so *happy* with me? Why are you kissing my ass? What is it, Goddamnit? I did terrible. I hurt them. Why did the *Daily Worker* keep silent until they were convicted? And look at their editorial today: 'Prayers are in order for that sweet little couple who are going to their doom.' How the fuck is that going to arouse the masses?"

Henky Rubin stared at the livid woman, rather attractive in her faded ruffian way. "My dear Mrs. Poffnick, to tell you the truth your button disturbs me terribly. How do you think you are going to reach the masses that way? The Party's position on the Rubells will be tested in the crucible of struggle. The crucible of struggle."

"But how can I help save the Rubells? I fucked up so bad at the trial."

"We do not feel that you did. You struck a blow against the Korean madness, your political perspective was perfect. You denied the Rubells did anything. You attested to their sweetness. This was good and proper. At a time when Wall Street's policies spell world disaster, we must develop correct tactics adapted to the concrete situation. The concrete situation. Subjectively you feel that you fucked up. Objectively you focused attention on the key issues on a high plane of political maturity."

"But what can I do to help?"

"We are planning a prayer vigil later in the week. If you take off that button, we'd love to have you."

When she was in the Party, she was really there. She looked with both eyes.

In the thirties she was an organizer for several groups helping the unemployed. They offered her ten dollars a week. She would not take it.

At one striking shop, a scab was trying to discourage the boss from settling with the union. The scab told the boss not to get discouraged and worked fifteen hours a day to set a good example. The strikers called Manya.

On a winter morning of snow, frost, and rain, the alarm clock awoke her at four. When Manya reached the subway station, a

worker was waiting for her. The worker would shake his umbrella
three times when the scab arrived.

He shook his umbrella. Manya hit the woman with a bottle of
Coca Cola wrapped in a *New York Times*.

A taxi was waiting at the station. The cab driver saw what had
happened and didn't want to let Manya into the cab. She pleaded
with him. "Is she fooling around with your husband?" he asked
Manya. "She's after him every day. My husband wouldn't do it if
she wouldn't make him do it," Manya said. They sped away.

Manya took the taxi to a friend with two babies. Manya sat on the
floor and played games with them.

The scab was in bed for six weeks. Manya felt guilty. But when
the woman came back to work with a bandaged head, she resumed
scabbing. Manya was relieved.

It wasn't easy for her to do a thing like that. She'd had to think of
all the hardships the scab had caused the workers. "So finally I got
her, so I gave it what I could."

It was always difficult for her to find steady work. She could never
push herself ahead of the other workers at the union hall. They came
with stories of starving children, sick husbands, and mothers. Some
of them lied, she suspected, but she couldn't compete with such
misery. After all, she was alone.

She would leave the hall and walk into the street. She often had
no carfare and no place to sleep. She went to a comrade's place, or
the public baths.

Bernie Nudelman, "that mincing little fairy," as the Rubell Committee
call him, raised arguments that persuaded the Supreme Court to stay
the Rubells' execution for a month. Henky Rubin had opposed every
effort Nudelman had made. But when the Supreme Court made its
announcement, Henky publicly kissed Nudelman on the lips to
show how happy he was. Nudelman swatted him off. Manya knew
little of Nudelman, as he was never mentioned in the *Daily Worker*.

The day after the execution, it was Nudelman who stood on a
soapbox in Union Square addressing a crowd of workers. He said,
"Workers and toilers, if you are happy about the murder of the
Rubells, you are all rotten to the core." Nudelman paused, looked

around at the effect his words had had, turned, and ran down the street, pursued by what he called this "band of maniacs." They chased him into a police station.

Three years later, Manya was seated in a bar frequented by progressives, nursing her third beer. A man with a ponytail, a shopping bag, and a smell of hunger to him, walked mincingly through the door. He said to the man seated beside Manya, "Wipe that silly smirk off your face."

Nudelman sat down beside Manya. "I am attracted by your button," he said. "If you don't touch me, everything will be all right."

She was silent.

"I will tell you about the day of July 8, 1954," he said. "That was the day this country was about to murder the Rubells. It didn't, because of me."

"Who are you?" Manya asked.

"My name is Bernard Nudelman. To certain Supreme Court justices, I am known as one with ulterior motives. To Judge Goldman, I was an interloper. To the Rubells' lawyer, I was an anathema. To Albert Einstein, I was a fresh mind. I will tell you of hideous truths, pernicious nobilities, and abominations."

"Sure," Manya said. "Why not?"

"I don't want to hear this Trotskyite garbage," one of the regulars said. The others gradually turned away and resumed talking to each other.

"Let us recall some smothered facts," Nudelman said to Manya. "I am talking about the moment in the trial when Henky Rubin asked Judge Goldman—that agent for a sinister cabal—to seal from public view, *in the interest of national security*, the diagram that Dolly's brother Hershie said he had composed. We heard from Hershie's soiled lips that the drawing was a true copy of a diagram he had composed five and a half years back.

"So what did the Rubells' lawyer do? Henky patriotically implored the judge to impound it so that it remained a secret. It was this trash that sealed the fate of the Rubells. Ooooh!" The rubber band around Nudelman's ponytail had snapped. His hair cascaded around him.

"The stay was granted on my point that the Rubells were tried under the wrong law: they should have been tried not under the Espionage Act of 1917, but the Atomic Energy Act of 1946. Under the 1946 act, a death sentence had to be specifically called for by the jury, and they could call for it only when intent was shown to injure the United States. The Rubells were accused of giving secrets to an ally. Henky Rubin said of my argument, 'it makes me want to throw up.'

"The majority overruled my point and the Rubells were rushed to their death."

Nudelman said, "The majority opinion referred to me as a 'peculiar champion with an odd record.' Those scumbags were speaking of my conviction on a charge of dissolute vagrancy. The police produced a witness who said I insulted the pope in Union Square, called for revolution, and pressed my rubber heels against a bench."

Nudelman popped up, stamped on the broken rubber band, and sat down again. "I was jailed six months after the Rubells were murdered.

"Henky Rubin was forty-nine when he died. He looked hale and hearty. We must leave to history the atrociously rich complexity of human nature—"

"You talk," Manya said, "like I don't know what—a dog with a college education."

"Remember," Nudelman said, "that the Rubell Committee, just like the Party, was shot through with F.B.I. agents. Rubin's death apparently came from a heart attack. But the police suspected foul play. Rubin's body was pajama clad, while his head was in a bathtub filled with water. A law officer told Rubin's law partner: 'We have to be sure that someone on your side didn't bump him off because he knew too much.' "

"This I don't know," Manya said. "They call you a pervert, an interloper, a provocateur, and a Trotskyite. If that's all that's wrong with you, in my opinion it's not so bad. Have a beer."

Later that night, the couple, he with his duffle bag filled with his pamphlets, petitions, ruminations, and autobiography: *Vomit-Provoking Thoughts*, and she with a shopping bag in each hand, trundled through Union Square. He shyly asked her if she had a place where he could stay. "No," she said, "but I was wondering if you got a place for me?"

They looked at each other, and took the subway to the all-night automat on 47th Street and Broadway.

At dawn, as the sky lightened over Broadway, over the RKO Palace and Jack Dempsey's and Lindy's and the Latin Quarter and Hubert's Flea Circus, the two Leninists thought it through and through, circling around and around their hunches and suspicions, how the Party fucked up and smelled rotten, but at dawn, their pale faces faint with fatigue, their berets falling over their faces, they knew for certain: it was the F.B.I. and the C.I.A. that had framed the Rubells. It was a close call, but still, as they gathered up their stuff, shooed out by the manager, they believed.

Judy Garland's picture was on the Palace marquee. "What disgusting displays," Nudelman said. "Lipstick, bosoms. This could never happen in the Soviet Union."

Manya bopped him on the side of the head. "You don't like Judy Garland? Mister, you gotta lighten up a little."

Nudelman jumped up in the air. "Sir, your accusations are fit for the machinations of the F.B.I. You've appeared pleasant enough, but the vicious nature of some humans accommodates both affection and outright betrayal. Goodnight."

Manya shrugged, and headed for the union hall. Perhaps he was a little unstable.

(In 1979, the reporter asked her: "What do you think you are?" Manya: "I don't know. I'm not interested in myself. I'm a human being with all the human shortcomings. So help yourself with a cookie.")

Sometimes she would go the whole day on the picket line without time to eat anything, drink a cup of coffee, go to the bathroom. The picket line began at 8 A.M. "The bosses are trying to choke it in the bud!" she shouted. When it was over, the strike committee met. Manya was chairman. Three hours remained for sleep. She slept on the bench in the union hall. At 6 A.M., she took a napkin out of her pocket, patted herself, and went back to the picket line. It went on for three months. Her mother said there were only three big Communists: Lenin, Trotsky, and Manya.

*   *   *

In 1928, the cafeteria workers had gone on strike. A court injunction was issued against the strikers. They decided they would have to break the injunction. Manya was chosen to go first. She could hold the line longer than anyone else.

She began picketing the cafeteria alone. A policeman said, "Madam, don't you know there is an injunction here?"

"What is an injunction?" Manya asked.

"I think it means you cannot strike. I'm not sure, frankly."

"Listen, Officer," Manya said, "you seem like a very nice person. I'll tell you: workers from this cafeteria are not allowed to strike. But I don't work here. So I don't think the injunction applies to me. Why don't you let me read it?"

The injunction was twenty-five pages long. It was mumbo jumbo to her, but she kept reading, walking slowly up and down with her picket sign up. The cafeteria manager stood by the door shaking with rage. No customers entered. The first policeman sought a second policeman, but he was also inexperienced in these matters.

After several more minutes, the first policeman said, "I'm afraid we're going to have to arrest you. The manager is distressed."

"All right, I'm arrested," said Manya. "Tow me away."

The policeman called the station and asked for reinforcements. Manya checked the clock. Another half hour passed. She was still walking.

Two officers from the station house arrived. Manya held on to the cafeteria pole "like two mules." They couldn't pull her away. They clubbed her arms. She thought she heard a bone being fractured.

It was noon. A large crowd formed. Traffic was halting on Fifth Avenue, a two-way street. The police frantically directed the cars to move on. Buses were rerouted. The crowd applauded Manya and booed the policemen.

The policemen used their nightsticks to beat her hands. She let go of the pole. They tried to pick her up. She kicked them and spat at them. She looked at the clock: ten minutes to one. Three more cops joined in and tried to pull her into the police car.

In the car the policemen hit her in the mouth. One of her teeth popped out, and a torrent of blood followed. It poured out on her coat, on the floor, on the men's uniforms. They socked her in the eye. It closed and swelled. They beat her on the nose. It bled. They beat her all over with their fists and heels, this bitch who had humiliated them.

She was unconscious when they brought her into the station. Four ribs were broken.

Bail was set at ten thousand dollars. Manya pleaded with the union rep to let her go to jail because the union couldn't afford that price. The rep was afraid of the condition of her eyes.

Manya said, "Look, no doctor can even find my eyes now because they're closed and swollen. I'm sure they won't beat me in jail. I'm okay there. I know everybody."

In jail she did know most of the girls: about forty prostitutes, one millinery worker, one dressmaker. A registered nurse looked at her eyes and said she must have ice. The women screamed until ice packs were brought.

That night the weather was hot. The windows were closed and the steam was turned on full blast. It was impossible to breathe in the cells.

The women pleaded for the guards to open the windows, but they refused. They screamed and yelled, "Open the windows, shut off the steam." During the midnight count, Manya led the women in singing, at the top of their voices, "Hold the Fort," the "Marseillaise," and the "Internationale."

Suddenly the women heard the steam being closed off, the windows being opened. One of the prostitutes said, "Can you beat that? 'Russia' gets the steam shut off and the windows opened in an American jail. We couldn't do it, but 'Russia' did it!"

Manya said, "You'll be very pleasantly surprised, sisters, at what the example of the Soviet Union will do for you in the future."

When Manya was six, her friends, most of whom were Christian, were discussing who would go to heaven. They didn't know. They asked a Greek Orthodox mother. She replied: Only the Greek Orthodox people would go to heaven.

The children, especially Manya, weren't satisfied. They went to a Catholic mother. She said only the Catholics would go to heaven. When they had tried all the other mothers, Manya said, "Well, let's try mine. What have we got to lose?" Manya's mother told them: "All the Jews will go to heaven, and everybody else will go to hell."

Manya led the children to her father. She said of him, "He's a very religious man, but he knows in the world everything." Her father sat in his study. "Papa," she asked, "how big is the Jewish population compared to the gentiles in the world?" He replied, "The Jews are a tiny fraction; maybe one percent." "My God," Manya said, "then heaven must be such a small place."

Her father said, "What makes you say that?"

Manya told him what all the mothers, including her own, had said.

"No, my child," he said, "not only the Jews will go to heaven. Any human being that cares for another human being will go there, regardless of his religion. Any human being that cares for an animal, that picks up a wounded dog, tries to help him, will go to heaven.

"So you see, Manya," he said, "heaven is not such a small place."

Her parents wanted her to fast on Yom Kippur from the age of thirteen. Her mother said, "If you eat on Yom Kippur, you die." When she was fourteen, Manya wanted to test God. So she secretly had a snack. She was terrified all day. By evening, she could not stop laughing.

Manya began printing and distributing Bolshevik literature at fifteen. She made leaflets on a press made out of gelatin, spreading the ink over and over again. She hid the gelatin stamp and the ink under a board under her bed.

Manya and the other young Bolsheviks organized a watch through the night to guard against a pogrom. They had two rifles that worked, but they paraded back and forth with six, as well as fifteen pinless grenades.

When the war ended, Manya left for America.

How could she leave the Party? At one time expulsion would have been worse than death.

After Stalin's death in 1953, the Soviet Central Committee said that in the future everything had to be voted on by a majority. In her club she shouted, "What means from now on? So what was before?"

After Khrushchev's speech in 1956, she claimed that she never slept again. Khrushchev said that if the other leaders, like himself, had protested, Stalin would have murdered them. "Where were their balls?" Manya shouted.

At first she had thought it was only the American Party that was at fault. One night at her club meeting, Sylvia Pollack said, "Isn't it wonderful how Brezhnev embraces Gus Hall? Gus told me that Brezhnev gave him a big hug and thanked him for doing such a marvelous job."

"Wait a fucking minute," Manya said. She walked up to Sylvia and spat at her. Sylvia spat back.

Manya ran out of the room, leaving her shopping bags behind.

She couldn't eat. She stopped looking for work.

She stopped going to Soviet movies, concerts, the Bolshoi.

She found a room of her own on the Upper West Side, a cot, a chair, and a table. She lined up seven bottles of beer on the floor at night, lay down on the cot, her eyes wide open. If she were in the Soviet Union, she would have one of three fates: shock therapy, an insane asylum, or a concentration camp.

"So now I know," she said, her voice thick by 3 A.M. "I even know why I never had a union job. What the hell's the point of even looking anymore? Even when the Party is in the union leadership. Somehow everybody gets a job except me. Even progressives want obedients. I took over jobs if somebody left sometimes . . . two months, three months . . . and then I had to give them up. Not only by the other side was I denied a job. I was denied by my own . . . nobody wants to stick their neck out . . . everybody wants quiet, Goddamnit . . ."

(She told the reporter in 1982: "There were sufferers in many other unions too. We are as we are, that's all. I couldn't sell myself for a job. It's not easy to be straight. It's not easy to try to better a shop. Everybody wants to have a smooth circle. In every shop there was something doing against the workers. Wherever I was, I couldn't tolerate it. That's all. There will be a time when people will be able to be free. And people will be able to straighten up. But so far, we haven't got it. We never had it.")

She looked around for a group that really believed in revolution. She found that even the most militant had a soft spot for Israel.

"Why is everybody so *hot* for Israel?" she asked in her thick Yiddish accent. "Goddamnit, what is it? What makes Israel so holy? The Israelis even have the American president in their pocket. In six or seven states there are almost a million Jews. And they can swing a president. So that's why all the American presidents handle the Israelis with silk gloves. Goddamnit, because of the Jews. And those six states don't only rule from Riverside Drive to West End Avenue. They rule America." At this point Manya lost some of her listeners, but she went on: "The formation of Israel didn't juice me up, I'll tell you the truth. The Israelis are worse than Hitler. If the czarist government or Brezhnev or Hitler chased me out and told me I could never come back, I would work my life, I would work to my death to kill all of those who did it."

Manya had a difficult time adjusting to some of the harsh new language of the sixties. "Kill the pigs" was a chant she found hard to digest. For years progressive Jews in the Party had expressed their admiration for pigs: their lovely taste, their working-class heft, their simplicity and unbourgeois brawn. "You look like a pig" had been a compliment, and Manya still found herself saying it by mistake.

It was the black militants who seemed to her to have kept their revolutionary purity.

Manya began selling copies of the *Black Panther* on Harlem street corners.

It was beautiful, the way this little Jewish activist understood, Lonnie Rose thought. She had come into the Panther office, given the black power salute, and handed out cartons of chopped liver. Flagrant lies had been espoused against them, yet Manya was always with them. When Lonnie lectured about the history of Palestine and the two alien pigs, British imperialism and kosher nationalism, there was Manya shouting, "That's right, shoot first!" When he explained that when the Jews were barbecued, they should have learned to behave themselves, Manya said, "Right on!"

When the Panthers were on trial, Manya would make a hissing sound in the courtroom. The judge couldn't pinpoint it. He spotted an old lady muttering in the first row and told her to come forward. Manya hobbled forth on two canes, and was told to keep her opinions to herself.

When the defendants were held in the Tombs, she would bring a little paper bag for each one, with chicken, fruit, and a piece of cake, all neatly wrapped, napkins, a small can of juice, and a can opener. "If I can't be behind bars with them," she said, "I can at least make things a little nicer for them."

If there was an acquittal, she shouted, "Hurray for the people's jury!" and tossed two canes in the air.

Manya helped Lonnie dissolve a lot of negative feelings he'd been harboring. And the checks she sent them with the notes: "This is to be used only for a fugitive from justice who shoots first."

Lonnie loved having Manya around when he talked about capitalism and imperialism and their running dogs, pork chop nationalism, kosher nationalism, taco nationalism, all that doomed shit imposing against the grain of history. They had two interpreters in the room, one doing sign language for the deaf, and Manya, translating Lonnie into Yiddish.

Lonnie wondered how she would react to the cartoon in the *Black Panther* that showed two pigs toe to toe, shaking hands and kissing, snout to snout. The pig labeled "Zionism" had an Israeli flag and wore a black eye patch. It held aloft in one arm a religious scepter crowned with a Star of David. The other pig was labeled "U.S.A." The front page also had a cartoon of a massive, bare-breasted pig labeled U.S.A. suckling two piglets, one called Israel, the other Germany. Grouped around the pig's feet, waiting their turn to be suckled, were ten other piglets: the countries of the Western world from France to Belgium.

"A little hyperbole there," Lonnie said defensively to Manya, testing her reaction. "I'll tell you the truth," Manya said, "I never thought pigs could be so ugly." Lonnie sparkled at this, roared, gave her an embrace that knocked out two of her last teeth.

By 1974, Manya thought she had asthma, ulcers, dozens of allergies (she fainted from plums), heart disease. She told friends that Dr. Reuben's book, *Everything You Always Wanted to Know About Sex but Were Afraid to Ask*, had come too late. If she had read it sooner, she would have married again. She heard psychiatrists talk on the radio about medication for depression, called them up and saw them for a few weeks. She tried acupuncture. She underwent a nutrition analysis. They took a strand of her hair and told her she was deficient in zinc.

Manya became a volunteer in the old-age home on Riverside Drive. She soon was shouting that the hospital needed to be "cleaned up from the waist," that it was neglecting the patients. The hospital barred her from the premises, but she kept coming back. In desperation they assigned her a social worker, Linda Pastoff. Manya tried to recruit the social worker into the Panthers, put up notices of demonstrations on the bulletin board, collected money for various causes when the social worker was out of the building.

Manya reminisced to Linda Pastoff about the years when she had raised two children. When she had been on a picket line, she said, and it had been a terrible day, before entering the house she would always compose herself and comb her hair and enter the apartment singing so that the children would not be upset. She said she never had much money, but she could always afford a couple of lemons and some sugar, and would make a big pitcher of lemonade for them and tell them to bring their friends to the house.

She had more and more blackouts from her allergies. Between blackouts she made Easter baskets for the children of the Panthers, stormed her way into the hospital to visit the elderly progressives, and was a full-time activist with the local welfare council, the Panthers, and a peace committee.

In 1975 Manya applied to live at the old-age home. "Over my dead body," Irving Bernstein, the director, told Linda Pastoff. "Now she's stealing food from the cafeteria to bring up to the patients."

Manya began to visit Linda Pastoff every few days.

In 1976 she blacked out for two days. When she awoke, she attempted suicide.

In a few weeks she was an activist again.

Linda Pastoff's Manya Poffnick File: 1974–1984

September 1974. Mrs. Poffnick complained that over the last few weeks she has become incontinent and has begun to sleep. She claimed that she had not slept at all for eighteen years prior to this. She is sleeping more and more, up to sixteen hours a night. Mrs. Poffnick had to stop taking Elavil as "it was tearing me apart," a feeling she could not describe in any other way and that she has never had before.

September 1975. Mrs. Poffnick is now taking 150 mg. of Synacon daily. She complains of weakness; at the same time the medication seems to have improved her appetite and feeling of well-being. She finds it difficult, for example, to climb onto a bus. She asked if this could be the result of depression. She also feels she can't leave the house anymore and go to meetings because of incontinence.

December 1976. Mrs. Poffnick has informed me that she has been diagnosed as having chronic leukemia. She feels that she may have to enter the home, if they will have her, but if so "I might as well be dead."

February 1977. Mrs. Poffnick seems to be very much improved. Taking 50 mg. of Elavil at bedtime, she says her fears of doing things, sleep problems, and difficulty getting up in the morning have been relieved. Today she dated the problem of fatigue and sleeplessness back to when she was in her mid-fifties. At that point she could no longer find work as a waitress or a restaurant worker. During this period she developed what she thought were allergies. She developed extreme sleeplessness, fatigue, and a dry mouth. At first she tried to sleep by drinking six to ten bottles of beer a night, and started taking barbiturates along with beer. At this point Mrs. Poffnick wondered if she had been depressed for the last twenty years, ever since she couldn't find work that was suitable for her and began to feel a sense of uselessness. She said she had also been very depressed over the Rubell case, but would not explain her feelings to me.

June 1978. Mrs. Poffnick's declining health and diagnosis of chronic leukemia have made it a continuous struggle for her to manage within the community and to maintain the independence she so fiercely holds on to.

Mrs. Poffnick's relationship with the social worker has been a source of support to her. In order to reach Mrs. Poffnick, an unorthodox approach is required. The social worker does not have regular appointments with Mrs. Poffnick, who usually drops in the office every three or four days. When she does come, Mrs. Poffnick makes it clear that she does not expect the social worker necessarily to be available to her.

December 1980. In recent weeks Mrs. Poffnick has shared more and more with the worker her fears regarding leukemia. Last week she was even more disturbed than usual. There was some incoherency; frequently she was unable to complete a sentence, because of a loss of thought process. She seemed to be overmedicated.

October 1982. Mrs. Poffnick continues to feed the patients and take care of them at the home. She carries a cane but refuses to use it. She helps everyone in need. She has thirteen gallons of apple juice and eighteen boxes of matzoh in her apartment because someone needed to sell them.

Mrs. Poffnick refuses to have a television set at home, although the worker indicated one could be made available to her. She considers many of the programs a waste of time, and has particularly strong negative reactions to daytime soap operas. She referred to them as "absolute bullshit."

January 1984. Mrs. Poffnick described at length the two children that she raised. They were orphaned when a nephew died fighting in the Korean War. She raised them with her late husband, a tailor. Mr. and Mrs. Poffnick cared for the children until they married and left home. Mrs. Poffnick was the children's only support subsequent to Mr. Poffnick's death. They never attempted to adopt the children since, in Mrs. Poffnick's own words, "No one else wanted them." Both children have turned out well, she reports, and are doctors. On the other hand, no one in the community who is close to Mrs. Poffnick recalls that she has ever had children or a husband living with her.

Mrs. Poffnick told the worker that with her strong interest in peace, Mrs. Poffnick refuses whenever possible to pay any federal taxes, and has done so since the beginning of the Vietnam War. In order to avoid the federal tax, she withdraws all her money at the end of the year and starts a savings account in a new bank. She also refuses to pay the subway fare since it has been raised, and swings through the gate.

June 5, 1984

Hi miss Pastoff,
Here is a check for what ever you want to use it.
Dont wory about ho much. Its anywy yours.

314

you are my beneficiary.
you may as well use it now then when I'll be in Heaven!!!
Let me tell you the Banks.
One is, Manufacturers Hanover Trust Co. located at 26st. &
Columb ave there I have 500.00 I dont need it.
The 2nd bank
East River savings bank located at 96 & amsterdam.
there I have now 200.00
this is a bank I use
3rd
Citibank located at 111 st and Bway. there I have only a
few dollars, that bank I use since I will not die any
more very yong.
you'll have to buy 3 death certificates and present your
Identification. plus a death certificate.
mark down for yourself where my banks are
Be Well—shoot first

Yours
Manya

Manya was invited to speak at the annual Rubell memorial rally at Town Hall. She had not heard from that crowd for a long time. They knew she was dying. True, she was a deviationist, but she had been the only person to testify on behalf of the Rubells.

Seated in the audience was the gang from Perry Street: Renée and Max Finger, Josh Moroze, Sophie Rich, Hermie Rich, a white-haired Maury Ballinzweig decked out in bell-bottoms.

Manya's beloved Lonnie Rose, who had been with the Panthers, was another guest speaker. Lonnie was one of the Morningside 3½, accused of a little mayhem. The Morningside 3½ thought the ½ made them sound warmer, less threatening. The ½ was Elton MacRaw. Elton had only one arm—the other was a meat hook.

The memorial meeting took place on the day the newspapers ran the photograph of Mrs. Klinghoffer being escorted off the Achille Lauro.

On the stage they talked of 1954, Union Square, masses of people united. Lovely Danny Michelle, Henky Rubin's successor, his moustache still black and red after all these years, stormed across the

315

stage, his tenor voice booming, holding stacks of pages about the Rubell case that fell from his hands. He suddenly threw the whole batch of pages on the floor in a heap and stomped on them with his spurred boots. "They're the wrong fucking pages!" he screamed.

"For years we fought the F.B.I. for these pages under the Freedom of Information Act. Now we got 'em, our offices are flooded with 'em, you can't move—and what do we get? F.B.I. plants telling us that Solly Rubell told an informer about the whole espionage operation! Now brothers and sisters, Solly Rubell was a very . . . careful . . . person. Would he have spilled the beans to a stranger in the House of Detention? In heaven's name, *give us the right pages*, the ones that prove we were right all along. Take this so-called spy, Walker. Dig the setup. A member of the Ku Klux Klan! Imagine such a reactionary working for the USSR! My friends, they're trying to do today what they did to the Rubells in the fifties. They don't call you a Communist anymore. Oh no. You're a—get this—now you're a *terrorist*! They use that buzz word, *K.G.B.*!" Michelle hopped on one foot in delight and the audience hooted. "A hijacker, a bomb-thrower. A threat to private property."

Michelle lowered his voice to a whisper, and wiped a tear from his eye. "Dolly and Solly." A large picture of the Rubells was raised on the stage. "Hello Dolly. Take a bow, Solly. It's so nice to see you back where you belong. You're looking swell, Dolly. I can tell, Solly. You're still growing, you're still crowing, you're still going strong. Dolly and Solly. Solly and Dolly. Dolly Solly, Solly Dolly," he intoned as a procession of men and women walked down the aisle with red roses. They knelt in front of the picture.

"Who were the Rubells? They were nobodies, for Christ's sake. And boy, were they ever reliable. Simple little progressive folk who drank deeply from the fountain of pure advanced thought. They would do anything you told them to do. Manya Poffnick, a guest speaker tonight, is another nobody." The audience applauded lustily.

"You may rise," Danny said to the kneeling group. "The beauty of it is that any one of you out there could have replaced them and no one would have known the difference. Goodbye, Solly and Dolly . . . goodbye noble folk . . ." Michelle blew kisses to the audience as he exited.

A Hollywood writer, his artistic career in ruins after being blacklisted for years, stepped to the podium. Bart London was best known for the brilliant "Bow Wow Goes to Hawaii" series at the peak of his creative powers, including the socially innovative "Bow Wow Goes to Leningrad." He had been cut down in his prime.

"I'd like to introduce the victims of a new frame-up, Lonnie Rose and Shirley Stirrup of the Morningside 3½." A tall, elegant man, a raincoat slung over his shoulder, holding a puppy by a leash and the Encyclopaedia Britannica in his other hand, walked dapperly to the microphone. He was accompanied by a plump woman with a snarl on her face. Shirley Stirrup spoke first. "This system been rapin' Mom Nature," she said, "gouging out the earth, mining, uprooting, butchering, robbin' her minerals, factories that's belchin' out poison in our air, killin' off the fish in the ocean, the birds in the sky and breedin' retardation, deformed babies. . . ."

"Tell it, sister!" Manya called out.

"We tell them to qualify, elabrofy," Shirley Stirrup continued, "back up their credentials with the facts or stop lyin', dupin' folks. . . . We was dragged down the steps by the guards, thrown on our stomachs in the prison vans while handcuffed and shackled, heat blasting, stifling, driven by speeding, callous drunken guards. . . . We been raped of our blood on a hunger strike, helded down by three-hundred-pound guards while nurses raped us of our blood and injected drugs into our bodies. . . ."

"What does she mean she was raped of her blood?" a prim young British woman said to Manya, but Manya had no time for bourgeois crap.

"Forced to eat commissary junk food—cookies! Potato chips! Crackers! Pretzels! They refused to give us our natural raw-food diet. We still suffering problems with our teeth, bleeding, swollen gums, cracked teeth, teeth falling out, crumbling at the root. They so bent on hurting us, taking away our health that they won't even give us a raw onion to help our gums—"

"Thank you, beautiful sister," said Lonnie, "and now perchance it's time for me to elabrofy on your statements." He gently moved her away from the microphone.

"It is historically known," he shouted, "that Reagan has decreed the death of all black babies. This is scientifically stated. Blacks are the targets because we're the spark for the prairie fire."

Manya, who was sitting in the front row, finished her fourth beer and put the bottle down on the floor beside her chair.

"We are 3½ black revolutionaries sprung from the depths of the people's struggle for freedom," Lonnie said. "We've been organizing for housing, education, health care, mass enlightenment, you know, fighting pig brutality. And they call us 'terrorists.' Our real crime, which I am prone to admit, is our exposure of the system. Just like with the Rubells, they wanted to extract from us here the names of our associates, who we knew, where we knew them, where we went, like that. And like the Rubells, we refused. They want to crush the vanguard, so they can go on raping Central America and Africa of their blood with no damn interference.

"Brothers and sisters, fascism is imminent, just as the beautiful Rubells realized over thirty years ago. Captured revolutionaries are buried in the camps, subject to isolation, harassment, physical abuse, electric-shock batons, murder, and loss of tranquility. Friends of the Rubells: the struggle is the same. Only the names have changed. Dolly and Solly, we are carrying on until victory."

There was ringing applause and a standing ovation.

Manya was introduced as the heroine of the Rubell trial. She walked to the podium with her two canes.

"When you invited me, I thought, my God, how did I get to the first act?" she said, peering nearsightedly across the hall. "But what the hell, I'll tell you what I know.

"When I think of the Rubells," she said, her voice breaking, "ordinary people like you and me, to become such heroes. I cried so much. I didn't cry for a very long time, but now that I speak of it, you see . . . parents of small children should do such a sacrifice, to show the world they were not guilty . . . it takes great courage. Great, great courage." The crowd applauded, led by Danny Michelle on the side of the stage.

"I was very active, but if I would have children, I would try to shield them. At one time we took small children on a hunger march, and the children were also beaten. At that time I thought to myself: I wouldn't take my child. If the Party would tell me to take my child, I wouldn't do it. A child is a child." Two people clapped.

"When I was in the Party, I was very critical about those who were trying to get away with murder doing nothing. I never bought new furniture. Instead I gave money to the Movement. For furniture, what I got, others gave away. For me it was enough. For Solly and Dolly Rubell, it was also enough. As little as it was, it was enough. To them their apartment on Catherine Street was a palace—steam heat. They felt kind of guilty that they knew so many people who needed apartments as badly as they did, and they had gotten this apartment. Not too many people in the Movement would feel that. They were real people.

"Dolly and Solly were very devoted to the Party. They never went underground. Hours before they were arrested, they were at a club meeting. They had gotten new subscriptions for the *Worker* and the *Morgen Freiheit*. If I hadn't been there, even I would wonder, because at one time I was for the Soviet Union more than a hundred percent, a thousand percent. Not now, but when it was a good Soviet Union, or when we didn't know what Stalin was doing, one of the two, you see. . . . At that time, if the Soviet Union would ask me to do something, I would do. I would endanger my life, I would do everything and anything. Being that Solly and Dolly were Communists, a good many of our own people suspected that maybe there is something." There was a loud stirring and rustling in the audience.

"But the only thing is, I can't understand why the Party murdered the Rubells. This I will take to the grave with me—why the Party officials crossed the street when the Rubell family came to plead for them, why the *Daily Worker* never mentioned the case, why Henky Rubin fucked up the defense—" Faces became foul and twisted, there were spitting and hissing noises, people turned to each other and began talking in loud voices about the weather and local restaurants.

"I don't understand it, Goddamnit—" Manya said, as the dashing, six-foot-eight Elton MacRaw came toward her smiling. He put his meat hook around Manya's shoulder and toward her throat. She kicked him. He lifted her up and carried her, her legs kicking in the air, off the stage.

In 1986 the reporter saw Manya for the last time. She had asked him to find an article, "A Cuban Lesson," in the *Times* written in 1980 by a Cuban poet, Heberto Padilla, who was exiled from Cuba. She referred to him as "an honest man." Manya had begun to refer to the United States with some surprise as a democracy. "You see, we live in a democracy," she would say.

Padilla wrote of his impressions on returning to New York City after living for twenty years in the Communist world: "In 1960, I wandered through the streets of New York, this city which exalted and fulfilled the self I was then. At that time, I couldn't even imagine a freedom as invisible, dependable, and natural as the air . . . Perhaps no one in the United States will ever have to go through my kind of apprenticeship, and never have the need to learn the lesson I now know."

Manya put the article down and said, "As rotten as Brezhnev was, as rotten as Gus Hall was, there was just . . . *nothing*."

Manya stood up from the bed in the monastic room in the gathering dusk and walked over to her broad window looking out on the garden and the majestic sweep of the Cathedral of St. John the Divine. "My life was very hard. Very hard." The reporter felt that he wanted to put his arm around her, and that she wanted nothing as much in the world as that. But he sensed that it was too late for Manya to begin to allow others to give to her.

Three months later, at the memorial meeting for Manya in a room of the old-age home, her nephew said, "During the Vietnam protests in Washington, I was watching the TV news. Here's the guard standing at the door to the Pentagon with the crowd of people as far back as you can see. And he's arguing with someone. I look at her. It was Aunt Manya. She was telling the guard to get out of her way, she wanted to talk to the Chief of Staff."

An older woman, Alix Werner, whose forty-year-old retarded son stared at her with a blissful smile, finished her speech about Manya. She said, "What did Manya stand for?" She dramatically removed her trench coat, revealing a second coat festooned with buttons: big buttons, small buttons, colored and black and white. The buttons said, "Fight White Violence," "Remember Allende," "Support Cuba," "Love Nicaragua," "Vindicate the Rubells," "People Before Profits," and "Shoot First."

"This," she said, pointing to each button, "is what Manya was."

Letters from Amerika

Me for you, you for me.
—G.L.

February 8, 1951

Solly darling,

As advanced people deeply involved in history's march, what have the Rubells done to deserve so much unhappiness? Torn asunder from their little ones, removed from the sunlight and laughter of the working class? I say to you, the Rubells are committed to virtue's dominion, and for this they are being singled out.

Only today, my friend, I chanced to be reading how a cross was burned in the Negro section of Suffolk, Virginia, and how the police escorted a motorcade of robed men bearing an electric cross and K.K.K. pennants in Tallahassee. And then too I perused a progressive daily that reported that a union leader was blinded after being beaten by police with blackjacks in Erie, Pennsylvania. I crieth, Fie!

Perhaps the persecution of a valiant Jewish couple like the Rubells will alert the world to the reality of conditions in "the home of the brave and the land of the free."

I wait with considerable interest for your wise thoughts on these subjects, hubby of mine.

Dolly

February 11, 1951

My sexy vixen,

You ring my bell with your passionate utterances of unity with the people. You are a woman truly worthy of the sweat of the masses. Let

323

me only state that it's a privilege to know you. That's how deeply you ring my chime, Miss Sublime! I am of the incontrovertible opinion that it is because we are informed people who have drunk deeply from the well of Those In the Know that we have the grit to stand up and be counted.

Just read *War and Peace*. Good book.

Those less informed and more backward may puzzle at our determination. Little do they understand how we have mingled our devotion to the People's Struggle for peace and pie with a healthy slice of our Jewish underdog background for a perfect blendship.

> Salud and Go In Peace,
> Solly

February 13, 1951

My friend,

I am so hot for you! Hot hot hot!

Do you like this frivolous tone, honey boy? Your Dolly has many tricks up her sleeve once we are united again.

Went to synagogue yesterday and really impressed at how wise our cultural heritage is and how relevant to us, fighting for our freedom, and oppressed as we are by latter-day pharoahs.

I am reading *A Lantern for Jeremy* by the noted advanced thinker, V.J. Jerome. A real contribution from the cultural front. Also the Declaration of Independence, the Bible, and Corliss Lamont's guide to a secular humanist funeral.

> Nutritious reading!
> Dolly

October 8, 1951

My Beloved Colleague,

The days darken early here in Sing Sing and I am compelled to render naught all intimations of negativity by thinking with a correct perspective. As the great Irish progressive Sean O'Connor has declared, "let hail the bright brambling children of Stalingrad, fresh bubbling stream of thistlebrook, so lush the leaves of red earth fulfilled, as I sing my comrades to fruitful hurrahs!"

The pit of degradation and horror lies in wait, but I shall summon forth within myself both perspective and confidence, knowing that the fresh greenery of proper thinking is enveloping the international working class, who will bury the braying jackals of hate who suck blood from the poor and the oppressed.

So your little Doll merrily laughs and hopes to dance on their graves.

Your progressive moll,
Doll

October 12, 1951

Dollface,

I just got your letter. Wow! What a woman! What a dame! Your political perspective ripens like a fresh peach! Holy cow, doll, what an animal you are! Frankly, you have a real working-class perspective and you can be in my shock brigade anytime.

Light of my life, the incarceration of Dolores Rubell in Sing Sing is a mean and destructive action. All America cries out at the torture of this progressive heroine, and I can only add my own cavil.

My wife, you humble me with your righteous anger and fortitude. Soon the people will wake up and the facts will reach them.

Just hold the fort, Dolly. I am your loving

Solly

December 3, 1951

Dear Dolores,

I was thinking today of the execution of Willie McGee in May. McGee, as you may recall, was the victim of a frame-up on a rape charge in Mississippi. The legal lynchings of Negroes were not enough for our "leaders"—now they are attempting to do the same thing to political prisoners. Surely the Rubells are sterling examples.

I am enclosing some recent pictures of lynchings for your files, my dear wife—and would like to also point out that bigotry in the good ole U.S.A. is not restricted to the South. A five-foot cross was burned recently in front of a school in New Jersey, where a meeting was held to protest the death sentence of the Trenton Six.

It is impossible to give tongue to all the frightful injustices that are going on in the gruesome new home of the swastika. If they succeed in burning us, they will paralyze other outspoken progressives who criticize the drive toward war. Therefore, my friend, our plight is of utmost importance and linked to the overall peace movement.

In friendly solidarity,
Sol

December 18, 1951

Hubby of mine,

How's this for a reply to all those smart alecks who tell us we should up and confess? I say to them the train of history doesn't go backward. The day the Hungarian People's Republic abandons socialism; the day the German Democratic Republic abandons socialism; the day the Polish People's Republic jettisons socialism—on that day the Rubells will say they're guilty!

Dolly

January 3, 1952

Dear Dolly,

You will be interested in a letter I received in the mail today from a rather backward and ignorant mine worker. He wrote: "You people talk with marbles in your mouths. Why don't you come out with it and tell people what you stand for and what you believe in?"

I was abashed to think of how dumb this poor lout really was. Have the Rubells not stated over and over again their unwavering faith in courage, confidence, and perspective? Have they not stated their belief in the ultimate triumph of decency and justice? Have they not said they stand with the sweet breaths of children, the rosy laughter of the workers, the fight for peace, bread, and roses? Have the Rubells not declared their hatred of the war profiteers, the munitions makers, the Southern Bourbons, the oligarchies and monopolies? Have we not written of how we found the answers to all of the complex riddles which a cold and exploitational society engendered? The answers we found are absolutely correct for all time. They have been proven by experience itself. Anyone who has the guts to explore and examine as we did will come up with exactly the same answers, and, surprisingly, in exactly the same language. Even the punctuation and grammar will be the same. *That's* the kind of people we are.

That is why we are indestructible, and why we are in prison today. When the people learn the truth, they too shall hearken and join the common clarion call.

Well, heck, Doll, if that isn't clear, this guy's some kind of an idiot, what say?

Golly!—
Solly

RED LOVE

(The following letters stay in the vault.—Henky Rubin)

May 23, 1954

Dear Friend,

In sooth, the Rubell case fascinates me. Here is an ordinary couple, their days filled with the little tasks common to their kind. When the time came, and vile disgusting lice spewed their filtheth uponest them, they stood up to be counted.

Lo, when Judgment Day cometh, these poisonous snakes will be ground into the dust where they belongeth.

Thou, my husband, share my profoundeth interest in this case.

Hy Briské laid his unclean hands upon our sacred family. My sister Americans by their inertia let his foul deeds go unchallenged. That little kike bastard, he had a field day with me. There is no creep on the face of the earth like Hy Briské.

Shall my heart forever be fraught with mute, abysmal anguish? What about yours, my husband? Well, it's almost over for us.

We have shared the best kind of love. I will say it aloud. Red love. The color of history, sex, blood, and revenge. We were not bound by the past, shackled by religious shit and superstition. Those fur traps on the rich bitches in the synagogues didn't interest us. The big *mochers* in the front rows in their jewelry and gold stolen from the workers.

There is only one Soviet Union in the world.

There—I've said it.

And one Communist Party, the true enemy of genocide and Nazism.

I enjoyed it. I die with glee at what I accomplished.

And you damn well better doeth the same.

Love,
Dolly

May 25, 1954

My dear children,

The system of thought that Mommy and I believe in teaches us that there are two ways of thinking: the subjective and the objective. It is the objective that allows us to see beyond our own narrow, petty concerns to the condition of all our fellow men and women.

And while at a time like this, I can well understand what my dearest children are feeling, I hope you, Joey, and you, Amy, will see the value of what I am trying to tell you.

327

You children must know that the sight of you, the feel and smell of you, having you on my lap asking me questions (like yours, Joey: "Where did your moustache go, Daddy?") are the dearest things I have ever experienced in my life.

Those are my subjective feelings. And I know very well that you love me as your Daddy every bit as much. If there was anything I could do—without sacrificing many other good people to stay with you—I would do it gladly.

But I do not have that choice. My objective thoughts are that what I am doing will benefit millions and millions of little boys and girls. We live in a period of history—and I hope with all my heart that you will someday study and learn this for yourselves—when for the very first time people will no longer live as slaves. They will control their own destinies. The system that has brought this about is the Soviet system. Don't ever let anyone try to bluff you into doubting this. Up to the very last minute liars have tried to convince Mommy and me that the Soviet Union is a bad place. But we *know* it is tops. Remember always: there is nothing more cunning than anti-Communism. It is the refuge of haters, scoundrels, and Nazis.

I could have lied and confessed to having done something evil, and betrayed everything that I believed in with all my heart. So could have Mommy. Many other people would have been arrested, and the Soviet Union would have been tarnished in the eyes of the world. The hyenas would have been unleashed.

Just know that your Daddy and Mommy were innocent. We helped the hungry, the downtrodden, the helpless, all over the world by our silence. You will live to see singing tomorrows. In all modesty, your Daddy and Mommy are part of those tomorrows.

Do not forget us. Do not forget why we died. And some day you will understand this as well:

It was for you, my children. For you.

Your loving father,
Solomon

The Catholic Boy

A different vigil.
—G.L.

He was nine years old. He lived between the Croton Falls Reservoir and Mahopac, New York, on Union Valley Road. There were all kinds of memories there connected with the Union Army. The imaginations of the farmers in that area were still linked to the Republican party, back to the Civil War. Even though two world wars had intervened, to them America was the Republican party. The Republican party had saved the Union.

They knew there were Democrats in places like New York City, but they were people who weren't like them. During the 1952 election he remembers standing at the bus stop with the farmers' kids and telling them his father supported Adlai Stevenson. They were all a little bit amazed and pissed off, calling him a Democrap. They had never even heard of one in the flesh before. Nor an Irish Catholic either.

The afternoon that the Rubells were executed, he was with the family of his friends. They were on the front lawn of the old farmhouse. The farmer had knocked off somewhat early after his day's work. He was out on the front porch with his wife. The boy was with the farmer's two sons, Chet and Mercer Hough. His father used to call him "Farmer Hough," so he doesn't recall his first name. It was a beautiful, spacious farmhouse with a big front lawn and huge oak and maple trees. The kids were playing catch and fooling around.

He remembers the Houghs' concern that the president might weaken, that he might give in and grant clemency to these people.

Now he finds it hard to remember if he knew they were the Rubells, if he knew they were Jewish, if he knew what they had been convicted of. He suspects he didn't. He thinks he knew they were spies, probably that they were Communists—primarily that they were traitors.

The Houghs thought there was a big danger right then: that very powerful influences might get to the president. The Rubells were people who deserved to be punished. The kids picked this up from the parents. The feeling was there had been a lot of weakness in the country, and that for the president to give clemency to these people would just be more weakness. They didn't think he would, because this was a tough guy. But the feeling was that there were enormous forces that made even the president somewhat weak in comparison.

Now he understands what they thought those "forces" were—the Jews, who somehow controlled the world—but he was just a kid then.

Real Americans wanted these people executed but real Americans were weak and beleaguered. They'd been pushed around and they were probably going to get pushed around again—but maybe the president had enough guts to hold out.

So it was a vigil. They were waiting, on this countryside. This house and farm were the only ones in sight. They had this little valley to themselves. There were no other human beings around. Farmer Hough's farm and cows and a few kids.

And a radio.

It was well known that there were people who lived up Lake Mahopac who would buy carp when you caught them. It was regarded as bad luck when you caught a carp. Because you didn't eat them. And they didn't fight, so you'd think you were just hauling out a log or a tire. But you could get a dollar for it.

They didn't know what the Jews did with them, but they'd heard that they ate the eyes. No one the boy knew was going to eat fish that lived down in the mud and ate all the garbage off the bottom of the pond.

Suddenly there was a hush and they drew around the crackling radio.

"The Rubells are dead at last," the announcer said.

There was a sense of relief, not exaltation: "Well, that's over," and it turned out all right. The radio was snapped off. They went back to playing catch.

Things hadn't gone wrong.

There were vigils going on at Union Square, at Sing Sing, in left-wing neighborhoods. They were participating in another kind of a vigil.

He remembers a very pleasant summer day and a very pleasant summer evening. A beautiful end to a beautiful day.

The House on the Hill

Close the door on your way out.

—G.L.

In 1949 the house on the hill was a jewel. Looking out over everything. You couldn't survey it; it surveyed you. Ziggy and Sarah Weissberger had immense wealth and standing in the world. Libraries and capsules were named after them. Their names connoted substantial values, commitment, and integrity.

The lighting of this house high on the hill was fantastic; if you looked up at it at night, the lights blinded you.

To this house came hunted figures. They drank out of goblets, slept in silk sheets and silk pajamas; little nips of caviar were offered to them on gold trays.

A personal tragedy occurred in this house: the death of a child; a tragedy that would send the family fleeing at night forever from this reminder of their mortality.

But in 1949 the house was still lit.

Sarah Weissberger, noted lawyer, skipping up and down, holding her butterfly dress and train so they wouldn't trail on the floor. A woman of principles could dress like a flibbertigibbet. Ziggy—tuxedo, bow tie, sneakers, that delicious touch. The servants wore tuxedos and shiny black shoes. They had official badges with the title, "Friend." The paintings were Picassos, Van Goghs, Matisses; in addition, Charles White, Hugo Gellert, Rockwell Kent, and William Gropper were in discreet alcoves. Supreme Court justices on arrival

337

saw Picasso, Utrillo, portraits of Franklin Delano Roosevelt. The pig imagery was muted, in darkened areas where the servants hunted for food and the dogs killed. Portraits of Robeson, Ben Davis, and Elizabeth Gurley Flynn resided in locked studies.

The famous senator stayed with the Weissbergers upon his return from his trip to Kolyma. He arrived aglow with stories of the "great experiment" and bearing the souvenir bones of counterrevolutionaries. He gave a small bone to the Weissbergers as a gift.

On the same night, a frightened Solly and Dolly Rubell appeared unexpectedly at the doorstep, stinking with terror. Solly had already been visited by the F.B.I. The smell was so strong that the Weissbergers were afraid it would reach the senator, three rooms and four vaults away. They were deeply conflicted; on the one hand, they looked at the couple in front of them as saints; on the other, as wretched runts. Their feelings were the dialectical contradictions of living under capitalism. They showed their proletarian solidarity by taking the stinking couple into their arms and embracing them, then spirited them away into the tower until the senator departed. They ordered the servants to delouse the couple and give them new togs.

The tower was reserved for political prisoners in flight, for progressives from around the world. Here everything was in the open: the pig imagery was forthright, the pictures of Stalin and Dmitrov and Lenin large and lustful. Soviet medals and rugs and medallions hung on every wall. Stalin's *Collected Works* were assembled on bookshelves in luscious red leather volumes.

The Weissbergers, with their Germanic culture, were not the ghetto Jews of Rivington Street, of Perry Street, the Jimmy Higginses. They revered the Rubells, but how common they seemed, the crumbs on their clothes, their accents. That whole little gang of engineers. They had heard Solly say: "They had no use for us as Jews. But others did. Good use, and we utilized our skills to the max."

Not being paranoid or poor themselves, they could not share the sentiments. A new university in Chicago had just been named after Ziggy; a nutrition drive was launched across America with Sarah's picture and name; the Weissbergers' weekly radio program was almost as popular as Howard Mayfield's.

They knew that many Americans bowed their heads when their names were spoken. Their money had softened people's brains and their hostility toward Jews. They gave away a thousand and got millions back in reputation. They were known for their philanthropy, their enlightened attitudes, and especially they were known for their money. The country knew of their special concern for children whose legs were of different sizes. Movietone News frequently ran shots of the bejeweled, befurred Sarah in her butterfly dress putting her arms around a little limping child, the two of them walking together (one walking, one hopping) into a sunlit forest, Sarah murmuring, "Come along, my child," or "Dear heart, you can do it. You can do anything you want to do." These movie vignettes often came at the end of segments about war, famine, bigotry, and anti-Semitism, and were a heartening windup to the news.

The servants were under the supervision of the lacquered, debonair, fur-and-feathered Howard Martin. A faint, wild, animal glint there. Martin, once Herb Winkelman, the cutthroat from the Bowery, Wink the Fink, Wink the Butcher, Wink the Harbor Pirate. If anyone recognized Wink, Ziggy said, "Yeah, he was a militant trade unionist. Ah, that's ancient history." The rat-faced woman by Wink's side was Sonya Stein. Stalin sent her to New York in 1937 to help Wink mop up some class enemies. She was a well-trained student of mesmerism from the Motnia College in Leningrad. Ziggy knew Wink since 1934, when he'd met him on a Party-run ship in Hamburg. Wink supplied him with cameras and instructions for photographing American harbors.

Sarah Weissberger was busy entertaining her guests, skipping up and down the steps. In the second basement, the red-hot light, the machines churned away day and night. People flew up and down the stairs with telegraphic instructions. The noise of the radio transmitters, the photography and microfilming was deafening; the machinery clanking against other machinery; slabs of concrete falling to the floor from overuse. Counterfeit money and passports were an extra drain; it was too much to do at one time. It was a life of exhilaration; men with hot messages screaming, *"Go for it."* The power made them horny; they plunged their faces into Sarah's breasts.

On the central floor the guests, the judges, the justices, the diplomats, the journalists, the whole slew—the senator was standing there in his gray suit and shiny shoes requesting, if possible, if she pleased, an autographed picture of Sarah with one of those short-legged creatures for his den, for his wife, for his daughter, for Congress, for the president, if only, if she could, if she would.

Beneath piles of rubble were covers of wood. Beneath the wood were cavities twenty inches long, eighteen inches wide, six inches deep. Packages were inside. In the middle was a gray metal box, covered by polyethylene bags. The box, the size of a small attaché case, was a radio transmitter that reached to Moscow. In another bag was a false torch battery with lenses to make microdots and a keying device for sending long messages quickly.

The transmitter had a single earpiece and no loudspeaker. It worked on a high-frequency band with a 150-watt output. It was used with the automatic keying device.

The photography equipment was superb: 35-millimeter cameras, a lens system, and the 35-millimeter negatives reduced to microdots. The microdots were inserted in letters, sealed behind the stamp on an envelope or sent out of the country in a book.

The Weissbergers visited the Rubells in the tower on the third day after the departure of the senator. "Be brave, be strong, it is too late to escape," they told Solly and Dolly.

You will be legends, you will be history, they told them. You must go back now to your little East Side hovel and you must remain true to your convictions. We are invincible. History is on our side. We love you. Your contribution has been enormous. We will never abandon you. Stalin loves you. You are steel rods. You will not break.

Solly said, his voice a trembling green reed, "I love my babies."

"Babies are born every minute, my dear Solly," said Sarah. "And now they will be free."